Tracking
the
Marvelous

Tracking the Marvelous

A Life in the New York Art World

John Bernard Myers

Random House · New York

All rights reserved under International and Pan-American Copyright Conventions. Published in the United States by Random House, Inc., New York, and simultaneously in Canada by Random House of Canada Limited, Toronto.

Portions of this work have previously appeared in the following publications: *Art in America, New Criterion, The New York Review of Books* and *Vanity Fair.*

Grateful acknowledgment is made to the following for permission to reprint previously published material:

Random House, Inc.: excerpt from "In Memoriam L.K.A." from W. H. Auden: *Collected Poems,* edited by Edward Mendelson, copyright © 1955 by W. H. Auden. Reprinted by permission of Random House, Inc.

Vanguard Press, Inc.: Excerpt from "Polka." Reprinted from *Collected Poems of Edith Sitwell* by permission of the publisher, Vanguard Press, Inc. Copyright © 1968 by Vanguard Press, Inc. Copyright 1949, 1953, 1954, © 1959, 1962, 1963 by Dame Edith Sitwell. Canadian and Open Market rights controlled by David Higham Associates Limited.

Library of Congress Cataloging in Publication Data
Myers, John Bernard.
   Tracking the marvelous.
Includes index.
1. Art—New York (N.Y.)—Anecdotes, facetiae, satire
etc.   2. Art, Modern—20th century—New York (N.Y.)—
Anecdotes, facetiae, satire, etc.   I. Title.
N6535.N5M93   1983   709'.747'1   83-42751
ISBN 0-394-53413-1

Manufactured in the United States of America
2   3   4   5   6   7   8   9
First Edition

For James Merrill and in memory of
Herbert Machiz and Arthur Cady

Acknowledgments

The possibilities for making mistakes in a chronicle-memoir such as this have been a source of worry, particularly the spelling of names, the dating of events, the naming of artworks. I am grateful to the many people who have been helpful with making corrections, since recent art history is elusive and sometimes memory does not speak clearly. No doubt there are still some errors in my story, and if there are, I should be grateful for the readers' forgiveness.

Michael Boodroo and Patrick Merla must be thanked for their patient assistance in the preparation of the manuscript. I should also like to express gratitude to Robert Cowley for his many suggestions in shaping the final version of my narrative.

Foreword

THIS IS AN ACCOUNT OF WHAT IT WAS LIKE TO BE AN ART DEALER OF A LITTLE fame but not much fortune, who managed to make a dent in the New York art world. It is also the story of a person who had to invent a self from a nobody and then become a plausible somebody without the aid of money, social connections or even a credible education.

To write a memoir is to betray considerable conceit, and to write a chronicle of recent art history seems particularly conceited. Yet I had developed a strong desire to tell what it was like to have been immersed in the art world of New York. Many other writers have attempted this story. Surely some of them succeeded because they possessed the cool detachment necessary for such a narrative. But was this not also a form of conceit? Were they not as motivated by likes and dislikes as I? Perhaps they were not sufficiently prejudiced. Indeed, how could anyone tell such a story without having been involved in the quarrels, the political and ideological differences, the clash of personalities, the loves and loathings, the greediness or the acts of selfless kindness?

I did not have to remind myself that art writers may be tempted to be sentimental or cynical, to pay off old scores, to punish enemies and, above all, to assert, pontificate and lay down rules as to what is Good and Bad in Art. The greatest temptation of all is to prove that one's tastes are superior and will last longer than those of other critics. Having lived all my adult life in a world devoted to shaping and controlling other people's tastes, I don't know anyone more aware of this final conceit than myself.

Is such a story worth telling? Art books are published *ad nauseam*, art being a fascinating commodity like oil or uranium. If there is any doubt that art is a commodity, the Department of Internal Revenue will happily explain that there is no difference between a painting or a piece of sculpture and a Cadillac or a diamond tiara. Art books of the popular sort are published to explain, to guide and to develop Art Love; they roll off the presses like confetti. There they are, this plethora, in ordinary bookshops, department stores, drugstores; in airports, bus stations, thrift shops, remainder outlets. Readers of such books like to know the "inside" view. We can learn from them the tragedy of Van Gogh, the kinky goings-on of Toulouse-Lautrec, the love life of Jackson Pollock, the genius of Michelangelo, the "avant-gardism" of Marcel Duchamp. For a few dollars we can read, enthralled, what it was that Degas said to Mary Cassatt, what Mary Cassatt said about Gertrude Stein and what Gertrude Stein said about the Museum of Modern Art. We can find out how many wives and mistresses Picasso had, what he liked to eat, how awful he was to his children, how much money he accrued, how he enjoyed gifts such as a cowboy suit or a white American roadster from Mr. Sam Kootz.

The rush to document "genius" knows few hesitations; more often than not, the reporter of such information (and hearsay) feels that some of the glitter has rubbed off on himself; in fact, he feels he has gained a form of superiority by presenting "the evidence." The tone of self-congratulation is at times startling. Do we need to quote authors who take such vertiginous delight in their expertise?

It is impossible to say why it is that art is a commodity. We can only recognize that it *is*, like forests, fishing grounds, coal deposits. The cathedrals, tombs, theaters, palaces, country houses go up, and art goes into them and upon them. The patrons pay, the artists complain, the historians document, the critics discriminate and the public is gently led into "appreciation." It is the sadness of art in the Western world, however, that it remains a commodity.

Those of us who have lived our lives with paintings and sculptures have two attitudes toward such inventions. The first is, "I must have, own and possess them." The other is, "I enjoy those things but I *don't* want to have, own or possess them." How pleasant to think of Rilke renting a room in a boarding house with one bed, a chair, an armoire, possibly a little desk. On the wall, some pinned-up postcards remind him of beauty: a photograph of a Rodin, a reproduction of a Dürer drawing, a view of the Adriatic Sea. Perhaps it is best to be reminded of beauty rather than to own it.

I believe the "art world" exists side by side with many groups of creative people. In the 1940s there was a give-and-take between the artists and the intellectuals, the poets and the entrepreneurs that seems hardly to exist today. What Sartre used to call the "others" in my chronicle are what I care about, above all, the amalgam. How else should I devote myself to tracking the marvelous?

One

A YOUNG PERSON SCRIBBLING IN HIS JOURNAL TENDS TO BE MORE SOLEMN than he has a right to be. My early scribbling attests to such earnestness, which often masked humorless self-regard and confusion. I trust it was the beginning of learning to be serious. But sometimes such journals reveal some small sense of what was going on; they are not altogether useless. Mine indicates how one person brought up in the provincial circumstances of Buffalo was conditioned *not* to stay put. I am surprised that anyone as hyperactive as I was could sit still long enough to write anything—even a messy journal—let alone stories, bad verse and half-baked "criticism." All the young people I knew at that time were full of high-flown notions, bursting with curiosity and a need to carry out what they thought they believed. It was in the air.

Over and over I've been asked, "How in the world did you become an art dealer?" The answer is, of course, elusive. Why does someone geared to carpentry become a skydiver or a professor of Greek literature? To become an art merchant was the last thing I could have imagined. But like Keats I seemed to have followed "my nose to the North."

Rumination Journal, 1939

"I is another," says Rimbaud. But who am I? I have three passions: poetry and puppets and painting. To which shall I turn? The way of poetry means being verbal, a saturation in more than one language, yet I could not learn Greek, Latin or French adequately. Poetry means precision, yet I never could get past algebra or geometry (even arithmetic) in school. Poetry is a way of distinguished and elevated speech, yet I cannot spell, punctuate or even be grammatical. I experience ideas (I hope), yet I never have any. English slips away from me.

I cannot learn to draw or paint. My hands do not connect with my eyes. My muscles do not behave with the harmonies I suspect lie below the surface of what is imagined, what are thought of as "images," what is put together in my "head." But that which is outside me, a detached image, is of no value. If there is no image, how will we know what is true?

I have become a puppeteer.

By wearing the mask of the marionette, I have become someone else. I am Jack with his beanstalk, the Frog Prince, Peter Rabbit, the child Mozart, the Blackamoor, a witch, a wicked sister, a butterfly, a balloonist, a high priest, a dragon.

The audience never sees *you*. *You* are behind the black masking drapes of your theater. You are the puller of strings and the master of fanciful destinies. You are also at the same time Jack and Peter and Mozart, the witch, the butterfly, even the dragon. You cannot be touched there, high up on your bridge above the stage, the lights shining down upon who *you* really are, whom no one can disturb or get at. You will never know a greater liberty.

Remembering Lafayette High School

I am grateful to my father who, in opposition to my mother, has built my beautiful theater that folds up and can be put in the trunk or on the roof of the car. My mother feels I should not be encouraged to play with dolls. She firmly believes it is unhealthy.

We have put on a marionette show in French class at Lafayette High School, called *L'Homme Sans Peur*. Our teacher, Miss Agnew, made the puppets and taught us to say the lines. The most thrilling moment came when the Man Without Fear cried out to the Ghost, *"Tombez, ou ne tombez pas?"* First the legs fell out of the ceiling, then the arms, then the torso, then the head—and *then*, with a pull of all the strings, the specter came together and danced about, his mirror eyes glistening!

* * *

I performed *Jack and the Beanstalk* at the Wellesley Club in North Street, where I met Mrs. Ernest Hill, a great lady who has invited me to have a cup of tea with her next Thursday.

I have at last been taught something of the world. Mrs. Hill lives in an apartment between Delaware Avenue and Irving Place that is handsomely appointed with good eighteenth-century furniture, a working fireplace, damask curtains on the high windows. The tea set is splendid English silver and the maid brings us watercress sandwiches and scones.

Mrs. Hill reads the *Yale Review*, the *New Republic* and English magazines. She wants to know about what the young poets are writing, but, alas, I can only tell her about what our own little group, writing for the little magazine we call *Upstate*, is doing. She is very amused when I tell her how one of our editors, Betty Cage, has used a line from Shakespeare, "springes to catch woodcocks," which not one of us could place as being from *Hamlet*. Mrs. Hill is beautiful and speaks with an Eastern accent; she has none of the flat Buffalo "a" 's that sound like snores or the baaing of sheep. But more than poetry, Mrs. Hill is curious about the young radicals I associate with. "Tell me," she asks, "about your Trotskyite friends." I, on the other hand, want to know about the society she frequents; reticence prevents her from divulging this aspect of her life.

Mrs. Hill and I have both heard the lecture given by Ananda Coomaraswamy at the Albright gallery. Gordon Washburn, the museum's director (whose art history courses I have taken for some time), introduced the great Indian art historian. Washburn was excited to be presenting the person with whom he had studied at Harvard and who was largely responsible for much of the astonishing collection of Oriental art in the Boston Museum of Fine Arts.

"And what," asked Mrs. Hill over our weekly Thursday afternoon tea, "did you get from Professor Coomaraswamy? What did he say that impressed you the most?"

I said I was fascinated that he felt the emergence of a work of art depended upon a threefold process: the maker, the purveyor and the receiver, all coming together to establish its presence.

"But," commented Mrs. Hill, "that would not include prehistoric or primitive art, would it?" I had to admit I couldn't see how the threefold process would apply to the Lascaux caves or Navaho sand painting or Kwakiutl totem poles.

Jotting, Journal, 1941

I look at whatever publications the Albright gallery library receives from Paris and New York relating to Dadaism and Surrealism. I am not sure I understand what either group is about; I do know their nihilism appeals to me. At the Waldorf Cafeteria under the *Upstate* "office" I have taken to saying things like, "Duchamp and Tristan Tzara were right in denouncing the art of the past. It is stifling to have all that art around. Let us paint mustaches, not only on the *Mona Lisa* but on all overpowering masterpieces that discourage new art from emerging!" Even my Trotskyite friends get the shivers. Alfred Giglierano nervously wants to know where we shall start. (He's thinking of his own rather sweet, lyrical figure paintings.) I then say, "With the academic artists of Buffalo. Down with the annual show of Western New York! Down with the Clay Club! Down with Charles Burchfield and Eugene Speicher!"

My friend Irving Janis glows with approval. His father and his whole family have no use for rear-guard art; his uncle Sidney is the advisor for the family collection and has seen to it that they buy the best School of Paris painting.

When Irving, our friend Edward Maisel and I were still in high school we made an excursion to New York to see Uncle Sidney's collection. It was he who also arranged for us to go down to Union Square to visit Arshile Gorky. We were received very pleasantly and shown many pictures. But one remains poignantly in my memory—the portrait Gorky had done of himself and his mother, re-created from memory and the aid of an old snapshot. It was almost life-size and we were deeply impressed because we thought Gorky only liked to paint abstractions. Uncle Sidney was out when we went to his Central Park West apartment to see his collection. But his two young sons, Karel and Conrad, greeted us and showed us everything; considering that they were not more than five or six years old, we were impressed by how much they knew about each item in the collection. Karel was particularly eloquent about Picasso's *Le Miroir,* and Conrad's favorite was *The Dream* by Le Douanier Rousseau.

The Buffalo Janises own Picassos, Gorkys, Gomaires, Mondrians and other abstractionists. (Uncle Sidney used to date my oldest sister, Evelyn, when they were in high school; the family name then was Janowitz, and Sidney was a champion ballroom dancer.) The Martin Janises have a shoe store on Main Street, whose façade was designed by the modern architect Frederick Kiesler.

Jotting, April 1942

The Albright library has received a magazine published in New York called *View*. I glanced at the editorial statement and discovered to my delight that one of the two editors is Parker Tyler, whom I have met on my numerous visits to Nancy and Philip Haydock, Communist party pals. They had warned me that Parker was a Trotskyite, a fellow traveler of the Socialist Workers, but they are very orthodox, especially Nancy. Philip fought in Spain with the Loyalists and detests what he calls the Counter-Revolutionary P.O.U.M.-ists, affiliated with the anarcho-syndicalists and Trotskyites, and, in his opinion, just as bad as the Falangist followers of Generalissimo Franco. It has been necessary that I not say too much about Parker when staying with the Haydocks. But I like him enormously and always look him up when I'm in New York. I used to meet him in a bar called George's, on the corner of Seventh Avenue and Bleecker Street, a hangout for intellectuals and poets. It was there that I met Margery Mason, Lionel Abel, Lou Swerling and Noah Greenberg, at that time conductor of a working-men's choral group. Parker is highly respected by these people because of his literary and film criticism and because, with his close friend Charles Henri Ford, he wrote a pornographic novel, *The Young and the Damned*, and (also with Ford) edited a magazine coming out of Columbus, Mississippi, called *Blues*. Both of them arrived in New York from Columbus in the early 1930s, but Ford moved on to Paris, and it was after his return from Europe that the two of them decided to further collaborate on a new magazine, this time *View*.

The first issue I saw was devoted to Max Ernst. It is not possible to describe the thrill that passed through me. Is it Keats who tells us that a poem should raise the hair at the back of the head? I seemed to feel as Keats wanted me to feel, a tangible thrill. I wrote a note to Miss Frances Steloff at the Gotham Book Mart asking for any or all back numbers of Parker's magazine. I felt an urge to send the editors of *View* copies of *Upstate*, but realized that our little Buffalo magazine was too provincial, too jejune, to make a satisfactory exchange with anything so refined and intelligent as *View*.

Journal, 1942

One has to be grateful to the Albright library. It is on those shelves that I have discovered *Minotaure*, *Cahiers d'Art* and the many catalogues of the only modern art I care about. It is there that I discovered the phantasmagoric landscapes of Max Ernst, which fascinate and repel me. I long to go to Paris and see more pictures by Picasso, Matisse, Juan Gris, Braque and Mondrian, among others. I long to sit in a café that artists frequent.

Since I have been rejected by both the Army and Navy because of ruptured eardrums (too many people died in army camps in World War I from highly infectious spinal meningitis), I must do something valuable, if possible, and fascinating. I have finally left the airplane plant where I was working. My friend Dave Weinstein decided we should both make ourselves scarce. As a member of the Socialist Workers party he had convinced me that the Negroes in the plant have been getting the worst jobs, such as floor sweeping or heavy labor in the heat-treatment department, for which they receive the lowest pay. The local of the Automobile Workers of America was preventing upgrading, thus ignoring the Mahoney Act, which makes discrimination due to color, race or religion unlawful.

We broached this injustice at the last union meeting; it created quite an uproar. The membership immediately took a vote and the proposal to upgrade Negroes qualified for higher paid skilled work was almost unanimously voted down. The officers were furious with Dave and me; some of the insults thrown at us as we left the meeting were frightening. Dave was less scared than I was. "Why," I asked, "couldn't we go to the management and tell them we are going to report the company to Albany and, at the same time, urge the colored workers to invoke the Mahoney Act?" Dave thought this a marvelous idea. He broached this plan to his comrades in the Socialist Workers party. They were against it on the grounds that Dave should not oppose the union, but rather keep trying to convince its members to understand the revolutionary role of the proletariat.

I said this would take years. What worker was going to give up his good salary and overtime to a Negro? Dave sorrowfully agreed. We did go to management and they instantly saw the point. Why should they care what color a worker is as long as the job gets done?

When we heard that the new upgrading system would go into effect almost immediately, I told Dave that he and I should skedaddle. Both of us were disillusioned with the trade unions as a step to revolution, since unions were just as much a part of the capitalist system as General Motors. No wonder Alexander Herzen, the Russian philosopher and theoretical socialist, continually brought up the question of how workers could rule themselves when invariably there springs up an elite that is quite positive of what is good for the masses. Shall we forget "dictatorship of the proletariat" in the USSR, with its stranglehold over millions of people by Stalin? My Trotskyite friends had certainly taught me not to, as did the Moscow trials. Anyway, I have seen some of the union's goons manhandle "strikebreakers." (I have seen one man's eye gouged out with a brass knuckle.) It was perfectly possible that once the union leadership found out it was we who had gone to the management, we might get "roughed up." The Young Communist League had by this time expelled me.

My contribution to World War II is therefore over. I now have a job at Ulbrich's bookstore. Ulbrich's is the Brentano's of Buffalo, a large, rambling store, well stocked, with additional departments carrying maps and globes, stationery and greeting cards. I am in charge of Poetry and Belles Lettres, Biography and Essays, my reward for being 4-F'd.

Mr. Otto Grauer, Jr., manages the book department; Mr. Grauer, Sr., manages the rest of the store and the money. Since I had met Otto, Jr., socially, I call him Otto. His father is awful—a tiresome, self-satisfied member of the Rotary Club, a law-abiding, churchgoing moralist who dislikes smoking and drinking. But I am fond of Otto, a most sympathetic boss, who went to Dartmouth College and has an Eastern accent, smokes cigars and drinks a martini before lunch, which he eats daily at the Hotel Lafayette. Once in a while he invites me to have lunch with him.

Old Mr. Grauer loathes me and would have me fired if it weren't for the fact that my sales record has been so high. I seem to have attracted a wholly new element into the store that Grauer *père* is repelled by. The book department at times looks like a convention of every radical and "bohemian" for miles around. Half my time is spent ardently gossiping with everyone who comes in; there's lots of unseemly laughter. Worst of all, outlandishly dressed young men, and girls who are considered "fast," come by the store almost daily. The young men are often "gay" as toys and the girls determined to be unconventional. I, of course, love every minute of the day. Otto has to continually remind his father that *no* salesman has ever sold so many books in the history of the store, especially books that people usually don't buy. He gets the giggles when he hears me say to one of my regulars, "My dear! Excitement beyond excitement. A *new* book by Wallace Stevens has just come in. Grab it. We only ordered *three."* Or, "Don't let on, but we have a copy of *Ulysses* stashed behind the limited editions. It's only twenty dollars. No, I can't *reveal* how we got it."

But perhaps what the elder Mr. Grauer finds most distressing (being a dyed-in-the-wool Republican) are the people he calls "The Bolsheviks," my radical friends from whom I take orders for books by Marx, Engels, Kautsky, Bakunin, Lenin and, of course, Leon Trotsky. "Why," he hisses to his son, "don't they go to that filthy bookstore on Chippewa Street?" He means the Workers' Bookshop, controlled by the Communist party, where I am quite unwelcome.

The nicest thing about working in a bookstore is the number of books I am able to read before anyone else and the books that I get for free. When the publishers' salesmen come around they like to butter me up with galley proofs and advance copies. It almost makes up for my small salary. I don't know how I live on it, since I give ten of the fourteen dollars to my mother, who calls this "board and keep." And sixty cents covers my daily bus fare six days of the week.

Journal, 1943

We have been trying, I suppose, by publishing *Upstate* magazine to escape the sad heaviness of the war. Our little "studio" at 639 Main Street is a refuge from banality and stupidity. We gather night after night in our "office," mimeographing the pages of each issue, reading our poems and stories to one another. Knowing that Miss Steloff of the Gotham Book Mart in New York likes and carries our magazine has given us courage to continue.

It is myopic for us to go on thinking that Buffalo is so provincial when in many ways it has been valuable. If it were as much of a backwater as we say, how then is it possible to have learned so much? The libraries are remarkable, especially the Grosvenor and Lockwood Memorial at the university. The Albright gallery is where we came to know modern painting and sculpture. The Albright acquired Brancusis, Picassos, Monets and Matisses long ago. The Chamber Music Society is one of the best in the world; most of the greatest chamber ensembles, including the Budapest String Quartet, come to Buffalo. There are several theaters, and many of the best productions play in Buffalo—the Lunts every year, Katharine Cornell, Eva Le Gallienne, Maurice Evans, Jane Cowl, Walter Hampden and many others. Even the local Little Theater run by Miss Jane Keeler constantly presents Shaw, Ibsen,

O'Neill, Galsworthy, Philip Barry, S. N. Behrman. Les Ballets Russes de Monte Carlo, Harald Kreutzberg, Mary Wigman, Martha Graham include Buffalo in their tours. There seems to be an audience.

All of the people in the group surrounding *Upstate* long to move away from Buffalo. They feel the future holds nothing for them if they stay here. The poet Waldemar Hansen works in a chemistry laboratory, Alfred Giglierano is a poster designer for the Public Library, Betty Cage is a secretary, Martha Mayer a schoolteacher, while George and Charlotte Poole work for the C.I.O. on the local labor newspaper. At eighteen George Poole went to Spain to fight with the Loyalists; he has an uneasy relationship with the Communist party and wants only to write novels that sound like Hemingway. Many of my friends from school have already gone to other places. They, too, dislike the Queen City of the Lakes.

Jotting, March 1943

At the Waldorf Cafeteria I have been explaining how the Unconscious contains the residue of all we know and that true freedom can come about only when the conscious mind and the Unconscious are aware of each other. I have managed to obtain the *manifestos* of André Breton,* the recognized leader of the Surrealist movement in which this truth is proclaimed.

I read aloud:

> Logical methods are applicable only to solving problems of secondary interest. The absolute radicalism that is still in vogue allows us to consider only facts relating directly to our experience. Logical ends, on the contrary, escape us. It is pointless to add that experience itself is increasingly circumscribed. It leans for support on what is most immediately expedient, protected by the sentinels of common sense. Under the pretense of civilization and progress, we have managed to banish from the mind everything that may rightly or wrongly be termed superstition or fancy: Forbidden is any kind of search for truth which is not in conformance with accepted practices. It was apparently by pure chance that a part of our mental world which we pretended not to be concerned with any longer and, in my opinion, by far the most important part, has been brought back to light. For this we must give thanks to the discoveries of Sigmund Freud. On the basis of these discoveries a current of opinion is finally forming by means of which the

---

* To spare the reader, I have used the brilliant translation of Richard Seaver and Helen R. Lane, *Manifestos of Surrealism* (University of Michigan Press, 1969, pp. 9–14).

human explorer will be able to carry his investigations much further, authorized, as he will henceforth be, not to confine himself solely to the most summary realities. The imagination is perhaps on the point of reasserting itself, of reclaiming its rights. If the depths of our mind contain within it strange forces capable of augmenting those on the surface or of waging a victorious battle against them, there is every reason to seize them and submit them to the control of our reason. The psychoanalysts have everything to gain but no means have been designated for carrying out this undertaking, thus, until further notice, it can be construed to be the province of poets as well as scholars . . .

I then quoted some random sentences that I thought important. "Freud very rightly brought his critical faculties to bear upon the dream."

"The time of pure dreaming, that is, the dreams of sleep, is not inferior to the sum of the moments of reality, the moments of being awake. I have always been amazed at the way an ordinary observer lends so much more credence and attaches so much more importance to waking events than to those occurring in dreams."

"Cannot dreams be used in solving the fundamental questions of life?"

"I believe in the future resolution of the two states, dream and reality, which are seemingly so contradictory, into a kind of absolute state of reality, a *surreality*, if one may so speak."

"Let us note the *hate of the marvelous* which rages in certain men. Let us not mince words: the marvelous is always beautiful, anything marvelous is beautiful, in fact, only the marvelous is beautiful."

I used the word *le merveilleux*. I said I could think of no more prodigious word and no greater goal in life than to seek *le merveilleux*.

Needless to say, the argument that followed went on for hours. I grew increasingly animated and I also found myself believing in a new absolute.

Jotting, April 1943

Mrs. Hill always surprises me; it is one of her greatest charms. She had heard from her friend Martha Visser t'Hooft while at lunch at the Garret Club in Cleveland Avenue that I was espousing a new cause. Mrs. Visser t'Hooft, a painter, is vaguely related to Mabel Dodge Luhan (a scandalous woman from Buffalo involved at one time in radical issues, devotee of D. H. Lawrence, a woman who had married a Navaho Indian named Tony Luhan and lived in Taos, New Mexico). Martha was enthusiastic, for she, too, had knowledge of Surrealism and was quite capable of embracing its dicta. But then, Martha Visser t'Hooft has for some time been my patroness for the Buffalo Cinema League and the Film Society and went so far as to give a reception for a Dutch film director I had invited to Buffalo, Joris Ivens (I showed several of his radical and avant-garde films). Tall, Junoesque, as they say, supremely elegant, Martha is married to the Dutch consul and lives a curiously split life between her own artistic activities and upper-class responsibilities. Her father, Chauncey Hamlin, is the president of the board of managers of the Buffalo Society of Natural Sciences. Her own tendencies have always been submerged in the necessities of family and class.

"Yes," I said to Mrs. Hill, "I would not be surprised if Martha was aware of the activities of Breton and his followers. She is always *au courant;* for instance, she once gave me a complete set of *Close-Up* magazine edited by Iris Barry."

"I thought," said Mrs. Hill, "the novelist Bryher and Kenneth MacPherson were the editors of *Close-Up.* Iris Barry went from the London Film Society to be curator of films at the Museum of Modern Art in New York. I don't think Miss Barry was *that* responsible for *Close-Up.*"

Good heavens! I thought to myself. How can this woman know so much about so many things?

"Did you know there's a lady in Oakland Place named Mrs. Mitchell who owns a painting by Salvador Dali? It's a picture of a spoon with an egg in it. I can arrange for you to see it if you like."

"André Breton calls Dali 'Avida Dollars,' " I exclaimed, hoping to be thought very "with it." "Breton says Dali loves only money and the Spanish Falange. He also says that Dali has gone back to the Roman Catholic Church."

"Is that so bad?" asked Mrs. Hill. "After all, Dali *is* Spanish."

I flushed with anger.

"My dear Mrs. Hill," I said, "surely you don't tolerate fascism or the horrors of the present Spanish regime?"

"Oh," she replied quickly, "I didn't mean the political squalor of such people as Dali. I meant that artists have the right to whatever religion they are comfortable with. And furthermore, most artists enjoy making lots of money. It's a sign, a symbol of appreciation." Her smile was enigmatic.

It was the first time I ever felt Mrs. Hill might be cynical. The awful tolerance, I thought, of the bourgeoisie. I must try to forgive her, since she has so many good aspects. On the other hand, I think she is typical of the liberals who support Roosevelt and cannot see that the embargo against the Spanish has meant the downfall of Spain and the beginning of World War II.

Jotting, May 1943

My dearest friend, Edward Maisel, who has been away at Harvard and now is only rarely in Buffalo, is amused by my fascination with Surrealism. He says jokingly that some Unconsciousnesses seem to be better supplied than others. I suppose he means that some of the Surrealists are more original than others, and the lesser talents seem to be using dream material already dreamed. But, of course, Edward ignores the art of children and the insane, the poetry of aboriginals, the anonymous art of working people.

Ruminations

I am plagued from time to time with a feeling of revulsion toward everything and everybody around me. It is as though life itself is a banality, a source of confusion, senselessness, dread. This feeling makes me melancholy; it is an admission of boredom. To experience ennui as did Baudelaire, detesting the everyday world, is also an admission of defeat—of a refusal to grow up and be more or less happy or unhappy. It is childish to seek only *le merveilleux*, yet it is the marvelous, the magical, the transcendent, that I most ardently desire. "Desire," says Breton, "is the dynamo of the Will." I know I cannot find *le merveilleux* in Buffalo. Reading books will not help me, or rather, books can only help me up to a point. It is the larger world that I long for, especially since I have learned that the French Surrealists have emigrated to New York to escape the oppression of the Vichy government.

Jotting, October 1943

Tea with Mrs. Mark De Wolfe Howe, Jr., was a failure. She was, under the name Mary Manning, a playwright with the Dublin Gate Theatre. I had read her *Youth's the Season?* in a collection of Irish plays and sought her out when I discovered she had married a professor of law at the University of Buffalo. Professor Howe is the son of a distinguished historian and theoretician of jurisprudence and a most elegant, well-turned-out man—a suitable choice for the dean of the Buffalo Law

School. Unfortunately, he joined Mrs. Howe and me in the middle of tea. I was spouting all sorts of radical nonsense that caused the professor to question me closely as to what I really know and believe. This caused me to make an even greater and more stubborn fool of myself as I became increasingly aware of my lack of seriousness. I was, as my mother would say, talking through my hat. Mary Howe was amused, since she was, no doubt, conditioned to hearing political *blague* of the most bizarre variety back in Dublin. But she is not what I think of as "Irish," since she is Anglo-Irish and Protestant. (A lady in the sense of Mrs. Hill.) Her husband found me a crashing bore and poseur. It is unlikely that I shall be invited back a second time.

Jotting, November 1943

I have just finished Stendhal's *The Red and the Black*. In my angry letters to the editors of the *Buffalo Evening News* I am signing myself "Julien Sorel." Actually, I am not certain whether I don't prefer Fabrizio in *The Charterhouse of Parma* to Julien. But how could I possibly sign my protests "Fabrizio"!

Jotting, November 1943 (Journal)

"The Collective Spirit of Individualism" is a phrase in Breton I think I understand, but do I? Does it mean we should all work together, but each one very separately? At *Upstate* we played the game of "exquisite corpses," where each person makes a part of a drawing, the paper is folded, no one knows what the previous person has drawn until the accordion of paper is unfolded. Perhaps this is a kind of "collective individualism"? We have also been doing automatic writing, but it either comes out sounding like Gertrude Stein's *Tender Buttons* or Breton's strings of bizarre images. Is this perhaps because there is a "collective unconscious"? Probably none of us is sufficiently liberated to do "free association," although I feel I am making progress. Edward Maisel is, of course, skeptical. He does not consider Freud scientific in the least, but he too loves parlor games and finds the "free associations" terribly funny. So do the rest of us—but then, who doesn't love word games, especially Twenty Questions, my favorite?

It must be thrilling to actually participate in one of the Surrealist "manifestations," where the games are done with utmost seriousness. I don't suppose anyone laughs, since Breton never does.

Journal Jotting, Spring 1944

When we decided that we would professionally print *Upstate* magazine, when we said goodbye to the silk-screen and the mimeograph, we knew that it would probably be the final issue. It was also a declaration that art and literature could not be "regional," that Buffalo could never be London or Paris or New York. We sent invitations to writers in Latin America; our final number contained work by such poets as Pablo Neruda and Gabriela Mistral. It turned out beautifully. The Gotham Book Mart took many copies. Frances Steloff sent a letter of congratulations. I mailed a copy to Parker Tyler, who wrote warmly how much he liked the issue and then, quite unexpectedly, wrote me another letter asking if I would be interested in becoming the managing editor of *View*. I replied that nothing could please me more, asking when I would be expected to begin work. A further letter informed me that there would be no activity during the summer months, but that I should arrive in time to work on the Fall number.

This invitation could not have arrived at a more propitious time. The ranks of *Upstate* are diminishing. Betty Cage and Waldemar Hansen have already left Buffalo to live in New York. The other editors have lost interest. I am finding myself increasingly alone in a city that has become alien to me. I no longer manage the Film Society. I rarely perform with my marionettes. Now I am a compulsive moviegoer and bookworm, reading eight to twelve books a week and rarely sleeping more than five hours a night. Living at home with my parents, three brothers and four sisters has become impossible. (It is true that two of my brothers and two of my sisters have for some time been married and also have children, but the nest is bulging; the comings and goings are not less but more frequent.) I am not very fond of any of them except my eldest sister, and none of them cares much for me, either. My unconventional behavior does not sit well; my two elder brothers have found me unspeakable and we rarely exchange words. Indeed, there is little I do or think that could be of any interest to any of them. The most unsympathetic aspect of my personality is my declared "atheism" and a total refusal to attend Mass, even at Easter. (It is difficult for people brought up in other religions to undersand how offensive this can be to devout Irish Catholics.) I should, in short, have fled the nest long before this.

Journal, September 15, 1944

At seven A.M., I stared out the bathroom window. I stared across the plant nursery next door, through the gardens beyond, at the elm-arched bridle path of Chapin Parkway. My bags are packed; I can hear my mother bustling about in the kitchen downstairs. I know for certain that I never shall return to this house. The night before last Martin Janis loaned me $50 to help me with my travel expenses. Being twenty-four years old I am aware that remaining in Buffalo another year would be the death of a still-uninvented self.

WALDEMAR HANSEN MET ME AT THE TRAIN AND CARRIED ONE OF MY TWO
heavy bags, since we were walking from Grand Central Station to Third
Avenue and Thirty-eighth Street. He had located a furnished apartment
for us, a third-floor walk-up right next to the Third Avenue El at 201
East Thirty-eighth Street. The apartment consisted of a living room,
two bedrooms, a tiny kitchen and a small bathroom. All the furniture
was by Hans Knoll—cheap, functional and neat-looking. Each room
had a Knoll-style lamp and gray-blue carpeting made of rope, which
was hard on the feet but easy to sweep. The rent seemed high, $90 a
month, but both of us had jobs and what was most attractive, we both
had the privacy of our own rooms.

"You'll get used to the noise of the El," explained Waldemar after
one had roared past the windows. Indeed, within a few days I learned
how not to hear it. Waldemar would pause in the middle of a sentence,
wait for the clang, crash, bang to die away and calmly finish what he
was saying. After midnight the trains ran once an hour until seven in
the morning and I cannot recall that they ever disturbed my sleep. In
fact, I learned to love the El with its old-fashioned station stops that had
coal-burning pot-bellied stoves and stained-glass decorations over the
doors and windows. I enjoyed the grocery stores, antiques shops, sa-
loons and restaurants along Third Avenue. I also loved the Murray Hill
neighborhood, with its handsome town houses and pretty trees. I could
take a bus at Park Avenue and Thirty-eighth Street that turned at

Forty-second Street and then went up Madison Avenue. And I could come home the same way. The fare was ten cents.

I reported to work a few days after my arrival, having telephoned Parker Tyler, who said he would meet me at the *View* office and explain what was expected of me. I was surprised at what I found; indeed, I thought I had come to the wrong address. A marquee over the sidewalk said the Stork Club, yet it was number One East Fifty-third Street. A side entrance finally revealed elevators. *View* occupied the front of the sixteenth floor, the penthouse of the building. How strange, I thought, for a highbrow publication to be located one door from Fifth Avenue, to be so close to the Museum of Modern Art and have Sherman Billingsly's Stork Club (the interior of which I never saw) as a downstairs neighbor.

Parker was waiting for me. There were two rooms, a small entrance area and a larger office space with a narrow balcony that overlooked midtown Manhattan, a breathtaking panorama for one who had just come from Buffalo.

Parker was amused by my star-struck expression; he had lived too long in New York to feel the kind of enthusiasm for a place that I considered Mecca. He was then in his early forties and strikingly handsome. But how does one describe a person for whom one feels deep affection? I recall a photograph of Parker taken of him when very young; he looked like a beautiful girl in male attire. Everything about him was delicate, sensitive, exquisite—qualities heightened by his quiet reserve, considered by those who did not know him to be an affectation of hauteur. He wore ascots or flowing cravats; his wavy black hair was long; his velvet or corduroy jackets somehow stamped upon him everyone's notion of a romantic poet. In fact, he considered poetry his vocation and lived what he considered the proper life of a poet.

Parker was a deep-dyed Greenwich Villager and what used to be known as a bohemian. Except for his early childhood he never lived too far from Sheridan Square; most of his close friends were Villagers—unconventional, radical, hysterically intelligent. For all that, he retained a slight Southern accent. His speech was decorous as only that of a gently bred person from Columbus, Mississippi, can be decorous. (He did not "eat dinner," he "dined.") Like his hero, Henry James, he avoided clichés and used slang only when it was effective. He felt it to be an incivility to address anyone with flaccid speech; this was a part of his almost rarefied courtesy, an inborn formality of manner. Had his sense of humor not been so sharp, his delight in the comic not so keen, he might have seemed stuffy. He loved fun and gossip. I never met a person whose laughter was so musical and catching.

"Look about," suggested Parker. "Charles will be here shortly." A mobile by Xenia Cage, John Cage's former wife, hung from the ceiling. An oil painting by Kurt Seligmann of Daedalus flying through a deep blue sky hung on one wall. Elsewhere were watercolors by Masson, Léger, Miró, and Pavel Tchelitchew.

Parker busied himself with ruler and T-square, laying out pages for the next issue of the magazine. There was an iron cot against one wall, on which were piled books, magazines, catalogues, announcements and whatever else landed on it. (A few weeks later my mother unexpectedly arrived in New York and visited the *View* office. What, she wanted to know, was a *bed* doing in an office?)

At eleven o'clock Charles Henri Ford, the editor, arrived, looking exactly the way I thought he would, though a trifle older than the marvelous portrait of him by Tchelitchew (I had been instructed by Parker to pronounce the name "Cheleet'-chev," with the accent on the middle syllable). Charles Ford was everything that Parker Tyler was not. It took me several days to observe the differences because during this first interview Charles was at his pragmatic, straightforward, no-nonsense best.

"Your title," said Charles, "will be managing editor and your duties will be to get advertising, check circulation, visit galleries, collect photographs and other material and to correct proofs." Later on I was to write a column informing readers what was happening in the Paris, London and New York art worlds. My salary would be $35 a week.

"The continued existence of *View* will depend on your ability to raise money through subscriptions, advertisements and circulation. There's a whole lot of legwork involved, honey." The word "honey" turned into pure syrup; it was accompanied by a smile that made a person feel that he and he alone existed. Among his many gifts, this was one of Charles Ford's most notable. He knew exactly what it was he wanted and was invariably determined to get it.

We went through lists of who must be seen, old supporters and possible new ones. He had thoroughly organized the tasks to be done. Just before he left to go home for lunch he said, "You will come for tea this afternoon and meet my friend Pavel Tchelitchew. Corner East Fifty-fifth and First Avenue. Southwest corner." It was another penthouse.

The main room was Tchelitchew's studio, with a ceiling perhaps fourteen feet high and tall windows along two sides. Outside the windows ran a terrace. Charles had a separate room with French doors opening onto the terrace. There was a view of the East River and the gardens of other people's terraces.

Tchelitchew received me amiably enough, but during the time I was with him I had the odd notion that I was supposed to feel fortunate to be in his presence. It was as though I were meeting not a painter but a Russian grand duke, for there was something aristocratic about him. Was it snobbery? He talked rapidly, volubly, randomly, and was often witty. Since I had never met anyone like him, I wasn't certain what I felt or thought. His facial expressions changed often, his eyes observed everything and obviously he was accustomed to occupying the center of attention wherever he might be. I could not decide whether he was good-looking or homely. Certainly he was both extremely clever and elegant.

Around the fireplace was an arrangement of driftwood, which I commented upon as beautiful and unusual.

"It is from the beach on Long Island," he said (it is difficult to record his Russian accent peppered with French). "Very simple and lovely, it is true. When I showed my *arrangement* to Edelgey Dinshaw—you know Edelgey? Of course not. He is son of richest untouchable Indian tycoon. As result, Edelgey and sister never lived in India so much as Switzerland and other places. Now, New York. Well, when Edelgey Dinshaw say my *arrangement*, he make his chauffeur take him to beach. Chauffeur collects driftwood. They bring back driftwood to New York. Then Edelgey Dinshaw telephones me to say, 'Pavlik, you must come for tea; I have something to show you.' I go for tea and there is driftwood in front of fireplace. But instead of *au naturel*, it has been gilded and then in different places he has put pearls, some diamonds, some rubies, even emeralds. I said to Edelgey Dinshaw, 'Edelgey, you have ruined the effect of nature.' He looked very hurt. 'Why did you do that?' I asked. 'Because,' he said, 'it looked too plain.' " At this Tchelitchew burst into a marvelous laugh and went out of the room to bring back tea. While he was gone I moved about looking at the few pictures he allowed to be visible. I was quite cheerful and without realizing it, I began to whistle a little tune. The door opened. Pavlik was looking at me rather angrily.

"Never whistle in house," he said loudly. "Every time you whistle in house, sailor dies at sea!" My sense of guilt was irrational and immediate.

Charles and Pavlik began a conversation that excluded me, as I did not know any of the people they were talking about. I did, however, realize that the names sounded grand and important. At one moment Charles went out of the room, and for lack of anything else to say, I asked Tchelitchew why he wore a band of red flannel around his wrist.

"Ah," he said, "it is very strong antidote against arthritis. I think I am having arthritis in right hand. This is the hand for painting. The red discourages the blood from bringing arthritis crystals into fingers. Old Russian knowledge." Then I was allowed to look at Tchelitchew's plants, his roof garden. The terrace was lovely with asters and marigolds blooming in boxes. On the windowsill in the kitchen was a jar of eggshells moldering, which was "very good mulch," also "old Russian knowledge."

I commented on a Joseph Cornell box in Charles' room. "Very strange man," said Tchelitchew. "One day I say to Joseph, after looking at object called *Pharmacie* that contained many little bottles on four shelves, in each bottle different substances—'Joseph,' I say, 'what is in this bottle?' In other bottles a little sand, old confetti, bits of coral and so forth. Easy to recognize. But in this bottle it looked like gray, dried-up, crumbly old putty. 'What is in *this* bottle?' And you know what Joseph said? 'Dog shit, dried dog shit.' Very serious he said it. I could not laugh."

Having been told the deadline for the October issue of *View,* I began visiting advertisers the very next day. Luckily, many ads were repeats and it was merely a question of checking the copy. The Ozenfant School, the bookseller Paul A. Strick, Braxton Frames and a few others were easy institutional ads. All of the others required copy changes and this meant visiting each gallery personally.

I arrived at the *View* offices at nine-thirty, went through the mail, made piles for each editor, then organized new subscriptions and discarded canceled ones. In a few days I found myself floundering with the checks coming in, the billing to be done and bills to be paid. I told Parker it was too much for me to handle and that the magazine badly needed a secretary to do those tasks as well as to handle correspondence. "Secretaries are hopeless for an operation like this one," said Charles. I told them I knew the perfect person, a former editor of our magazine in Buffalo, *Upstate,* whose name was Betty Cage.

Shortly after I moved to East Thirty-eighth Street, the apartment downstairs became vacant. Betty Cage was looking for a place to live. Two weeks later, Betty took the apartment below us. She was fed up with her job, and she, no more than we, had not come to the metropolis to be bored. When I told her about *View,* she agreed to join forces with us. In less than a week she completely reorganized the files, correspondence, billing and deposits. Charles Ford and Parker were delighted with her because they immediately recognized how practical and bright she was; she was also beautiful.

201 East Thirty-eighth Street became a little part of Buffalo away from Buffalo. Edward Maisel arrived sometime later. He was no longer in the army, and his brilliant biography of the composer Charles Tomlinson Griffes had been published. Shortly thereafter Martha Mayer, another *Upstate* editor, who was tired of being a schoolteacher, joined Betty. Martha had lived on Peach Street in Buffalo in one of those huge rambling old houses with her German parents, her sisters and a brother. She had a friend named Robert Frost—not the famous poet— who was away at the war. Tall, with Titian-red hair, she had the talent to be amused and amusing. She also had a tendency toward melancholia and worried about her friend Robert. Two cats, a huge black one named Sabastian and a gray one, Hissey-belle, completed the ménage.

None of us earned much money. Meat rationing still continued, and often the four or five of us shared dinner. Waldemar hated his job as a chemist for a company called New Jersey Zinc. After all, he had come to New York to be a poet, and so far nothing had occurred to help him. We tried to sympathize with his frustration and read whatever new verses he showed us.

My first call on a gallery was the Bonestell at 17 East Fifty-seventh Street. Charles Ford's mother, Gertrude Cato, had an exhibition opening there October 30. Miss Bonestell was a polite, finicky lady whose taste in art I was unable to determine. Gertrude Cato was given gratis a full-page ad with a reproduction and a list of all the picture titles. I noticed that several pictures were loaned by the English multimillionaire Edward James and by Ruth Ford the actress. Charles called Ruth "sistah" and Ruth called Charles "bubbah." (No one else called Charles anything but Charles or Charlie.)

My next call was at Art of This Century, 30 West Fifty-seventh Street, Peggy Guggenheim's gallery. I had only heard of this gallery and was seeing it for the first time. It occupied the whole of the second floor. A little over half the space was devoted to Miss Guggenheim's personal collection of Cubists and Surrealists. The rest was taken up by exhibitions of New York artists, and by a large office. The office was in the front: two big desks backed by windows. The desks were for Miss Guggenheim and her secretary, Marius Bewley. Miss Guggenheim was out but Marius cordially invited me to sit down. I remarked immediately on the permanent installation and the unusual design of the gallery. Indeed, I had seen no gallery like it; many of the walls curved convexly or concavely. Pictures were not hung, but thrust forward on wooden arms.

"Thank goodness," said Marius, "the temporary shows are on flat walls and the pictures are hung on hooks."

We immediately "hit it off," as people say. I asked Marius where he found the buttons for his elegant black suit, since they were covered with the same material as the suit itself. He explained that bone buttons gave him the shivers if he touched them, rather the way down on peaches can give other people the shivers. His suit looked clerical, as though Marius were an English vicar. His accent was decidedly English, the result of having been educated at Cambridge, where he had studied with Professor Leavis. How in the world had he become the secretary to Miss Guggenheim? It seems he had gone back to intolerable St. Louis, had met Miss Guggenheim through her former assistant, Howard Putzel, and abandoned academia for the art world. Howard Putzel was forming his own gallery.

"I have," said Marius, "a *special* friend who will soon exhibit his work here. His name is Julian Beck. Let me show you a few." The Becks were abstract and indicated a strong talent. Shortly after the Guggenheim exhibition Julian met an actress named Judith Malina, whom he married. Together they founded The Living Theatre, and Julian from then on bent his skill as a painter to the designing and construction of stage sets. The Becks' long and stormy career has been much written about by devoted disciples.

While I was visiting, two artists dropped in for a few moments. The first was Mark Rothko and the second was Robert Motherwell. At last Peggy Guggenheim arrived. She had dyed black hair, wore extraordinary jewelry—including dangling earrings—that did not, however, distract one from her unfortunate nose, a putty-shaped blob that was the result of bad plastic surgery. She was highly nervous, and moved her hands and face more than she should have. This was because she became easily distracted. Her mind was always elsewhere. However, she was nice to me, since as she said, "I am devoted to Charles and Parker and their wonderful magazine." The copy for her latest ad publicized Motherwell and Rothko during late October and December,

with further exhibitions by Giacometti, David Hare and Isabelle Wald-
berg. Then in special "boxes," there was publicity for a recording by
Paul Bowles and a gallery anthology with a cover by Max Ernst and
essays by Breton, Arp and Mondrian.

Miss Guggenheim looked peevish and put off when I said, after
she asked me how I liked Kiesler's "interior architecture," that I was
acquainted with Kiesler's work since he had done a shoe-store façade in
Buffalo for Martin Janis.

That afternoon I went to Julien Levy's at 42 East Fifty-seventh
Street, which would be featuring paintings by Kay Sage and works by
Leon Kelly, Giorgio de Chirico and Eugene Berman. I crossed the
street and went to Pierre Matisse, who would be showing Marc Chagall.
Miss Catherine Viviano received me there and treated me with great
courtesy. The last place I stopped was 11 East Fifty-seventh Street,
Durlacher Brothers, whose director was Kirk Askew, Jr. This was the
gallery where Pavel Tchelitchew exhibited along with Esteban Frances
and Kurt Seligmann.

As the days went by, I accumulated the rest of the advertisements.
Probably the six most important were those we got from cosmetics
companies, which took full-page ads that brought us considerable and
necessary revenues. I asked Parker how this came about, and he explained that Marcel Duchamp was friendly to the magazine and that
one of his great friends was Enrico Donati, the art director for a large
publicity firm. Donati usually managed to slip a few full pages. The
Helena Rubinstein ones came from "Madame" herself, since she was a
collector of Tchelitchews and admired *View*. It was rather peculiar to
see so many perfume ads in a highbrow art magazine, but they did no
harm and helped to keep us going. Madame Schiaparelli said that the
inspiration for her "shocking pink" came from Tchelitchew's painting
Strawberries. She, too, was loyal.

As we moved toward the deadline for the fall issue, my excitement
grew. I could hardly wait to see my name on the masthead of *View* as
managing editor; it would be one of the best issues yet assembled. I had
to call on Mr. Dudensing of the Valentine Gallery to collect the necessary photographs for an article by James Johnson Sweeney of the Museum of Modern Art. The article, "Léger and the Search for Order,"
seemed to me brilliant in its examination of Léger's so-called crude
strength or forcefulness, as balanced with his exquisite, even refined,
flat structures whose harmonies I so much admired. While waiting for
Mr. Dudensing to give me the photos for Sweeney's essay, Léger him-

self appeared from the back room—a huge mustachioed, powerful-looking man who might be mistaken for a butcher. He spoke almost no English, but somehow he managed to communicate warm interest and concern for me, for *View*, for Dudensing and for his good friend Sweeney. A few days later, at M. Léger's invitation, I went to a working-men's hall off Union Square. It was a gathering organized by the artists' section of the Communist party. Léger, who was awkward, stumbled at one point and nearly fell off the platform. He gave a brief speech, rather in the nature of a fraternal greeting, and concluded with the exhortation that all artists everywhere should combat the fascist brutes who were destroying civilization. One of the comrades translated. It was a sincere speech but not very cerebral. I especially enjoyed hearing his deep Norman peasant voice.

Léger donated a superb cover for the Fall number. The colors were bright red, yellow, black and white. Who could fail to be moved by the continuous generosity of painters who never asked a fee, even when they created original covers or special drawings to go with articles or poems? Several of these works were sold and were a source of income even though contemporary art at that time did not bring in much money. (For instance, it seemed doubtful that we could get much more than $100 for the Léger cover design!)

The whole issue was remarkable. What American magazine would have published a section of Giorgio de Chirico's fantastical "novel," *Hebdomeros?* We also featured Paul Bowles' translation of this strange prose masterpiece published in Paris in 1929. It is a novel containing a series of enigmatic, changing images and incidents that reveal de Chirico's imagination as it existed during the period of his finest work, the decade between 1908 and 1918.

There was a bizarre essay by Parker Tyler called "The Erotic Spectator," in which a painting by an unknown artist, Audrey Buller, was compared to a photograph of the movie star Veronica Lake. The subtitle, "The Eye of Libido," emphasized Parker's argument that metamorphoses result from voyeurism, that seeing is an erotic action. Parker's arguments were often weird, which may be why his book *The Hollywood Hallucination* later made him a cult figure among movie fans.

At the last minute, Charles obtained a full-page, back-cover ad from the Marquis de Cuevas, publicizing the opening of the Ballet International at Columbus Circle. The Marquis de Cuevas had an extremely rich wife (one of the Rockefellers), whose money he was going through with exemplary speed.

When it was time to pick up the proofs, Parker invited me to go with him to the Liberal Press at 80 Fourth Avenue. The printers were all of the anarchist-pacifist persuasion and fond of anything involving poetry and art. Thus, it was quite logical that they also printed *Partisan Review* and *Dance Index*. When we arrived, Donald Windham, editor of *Dance Index*, was poring over some pages. I was delighted to meet him because I had read some of his work—a few stories and some short contributions to *View*. He had a fresh, countryish complexion and prematurely white hair. Like Parker, Windham had beautiful Southern manners and a most ingratiating style of speech. Lincoln Kirstein was the nominal boss of *Dance Index*, but Windham did all the work.

As we were about to leave, William Phillips, one of the editors for *Partisan Review*, came in. I wondered when I would meet Philip Rahv, the other editor; not that I really liked his criticism—it was too political for me. I had become quite certain that art and politics did not go hand-in-hand as some critics chose to believe. The connection was too often ambiguous or contradictory. When I got to know Rahv I found him a warmhearted, charming and rather worldly person.

I learned many things from Parker, but I don't think I shall ever be able to match his diligence. From the minute he arrived in the office until he left, he sat at his drawing board with ruler and T-square, scissors and rubber cement, designing page after page with absolute concentration. Nothing disturbed him—telephones ringing, people talking or walking in and out. His feeling for design was innate and he was self-taught. Parker never went to school. Though descended from the old Southern aristocracy—descended, in fact, from two Presidents—the Tylers were very poor. Parker left home early, shifting for himself in New York, and was self-educated through omnivorous reading. Once I noted, scribbled in his own hand on the title page of Breton's *Nadja*, "What a terribly designed page!" Many commercial artists have commented on the elegance of *View*'s physical appearance. It was certainly unorthodox; no one in the commercial-art world would have dreamed of making such strange layouts. But then, no one since the Dadaists had Parker's flair for *mise-en-pages*—layouts.

Finally my great day arrived: the Fall *View*. The price was fifty cents per copy or $2 a year. I took three copies home with me and showed one to Waldemar Hansen. After reading it he said, "I don't think much of that poem by Charles Henri Ford called 'The Fortunes of Edith Sitwell.' Warmed-over Surrealism, warmed-over André Breton, full of affectation and conceit. As for *Hebdomeros*, it's simply a string of nutty images from de Chirico's nightmares and doesn't signify very much. As a matter of fact, I don't go along with your obsession with Surrealism." He was quite sour, and I was dismayed. My first thought was, How can I possibly share an apartment with someone who is *anti-*Surrealist? I tried to remember how unhappy Waldemar was working at New Jersey Zinc and how frustrated with his own writing. Then I reread the last stanza of Charles' poem:

> Oh the harp we hear is like the nightlong rain
> Plucked from the wind as you walked on Cape Cod
> The lady in the mirror with the otherworldly air
> Shudders and is silent as she combs her singing hair

And I was comforted because Charles believed as I did in *le merveilleux*.

Shortly after the Fall issue appeared, Parker, Charles and I were invited by Peggy Guggenheim to a large party at her apartment in the East Sixties. She lived in a duplex, the upper floor of which was occupied by the rich Englishman and art patron Kenneth MacPherson. A curving staircase connected upstairs with downstairs. When you first entered the house there was a hall; on one wall was a mural-sized canvas full of globs and streaks of bright paint by Peggy's favorite artist of that moment, Jackson Pollock. I found the picture quite startling and Parker said it looked like a plate of baked macaroni. I had never seen so many extraordinary people gathered together at the same time. There was lots to drink, not too much to eat.

Marius Bewley, noticing my bewilderment, took me about, introducing me to people I did not know except by reputation. By the end of the evening most of the faces had blurred together and I couldn't distinguish one from another. It seemed to me that almost everyone got terribly drunk, including me. But two people in particular did remain vividly in mind, Jackson Pollock and his wife, Lee Krasner. Within minutes after talking with Lee, I found both of us laughing wildly. As for Jackson, the impact of his personality was almost completely chemical. Shall I call it sex appeal, personal magnetism, inner radiance? I don't know. Lee told me that they were moving to East Hampton, Long Island, to a place called the Springs, and invited me to pay a call if I was ever out that way. Parker told me later that Jackson was a heavy drinker and that the move to Long Island was perhaps a way to keep him on the straight and narrow.

The next day Charles commented that he noticed I had seemed to be getting along with "that Jackson Pollock." I admitted liking him and

Lee. "Well," said Charles,"he didn't behave as badly as usual. Last year at Peggy's big party he pissed in the fireplace in front of everybody. God knows what Peggy sees in those sloppy pictures of his."

We all lost interest in the Fall issue the day after it came out, since everything was now geared to the December number and Charles' scheme to raise money by presenting a jazz concert. The idea originated with Barry Ulanov, who wrote about jazz for several magazines, including ours. Ulanov regarded himself as a "conservative," preferring an older, sweeter style of jazz to the newer "bop" freneticism. (I didn't agree with this opinion, since I was especially partial to Charlie Parker and an obscure pianist called Thelonius Monk.) The musicians who would be participating were the singer Pearl Bailey, clarinetist Barney Bigard, pianist Erroll Garner, and jazz violinist Stuff Smith. Red Norvo, Don Byas and several other good players agreed to sit in.

The December cover, a glorious, splashy, agitated design in reds, blacks and blue-grays was by Esteban Frances. This design was enlarged to fill the entire back wall of the stage at Times Hall on West Forty-third Street, a perfect theater for a jazz concert. Charles Ford managed to get some terribly grand people to be patrons and sponsors: Mrs. Vincent Astor, the Marquis De Cuevas, Princess Gourielli (otherwise known as Helena Rubinstein), Mr. Arthur Lopez-Wilshaw (the South American multimillionaire), the Marquise De Montferrier, the beautiful Mrs. Huddleston Rogers (all of whose clothes were made for her by the American designer Charles James), Mrs. Robert Sarnoff (electronics), the Princess Zalstem-Zalesky (Johnson bandages).

The list of other backers also read impressively: Alexander Calder, Marcel Duchamp, Aaron Copland, André Eglevsky, Gian-Carlo Menotti, Georgia O'Keeffe, Tamara Toumanova, Carl Van Vechten, Glenway Wescott, Monroe Wheeler, Stark Young, Vera Zorina, several art dealers, writers, critics and the celebrated striptease artist Gypsy Rose Lee. Many of these people had been induced to participate by Tchelitchew, who was much admired by *le gratin* of Paris and New York. Our motto from Rimbaud, *"Il faut être absolument moderne,"* had become chic.

The jazz concert went off very well. The house was filled with glamorous people. The music was delightful. But, alas, it turned out to be a big expense and *View* realized almost no profit.

The new issue was a big job: we had more pages, more reproductions and more advertisements. Lionel Abel brought us a longish piece about Lautréamont, the ferocious nineteenth-century author who ranked high with the Surrealists. To illustrate the piece Parker used an engraving by Gustave Doré of the Grim Reaper sitting on a globe of the world. Ossip Zadkine sent us a drawing to illustrate an essay, "Tie the Gordian Knot Again!," by the Swiss writer Denis de Rougemont. (De Rougemont's wife, Simone, taught at the École Française and one of the children in her first-grade class was Breton's daughter, Aube. One day, fifteen minutes before the dismissal bell, Mme. de Rougemont told the six-year-olds that they could discuss any subject they wiṣhed. Little Aube's hand shot into the air and she cried, *"Oh, discutons nous la mort! J'adore ça!"* Said Waldemar Hansen: "Truly her father's daughter.")

We were given a two-page-spread drawing by Jean Hélion, a long poem called "Full Margin" by André Breton translated by Edouard Roditi, a speculative article on graphics by William Stanley Hayter. Nicolas Calas, Paul Goodman and Marius Bewley contributed book reviews and Kurt Seligmann contributed the "Microcosmological Chart of Man," a drawing with a deliciously occult explanation.

Paul Goodman was one of the regular visitors to the office, a most talkative and pleasant person. I asked him one day how he managed to get so much writing done in addition to everything else he did. The answer was simple, although hard to believe: "I never rewrite." But then, it was hard to believe a Paul Goodman existed. He was such a combination of ragamuffin (a cowlick of hair hanging over his forehead, old sweaters and baggy pants) and superintellectual. He seemed to have read everything, particularly Latin, Greek and Hebrew texts. Within minutes of meeting him you felt as if you had known Paul for years. Informal, friendly, childlike, candid and sympathetic on the one hand, he was also pedantic, professorial and (intermittently) abstracted, even distant. Somehow he didn't fit the category of "New York Jewish Intellectual," probably because he saw life and art in such a highly personal manner. Anyway, "Jewish Intellectuals" didn't quote Aristotle and also adore Jean Cocteau (Waldemar Hansen said Paul Goodman's enthusiasm for Cocteau proved that he was "essentially superficial"). The range of Paul's interests was extraordinary. When we first met, he was engaged in a book-length essay entitled *Kafka's Prayer*. With his brother Percy, an architect, he was also speculating about city planning. Not being a Marxist (can an Aristotelian be a Marxist?), he was concerned with such libertarian notions as "mutual aid" and what he called "communitas." He also had a variety of ideas about education and sex that I suppose most people found scandalous. There was, however, one area of Paul's beliefs that I found peculiar—his penchant for a couple of schools of psychoanalysis that I could only think of as lunatic. They were those of Wilhelm Reich and the bite-chew-and-swallow shaman, Dr. Frederich Perls. Waldemar Hansen once met Perls at a party. "Can you imagine? Dr. Perls saw me chewing a pretzel and he told me I had schizophrenia!" "And what did you answer, Waldemar?" "I told him to go swallow an old corn cob." The most hilarious aspect of Reichian therapy was the large wooden cube called an orgone box in which the "patient" sat and obtained orgone energy from the atmosphere. Waldemar said he met a girl at the same party who told him that she experienced the orgone rays so pulsatingly that when she stepped out of her box she looked as though she had been sunburned. "I did not feel," said Waldemar, "that any comment was necessary."

Who knew where Paul Goodman's interests would lead him? I didn't think his psychoanalytic preoccupations were any more harmful or silly than W. B. Yeats' intimacy with spooks. It was a form of hocus-pocus which seemed to be "useful" to Paul as a writer, and no one I knew was so prolific. I was particularly fond of his lyric poems and short stories, which were beautiful.

On some days the wheeler-dealer poet Edouard Roditi stopped by. He looked a little bit like Dracula as played by Bela Lugosi in the movies. Paul Goodman, who was fond of Edouard, said he was the only person he'd ever met who could "camp" in five languages. Edouard was indeed terribly funny and loved to give the impression of being wicked, which of course he wasn't. The instant he stepped into the office he proceeded to tease the editors in the most extravagant ways. He would tell Charles, who was a health fanatic, not to get near him, since he still carried a touch of the oldest disease in the world. "Just a few cocci linger, my dear." Edouard had a talent for leering. Because he thought Roditi was a good translator, Breton allowed him to translate many of his poems, and Charles decided to make a special publication of them in a series to be called View Editions.

The 1946 Spring issue was devoted completely to Marcel Duchamp; I had been picking up material for this from various sources ever since I began work. Without doubt it was the most ambitious project Charles had yet attempted. It would be difficult to explain to anyone who has not been enthralled by Duchamp's audacity and wit why it is that he occupies such an extraordinary position in the history of modern art. For those who feel "committed" to an avant-garde, Duchamp is regarded as a secular deity. I numbered myself among his worshippers, although, considering his sense of fun, Duchamp should *not* have become a sacred cow.

My feelings about Surrealism were stronger than ever, perhaps because my need to "believe," as when I joined the Young Communist League, might have been a substitute for my discarded Roman Catholicism. Perhaps my addiction to Freud and Surrealism was yet another substitute. I was not certain of that, but I did know that I could not learn anything without active participation. This required belief.

Meeting Breton in the *View* office the day he brought in his essay on Duchamp was for me a religious experience. He refused to speak English; I was tongue-tied. But an odd thing happened: as he spoke (and his low voice and solemn face were awe-inspiring), I seemed to apprehend everything he was saying. Was my school French perhaps coming to my rescue? I quite understand why he attracted artists to his movement, for he reminded me of a cardinal or some other prince of the Roman Church. The head was magnificent. The great shock of white hair and the large probing eyes combined to make you believe that he was indeed a leader, a chieftain, a pasha, a mandarin, a condottiere.

He spent most of his time during this appointment with Charles Ford, but I saw Breton again a few weeks later at an opening at the Pierre Matisse gallery. I was puzzling over an object in a shallow box, a profile of George Washington made of what I thought was white cotton batting streaked with red and blue stripes. M. Breton was standing nearby with a trace of a smile on his otherwise grave countenance. He was friendly and spoke in French of Duchamp's object, which I suddenly realized was made of Kotex! For whatever reason I blushed. I felt genuinely embarrassed but suspected that Breton was pleased, since he advocated shock and surprise and I was registering both.

Pierre Matisse and his wife, Tini, moved among the people at the *vernissage* as though it were a party in their apartment. Like most of the women who were in attendance, Madame Matisse was very handsome and stylish. Unlike the other women, however, she did not cut a figure; her clothes were simple and cunningly made, whereas Madame Breton (known as an artist by the name of Jacqueline Lamba) wore striking Navaho beads and slippers, a brightly colored thick string to keep her hair in place, and a dress that might be Mexican. Similar attire was affected by other women, including Jeanne Reynal, Mrs. Arshile Gorky, the wealthy painter Ethel Schwabacher, the ambassadress from Brazil known as Maria and the sculptor Mary Callery. Most wore extraordinary jewelry—Mrs. Bernard Reis had on a huge necklace by Calder and carried a delicate silver lorgnette. I had never seen women quite like them. They seemed to have total self-possession, and moved with ease while holding themselves erect. They did not have conventional coiffures, but, for all that, looked very well groomed. Almost everyone spoke French. Many of the men were artists, and thus I met for the first time Yves Tanguy and his wife, as well as Kay Sage, Matta, Zadkine, Eugene Berman, Jacques Lipchitz, William Stanley Hayter, Max Ernst and many others.

I saw a good deal of Marcel Duchamp in the weeks preceding the next issue. We soon were using first names (even Waldemar liked Marcel the day he met him). He didn't talk much, loved to smoke a pipe, listened carefully when spoken to and had a wonderful enigmatic smile. One day I asked him how many people he thought *really* liked avant-garde art and he replied, "Oh, maybe ten in New York and one or two in New Jersey." He had a beautiful woman friend who was visiting him named Mary Reynolds, but I doubt she visited him in his extremely messy studio, which was over a beauty parlor on Fourteenth Street (the last line of Charles Ford's poem of homage to Duchamp called "Flag of Ecstasy" ends with "Marcel, wave!").

Even after many weeks with Duchamp, I could not decide whether he was being serious. His very earliest paintings did not seem to me distinguished; I was, however, fond of his work after 1911—*Nude Descending a Staircase, The King and Queen Surrounded by Swift Nudes* and, above all, the glass panels called *La Marieé Mise à Nu . . . (The Bride Stripped Bare by Her Bachelors),* and *The Watermill.* By 1919 Duchamp had given up painting and become "anti-art," a phrase I was not certain I understood. If he had indeed given up art, why then did he from time to time go on making what have been called "experiments" with, for instance, his "found objects"—a bicycle wheel, a coat hanger, a wine rack, a snow shovel. And his visual jokes, the latrine, the leather door, the bottle of air from Paris, the cage of sugar cubes, the "ready-mades," all of these accompanied by puns and hermetic drolleries. Why, if he was against art, was he so helpful to other artists and such collectors as Walter Arensberg, Katherine Dreier and Peggy Guggenheim? Certainly he maintained his friendships with the widest variety of painters, poets, sculptors, writers, even critics. Why did he collaborate with a movement like Surrealism? Breton firmly believed Duchamp was the greatest of them all. Our whole Duchamp issue was a rhapsody of praise.

Duchamp himself remained completely elusive. One day I met him at the elevator of the *View* office. He had arrived a bit earlier than I and was waiting for me. I noticed he had in his hand a pocket chess set, the black and white men arrayed against each other. I asked him whom he might be playing against and he answered, "Marcel versus Duchamp."

Not many people who passed through the office ever inquired how things were going. I suppose it was because people took it for granted that *View* was supported by Charles Ford's rich friends. One day Marcel *did* ask and I explained that we raised most of the money ourselves through advertising, circulation and gifts from artists. Duchamp later urged his friend Enrico Donati, the advertising executive, to get us still more perfume ads. He realized the Duchamp issue was the most expensive to date, the largest cost being a three-page centerfold with a cutout designed by the architect Frederick Kiesler. Nothing we had ever printed before caused so many problems or cost as much money as what Parker referred to as "Kiesler's Folly."

It was, I suppose, Duchamp's character that was so much admired. He dressed very conventionally and was not in the slightest way bohemian or pretentious. His courtesy was innate and sprang from a deep well of kindness. I could not imagine Marcel ever being cheap or rude, no doubt the reason he had friends among all classes of people.

I asked him one day why he did not work and was against working. "Lazy people like myself," he said, "cause the least trouble." But was Marcel really lazy? He went to enormous lengths to make certain that the Duchamp cover of *View*, a wine bottle with smoke coming out of it and his *Livret Militaire* pasted on it as though it were a label, would be technically possible for our printer. This was also true for the book jacket he was making for View Editions, a blown-up postcard of the Statue of Liberty with Breton's face pasted over Miss Liberty's visage.

Peter Lindamood, an old friend of both Charles and Parker from Columbus, Mississippi, has written a description of how he, Marcel and Breton decided at dinner to use the wine bottle that had been emptied to make the *View* cover. "Duchamp rigged up a smoke-pipe (now invisible) under the bottle, the pipe's end coincided with the bottle's neck and was held thereto by a clip extending from the cork's customary 'cove.'"

A sigh of relief went up after the Duchamp issue came out. The coterie surrounding Breton was pleased—something that was not easy to accomplish considering that Breton had a quarterly of his own, *VVV*, beautifully printed, edited, and carefully managed on the practical level by Bernard and Becky Reis. Mrs. Reis herself carried *VVV* in a satchel to bookstores and galleries to avoid commercial distribution. Bernard Reis, the accountant, handled the money-raising efficiently and prudently. The concern of the Reises for all the European "artists in exile" was admirable. Max Ernst sometimes lived with them for weeks on end, and many of the others were house guests until they had found accommodations of their own. Their concern was particularly noticeable at the large benefit show for French Refugee Aid, for which Duchamp made a dramatic labyrinth of string. The Reises' good sense and organizational talents earned them great affection among the European artists.

Despite the Duchamp issue, Breton was not altogether convinced that *View* was up to his standards. He at best tolerated it. He did not, for instance, much approve of Neo-Romantics like Berman, Leonid, Bérard, Tchelitchew or Parker Tyler. Nor did he approve of jazz. Certainly I thought he was suspicious of Charles Ford, since Breton had extremely rigorous sexual ideas, among them a strong antihomosexual bias. Breton was a snob and thought Americans were essentially crass and somewhat childish. He dismissed Robert Motherwell after their first few months of friendship as *"un naif,"* referring to him ironically as *"le petit philosophe."* Motherwell's intellectual pretensions did not sit well on Breton's very high brow. He was also quite upset with the fact that his wife, Jacqueline Lamba, was keeping company with the sculptor and co-editor of *VVV*, David Hare. The View Editions volume of Breton's poems was called, using a quotation from Goethe, *Young Cherry Trees Secured Against Hares.* Wiseacres repeated the word "hares" and said, "*Correspondence?*"—a pet Surrealist word taken from Baudelaire. Breton was very sad about the break-up with his wife, but soon after he found a pleasant new woman friend.

I did not meet one of our contributing editors, Paul Bowles, until we began work on Volume 5, Number 2 of *View*. This issue was called "Tropical Americans." Paul was invited to be guest editor because he had been living in the Caribbean, Mexico and other places in Latin America and knew that part of the world from an angle peculiarly his own. Eschewing politics, journalism, so-called objectivity, Bowles wrote in his foreword, "The aim of this issue of *View* is to present a poetically apt version of life as it is lived by the peoples of Tropical America." He was particularly interested in "the existence, alongside the Church, of a widespread system of practical magic . . . which keeps the minds of its participants in a healthy state of pesonalized anarchy."

Looking at him in his finely tailored suit and custom-made shoes, seeing the high, clear color of his complexion—a Hollywood pinkish tan—and the blond hair cut close to the head, and above all, noticing the neatness of his every gesture and movement, it would have been hard to guess that here was a man who loathed modern "civilization" and spent as much time as he could among primitive people, the less civilized the better. I can think of no one I've met who seemed more of a dandy. I'm thinking particularly of the dandies of Paris, circa 1830, such as Petrus Borel, Alfred de Musset and other members of *"le Cénacle."* Paul was neither foppish nor bizarre, being too practical and hard-working to waste his time on fripperies. That a composer of some repute should also be a linguist, an amateur anthropologist, a serious writer and a performing musician was, for me, impressive. Little wonder that the entire "Tropical Americans" issue was both original and exciting. The Surrealists were also impressed, probably because of Breton's friendship with Claude Lévi-Strauss, who worked with him on the Free French Radio and liked what Paul had put together. After all, had he not written the celebrated *Triste Tropiques?*

3

*T*HE FIGHTING IN EUROPE WAS IN ITS FINAL STAGES AND I BEGAN TO SUSPECT that many of the European artists would return home. I couldn't imagine Breton continuing to live in New York City; he remained totally French, untouched by his residence in America, almost as though he had never left Paris. He still would not learn to speak English for fear it would corrupt the perfection of his written French—a curious notion, but Breton believed it. William Carlos Williams maintained that Breton wrote the classic French of a Racine or a Pascal. I would have been a little dubious of this had Edouard Roditi not supported the same opinion in his own fashion. "It's awfully classy, such awfully classy French," he remarked one day.

Other artists, such as Léger, regarded their stay as little more than a long visit. The pickings were not as yet very good. Poor Mondrian lived in a cold-water flat, helped by friends like Harry Holtzman and Katherine Dreier. His pictures were emerging slowly; sales were occasional. André Masson, with his wife and two children, lived in Connecticut near the Calders and other artists of a vanguard persuasion. But he was having a difficult time. Curt Valentine was paying him $300 a month in advance of future sales and Louisa Calder was sometimes helpful. His disturbingly Surrealist images of this period were not to the liking of many collectors. On top of that, Masson was so uncomfortable in America that he never learned a word of English.

But my presentiments about the Europeans were fleeting, for life at

View was a daily delight. My friend Waldemar Hansen had quit his job at New Jersey Zinc and persisted as a poet even though dissatisfied with what he was writing. He joined a poetry workshop directed by John Malcolm Brinnin, whose work he did not particularly approve of or like, but in truth Brinnin was a fine teacher and a distinguished poet. I admired Waldemar's determination to improve, since he was convinced that expert technical means guaranteed the composition of good verse. The bravura of W. H. Auden dazzled him. "Automatic writing, free association, accident and all the rest of the Surrealist goings-on are silly nonsense," Waldemar would declare with some heat. "It's empty-headed prattling!" Much later I discovered that Auden quite shared this opinion and thought Breton was an ass.

In June 1945, Charles Ford decided *View* would become a monthly, beginning with the October issue. The art galleries were closed for the summer. Not being able to go abroad, most of the artists and the people who surrounded them moved to the Hamptons. Matta had a house in Amagansett, Motherwell lived in East Hampton and the Pollocks had their little farmhouse in the Springs. May and Harold Rosenberg had a house not far from the Pollocks. Peggy Guggenheim was everybody's house guest, since she did not like renting. Charles Ford and Pavel Tchelitchew had a guest house on the estate of Alice De Lamar, who was reputed to be the richest woman in the world, but no one knew of her because she employed a public relations expert to prevent her name from appearing anywhere.

It was easy to keep the *View* office open mornings, but my salary in those summer months had diminished to a trickle and I had to find fresh ways to survive. Luckily, I met William Lieberman, a tall, blond, neat young man with a tendency to giggle. He worked for Alfred Barr at the Museum of Modern Art, holding the position of assistant curator in drawings and prints. He had learned much of what he knew from Paul Sachs, the great professor in the graduate school of fine arts at Harvard. Knowing I was hard up, he took me to meet a former Swarthmore friend, Diana Dodge, a charming girl who was very fond of Billy. She had prepared us a little dinner. Diana had an admirer of a kind, a married man named Mel Pitzele, who joined us shortly after we arrived. During dinner Diana said that Pitzele was interested in collecting art. Indeed, he was in a position to do so, since he was a highly paid editor and executive of *Business Week* and owned a fine town house in Henderson Place next door to Edmund and Mary (McCarthy) Wilson. Perhaps we could give him advice as to what was available at good prices? I told him of a few nice pictures we had at the *View* office, including the wonderful *Icarus*, an oil painting by Kurt Seligmann that he did later buy, helping *View*'s exchequer. However, what fascinated me more than anything else during the evening was to learn over our coffee that both Diana and Billy had been students of W. H. Auden at Swarthmore and that Billy had become a good friend of his, as later I did.

The upshot of the little party was that Mel Pitzele, using his influence, got me a part-time job working in an office that published a labor-management newsletter. The job entailed reading large batches of labor newspapers and clipping items of special interest to subscribers. The subscribers, needless to say, were mostly on the managerial side, anxious to be informed about the unions and their discontents. Luckily the job did not last long; I became exceedingly bored.

At last the summer was over. The chilly winds of September brought both the art world and high society back to Manhattan; the new season was in full swing. Edouard Roditi appeared in the office in his usual black suit, resembling a disdainful floor manager at Cartier's. In those days one said Cartier's, pronouncing the hard *"er"* sound.

"I see," Edouard declared, "that you have a review *right under* an article of mine of that tiny novella called—ha!—*Age of Thunder*." (He was referring to a book by Frederick Prokosch.) "I was pleased to see Marius Bewley's review was less than approving.

"Did I ever tell you, my dears," he went on, "of the time I was sitting with a friend having coffee in Florian's, when suddenly upon looking up across the Piazza San Marco I saw this tall figure, wearing impeccable white Bermudas, sneakers and a short-sleeved shirt with a small lizard design sewn over the breast pocket, rushing toward the vaporetto stop swinging a tennis racket? The following jingle issued instantly from my mouth: 'How posh / Of Prokosch / To play tennis / In Venice!' "

Edouard looked pleased with himself, smiling like a naughty satyr. "Surely," commented Parker, "you could choose a better bête noire than Prokosch."

"Oh," replied Edouard, "it isn't his talent that bothers me; it's his success."

The afternoon of that same day Tennessee Williams paid a visit. We were all gathered in Charles Ford's room, Charles sitting on his desk, a pile of books to be reviewed at his side, while in his hand he held a copy of *Nevertheless* by Marianne Moore. "Who," he was asking, "should write a piece about this?"

Tennessee spoke up. "You know, Charlie," he said, "I think I could do a real nice review of Marianne Moore."

Charles looked at him in astonishment and then in deepest Columbus, Mississippi, drawl he said, "Why, Tinn, can yew *read?*"

There was silence.

"No, my dear," he continued, "this goes to our best reviewer, Marius Bewley, who studied in Cambridge, England."

Many of our contributors enjoyed bringing their drawings or manuscripts to the office in person, and as a result, the ambience tended to be lively; new friendships were established. The October issue emphasized "Americana" with another essay by Marius Bewley concerning what he called the "American macabre." Lowell Naeve, a conscientious objector who was in a federal prison, described what it was like to be in solitary confinement for refusing to do any work except his own work as an artist. There was a poem by Wallace Stevens, an article about Florine Stettheimer by the delightful elderly art critic Henry McBride and a story by James T. Farrell. Little did we know that the Farrell story, "Lunch Hour: 1923," would be the cause of Breton's severing all future relations with *View*. Nor could we have known that Breton would be so angry when he heard André Masson was going to do a cover design that he demanded that Masson not collaborate with us. Masson, however, paid no attention to Breton's orders and contributed his design anyway. They never spoke to each other again during their lifetimes.

Charles Ford had been down to Chinatown and saw a sign that read PHOTOGRAPH YOUR INJURIES AT ONCE. Under this was the message, "You cannot photograph your pain but you can photograph the wound. Time heals everything, so photograph it now." The proprietor of the shop was a Mr. A. J. Drummond, whose profession it was to document accidents, especially personal injuries. Mr. Drummond was pleased to give a few samples of his craft to our magazine. Two were used on the page of the Farrell story. They depicted a girl with a gash over her right eye and a nasty wound above her right knee. What the photographs had to do with the story, I do not know. At any rate, I found them unpleasant but moving.

Breton's reaction was one of angry distaste. He let us know that *View* was "antiwoman," that such images depicted woman in a disgusting light and that this was contrary to the most basic tenets of Surrealism, by which Woman is at all times to be exalted. Parker took Breton's reaction more seriously than Charles, who simply dismissed the charge as capricious. "How," asked Parker, "could Breton maintain that *View* is antiwoman when half the world's population and half our readers are female?" I pointed out that throughout Breton's poetry the ideal of woman is stressed repeatedly. "But," said Parker, "it is Breton who asks the question of who could love Ophelia after she went mad. I am not really convinced that he loved his character Nadja, whose madness he extols."

I was considerably shaken by this small incident because it caused me to think more carefully about Breton's constantly shifting yet intransigent attitudes. I was told, for instance, that there was a rift between Breton and Max Ernst, which had not as yet been publicly manifested. Kurt Seligmann was tolerated because his source material was useful, but I could not see why he was not as strongly entrenched as Yves Tanguy. As for Breton's policies, I didn't quite know where he stood. Anti-Stalinist, of course, but in what ways he supported the Trotskyites or how seriously he was committed to *any* political program, I was unsure.

My journals of this period are full of sketches of other contributors as I perceived them on Fifty-third Street and gradually came to know them socially. The "ideas" put forth in some of these pages are a record of ruminations about the world, politics, literature and art as they were generally discussed and argued among this tiny group of "literati" in which I moved.

Journal, October 1945

Nicolas Calas has been contributing regularly to the magazine since it first began. To an early issue he had contributed a derisive polemic against Dali called "I Say His Flies Are Ersatz." He had associated with Breton in Paris in the late thirties, before expatriating himself from Greece and Europe to live permanently in New York. In Paris he published a book called *Foyers d'Incendie* that was highly thought of by the Surrealists, and the legend had grown up that Calas occupied the position of *éminence grise* to Breton. (Anti-Surrealists call Breton the "black pope.") If one were to ask me what a Surrealist looked like, I think I would point to Nico. He is extremely tall and lanky and makes nervous movements when excited. At such moments his speech accelerates and occasionally hits a falsetto note. When he makes a pun or a witty remark he chuckles loudly and looks you straight in the eye to see (a) if you got it, and (b) if you enjoyed it. When Nico's speech reaches its highest velocity he spits slightly, which has caused Tchelitchew to call him "The Camel."

At the moment Nico has the attention of Florence Codman, a rich lady who lives in Maine. She is publishing his second book of essays, called *Confound the Wise*. I admire her for doing so because the essays are audacious, sometimes bizarre, but the prose style is somewhat clogged; although the words are in English, the thought seems either French or Greek. Gossip has it that Breton does not approve of Calas' continuing bacherlorhood. (I saw him recently in an all-male bar. At one point he put down his beer and took a small, live green snake out of his pocket, which he said was a pet.) Others in the know say Calas is about to marry a Russian girl named Lolya, who works as a psychologist. She is apparently extremely intelligent and adores Nico.

Diary

Now the war is over. Our lives can never again be the same; people everywhere must live with the A-bomb. What Paul Goodman fears most is that one will go off "accidentally," just as so many places were "accidentally" bombed in Italy (Monte Cassino) because orders were misunderstood due to incorrect spelling or pronunciation of names.

When I went downstairs yesterday to visit with Martha Mayer and Betty Cage, Martha had closed herself in her bedroom to be alone. She is sad because she has learned that her dear friend Robert Frost was killed in action some months back. He was such a nice person and so young.

I also had learned from George Poole of the death of a special friend, Dino Casagrande. Before he went to the war he had worked in the Lackawanna Steel Plant as a furnace cleaner—a dangerous and unpleasant job that required the wearing of a thick asbestos suit and mask, since the furnaces, even after they are emptied of molten metal, can be cooled only partially for cleaning. Dino wanted to be a composer of popular songs and asked me to write some lyrics for him, a talent it turned out I did not possess. He worked in the ovens of the steel plant because the pay was high and he had a mother and sisters to support. The irony of Dino's death is that he was serving in the tank corps and was burned alive in an armored tank that had been hit.

Journal, October 1945

Edouard Roditi announced that Breton had managed to pull another rabbit out of his hat. "He is ecstatic about the pictures of Arshile Gorky." I went to see them at Julien Levy's gallery, a Duchamp-Breton stronghold. Gorky's new work now looked to me like Miró's, but I was instantly told that it was "anthropomorphic" and that the images were conceived from nature: birds and insects, strange flora and fauna.

Julien Levy reminds me of Antonin Artaud, probably because I had seen a photograph of Julien with a shaved head, which Berenice Abbott had taken years before in Paris. He is intelligent and handsome, with a profile rivaling that of the great actor John Barrymore. It was Julien who explained Gorky's great talents, after which I told him I had heard that he did fortune-telling with Tarot cards—a parlor game that all the Surrealists are doing now.

"Ouspensky," said Julien, "thinks that the Tarot provides an occasion for philosophizing." He then offered to read my fortune, which made me feel uneasy. I needn't have been, for my fortune didn't seem to me much different from a tea-leaf reading. The symbols on the cards are, however, fascinating.

Journal, October 1945

Our activity has been doubled because we have been invited to select an exhibition called *The Fantastic in Modern Art* for a new gallery on East Fifty-fifth Street, the Hugo. It is managed by Alexander Iolas, who, after his ruinous pratfall with the De Cuevas ballet, has retired from dancing and taken for a partner in this new venture a Madame Hugo, who has financial resources and who is also known as the Duchess de Gramont. Iolas wants a splashy, controversial opening, and it seems to him that *View* might be the right sponsor. Kiesler is to do the installation, with a sculpture of a horse as seen from below attached to the ceiling. The selection is a mixed bag that includes the Neo-Romantics, Lam, Léger, Georgia O'Keeffe, Noguchi, Seligmann, Zadkine, and such oddities as Charles Ford's mother, Gertrude Cato and a boyfriend from Columbus, Mississippi, Kennedy Blanchard. I personally think there are too many things in the show and that the viewpoint is too disparate to make any sort of clear statement.

Iolas was once painted by his friend Leonor Fini—a portrait that depicts him as more beautiful than Ganymede—and he is convinced that that is how he still looks. He is immensely vain, loves jewelry and wears extraordinary rings. He is also very Greek, and when one goes to his place on First Avenue, one forgets it's a cold-water flat, so struck is one by the number of gilt-framed mirrors and gilt cherubim on every wall. The furniture tends to be brocaded and gilded, the carpets Oriental. Iolas loves to entertain, and he cooks vast Greco-Italian meals full of pinenuts, feta cheese, black olives and black cherries. He prides himself on knowing everyone in the Great World and I suppose he does.

One day in the gallery Iolas asked me, Who is this Freud that people mention? I answered that he is an Austrian psychiatrist, whereupon he brightened and said, "Oh, I know who you mean. He is the little Jew from Vienna who my friend Princess Bonaparte has patronized!"

Journal, October 1945

I have been running faster and faster. The *Fantastic* exhibition opens November 15 and meanwhile we are behind schedule. Picking up photographic material has been at times frustrating; for instance, dancing attention on the unpleasant Edith Halpert at the Downtown gallery to obtain Harnett photos (Roditi has done an excellent article on William Harnett, whom he calls an "American Necromantic"). Of course, the good side of daily gallery rounds is the amount of art one sees. It is particularly good for me, since I neither draw nor paint, and so-called art appreciation inevitably has to do with directly experiencing works of art and memorizing them. I have, however, again begun studying art history by attending the lectures of Meyer Schapiro at the New School. There are times when I feel painfully ignorant, and listening to him has given me the stimulus to fuller and better reading. For instance, I am enjoying and learning from Erwin Panofsky's *Abbot Suger: On the Abbey-Church of St.-Denis and its Art Treasures*. Schapiro is generous in supplying his auditors with an excellent list of supplementary books, although I feel that what I get from his lectures is material uniquely his own.

And what a spellbinder he is! I listen to him the way I used to listen to the storyteller in the children's room of the Buffalo Public Library. He refers to notes rarely and only reads from a book when there is a necessary quotation. Meanwhile, he uses two magic-lantern screens on which to show his slides. Often the slides will indicate several details of one painting. By this method I have learned better how to "read" pictures, how to relate the details to the whole and, above all, where symbols are utilized, what it is they mean. I suppose Schapiro is more interested in the "subject matter" of pictures, statues and architecture than he is in their "formal" aspects. But one is quickly made aware that he is more than a historian, more than an iconologist, that his aesthetic sense is keen and sophisticated. I long to become a friend of his. Already he has shown warmth upon hearing I work at *View*; he has been a contributor and is very close to Parker Tyler.

I have been going often to Curt Valentine at 32 East Fifty-seventh Street and to Marian Willard, who occupies the rooms adjacent. Miss Willard (in private life Mrs. Dan Johnson) is the enthusiastic sponsor of two American painters, Mark Tobey and Morris Graves (neither of whom I appreciate), and a remarkable sculptor named David Smith, whose work reminds me of the Spaniard Julio González. The Valentine gallery is more European and glamorous. Here one finds Picasso, Gris, Lipchitz, Moore and huge amounts of Paul Klee. Mr. Valentine has a couple of enthusiasms I agree with. One is for André Masson and the other is for Alexander Calder. But the breadth of his taste is remarkable. He is an authority on German Expressionist painting and sculpture and carries a large stock of such art. Talking with Curt, who seems always ready for a good chat, is a pleasure because he's amusing and informative and full of Middle-European charm. Little wonder that Alfred Barr and many of the members of the Museum of Modern Art's board of trustees heed his suggestions as to what they should acquire. He has a special talent for making catalogues, and aside from publishing *éditions de luxe* of prints by artists he represents, the little catalogues are in themselves works of the printer's art.

Even going back still again to the awful Edith Halpert—she had given me a wrong photograph—I cannot help but respect her as a knowledgeable dealer. Despite her crude and, for me, totally unsympathetic personality, she simply knows more about American folk art than any other person in the field. It takes a certain kind of eye to discern the value of such "magic realist" painters of the nineteenth century as John Peto and Harnett. I know only one other person with a similar "eye," the collector Paul Magriel.

The opening of the Hugo gallery could not have been more gala. Naturally the world of the ballet turned out, as much for Tchelitchew as for Iolas. The European dancers revere Tchelitchew and regard him as the greatest of all designers for the ballet. No doubt, too, this is why one of Tchelitchew's closest friends is the rich balletomaine Lincoln Kirstein. George Balanchine is also an old friend. It was a pleasure to see up close the ballerina Tamara Toumanova, who dotes on Tchelitchew, as do other dancers. And, indeed, he is sweetly cordial to them.

I finally met Tchelitchew's friend Edelgey Dinshaw. Thin, tall, dark-skinned, he seemed more like a rare species of gazelle than a person. His eyes are abnormally large, deerlike, and his nostrils seemed to tremble. He was perfectly dressed in a black silk suit.

"What beautiful shoes you are wearing," I said.

He glanced down at them critically and answered, "Is it true. They are very beautiful. But in order to have such shoes I must go to immense trouble because I have such delicate feet. I try to have shoes as close to ballet slippers as possible. But I know quite well that I cannot walk on the streets of the city with such slippers. At last I was so fortunate as to find a bootmaker in London who appreciates my problem. He is more than a bootmaker. He is a sculptor, for he makes what they call lasts of plaster of my feet. Then with considerable care he molds the leather about the lasts."

"They seem to be very lightweight," I observed.

"They are. They are very light. Shoes must be made with a special kid so that I am only barely aware that I am wearing any shoes at all." He lowered his eyes and gave me a delicate smile as though he were a character in an Indian print.

The architect Frederick Kiesler was on hand, accepting homage from the guests, who kept exclaiming on the brilliance of his installation and the splayed horse on the ceiling. He is extremely short, seemingly less than five feet, but Napoleonic in manner. He doesn't converse, he announces whatever it is he has to say. This impresses almost everyone he meets and he is referred to as the "great architect Kiesler." I feel skeptical because to my knowledge he's never done a building with the exception of the Janis shoe-store façade in Buffalo.

Once again the differences between the artistic tendencies now prevalent were buried at this *vernissage.* This celebrated ballet designer Eugene Berman bowed cordially to Surrealist rivals, gravely kissed Miss Guggenheim's hand (one half inch above the flesh) and respectfully shook the hand of Nico Calas. The Europeans remain civil even when they detest each other.

Of all the artists I have come to know, the one I am most fond of is Kurt Seligmann. It is a joy to visit him in his studio at 40 West Fortieth Street (the same building where Florine Stettheimer used to have hers) high above Bryant Park. It is a studio with gigantic windows, and the park below, with its greensward, fountain, allées of trees leading to the lovely terrace of the Public Library, seems more Parisian than New York. He and his wife, Arlette, who is the neice of Wildenstein, both live and work in the studio. In one corner Kurt has a large press for making etchings, a technique at which he is highly proficient. In another space he does his oil painting. One wall is completely covered with shelves, upon which are grouped hundreds of books—old and strange editions dealing largely with alchemy, astrology, and other forms of prescientific injury. Seligmann has spent years collecting these volumes, many of which are extremely rare. His attitude toward superstition is clinical; he studies the life and work of magicians in the same way he might study the wing of a fruit fly under a microscope. Yet he is aware of the possible truths a Paracelsus or an Agrippa might be telling him, as he would be of the truths in a myth or fairy story. No one more than Seligmann, among the Surrealists, has been so in touch with "the marvelous."

One of Kurt's dearest friends is Meyer Schapiro, who is impressed by Kurt's scholarship and enthusiasm in a field that is of the highest value to art historical studies. I am delighted to learn that the two of them are collaborating on a book—text and pictures—dealing with the myth of Oedipus.

Arlette Seligmann offers me tea and candy whenever I visit. Kurt tells me stories and once again I have the delicious feeling of being a child listening to one of my older sisters repeating the tale of Jack and the Beanstalk or the Three Bears. Except that Kurt's stories are apt to be hair raising, dealing as they do in diabolism, witchcraft, incest, blood sacrifice, two-headed monsters, the evil eye and other shockers.

Diary, October 1945

Thank God I keep a dark-blue suit jacket, gray flannel trousers and my brown Brooks Brothers oxfords in decent shape. My wardrobe grows ever more meager, but with my blue-and-gray uniform (Waldemar Hansen wears similar attire) it is possible to go into society. And go into it I do, for as in the I.L.G.W.U. (garment workers') musical, I must "sing for my supper." I suppose both Waldemar and I are amusing and get invited out to dinner as often as we do for our entertainment potential. Waldemar is good for at least an hour of laughs and I am an inveterate gossip. This doesn't bother me, since people never tell me they don't want to hear the latest "dish" and everybody seems to want to tell *me* things they ought not to. Since I seem to see a lot of people who tell me many things, I sometimes am described as "central clearing." But like all good gossips, I *do* have a sense of what *not* to tell.

We are publishing an editorial in the next issue of *View*, on the subject of the bad conduct of a poet I admire, Ezra Pound. The editors state that inasmuch as Pound's behavior was political and not aesthetic, he must take the consequences due a traitor and a fascist. I find this opinion so painful that I cannot discuss the case of the poet. It is said he is crazy. I hope so, I cannot bear to see him executed.

Letter from Buffalo friend George Poole, October 1945

Do you think dreams are class-determined? For instance, when the really poor have dreams, do they dream of eating? Are their nightmares filled with dread of cold, of exposure, of sickness and death? Or do you think their anxieties are so great that they don't bother to dream? Maybe they just black out when they go to sleep.

When I look at Surrealist pictures, quite aside from their aesthetic merit, it seems to me that they reveal a world of luxurious pain and pleasure, even the fears depicted are rather well cushioned. I don't think any Surrealist can top the nightmare horrors of the real world—Hitler's death camps, Stalin's prisons, the bombing of Hiroshima.

Breton's idea of bringing the Conscious and the Unconscious into unity implies a world made up of good children and bad children, estranged from nature and reality. Little wonder Freud thinks the Surrealists are eccentric abscurantists.

You understand, my dear John, it is their ideology and political silliness that makes me impatient. But then, no one takes them seriously on this level. Nor does it interfere with my delight when seeing a Magritte or an Ernst.

> Blessings!
> George

Journal, October 1945

Alice De Lamar thought it would be nice if the fifth birthday of *View* was to be celebrated on her estate in Weston, Connecticut. Charles Ford thought it a wonderful notion, and since it would be near Halloween, the celebration should be a costume ball with Tchelitchew creating the decorations. Miss De Lemar had had one of the barns completely renovated, putting in a kitchen, bathrooms and a hardwood floor for dancing. About two hundred people were invited, but even more came. The party began at ten. In a field near the barn a gigantic bonfire was lighted that could be seen from some distance and made it easy for the guests to find their way. Another field was devoted to parking. The dance band was perfect—musicians chosen by Barry Ulanov. Tchelitchew used corn stalks and blades of wheat and paper streamers to make the place seem a setting for a rustic ballet. On one wall he created a glorious paper owl.

The costumes were bizarre—some beautiful, others hilarious: two boys arrived on roller skates dressed in nuns' habits; ten young men and women made an entrance single file all dressed as Santa Claus. My costume was demure by comparison; I was impersonating Alfred de Musset and I wore a laurel wreath on my head—since I wanted to look attractive rather than eccentric. I was standing near the door when suddenly there was a roll of drums and a large man in pirate's clothes with a huge plumed hat and a frightening skeleton face mask appeared. "Oh, Death!" I shouted, "Thou comest when least we expect thee." There was applause and music. When Peggy Guggenheim whirled by, wearing a Venetian gown with a tricorn on her head, the skirt billowed out revealing not only her bare legs but also the fact that she had absolutely nothing on beneath her dress. Charles Ford and Parker Tyler, taking their cue from Tchelitchew's beautiful drawings for *Hide and Seek*, were dressed as leaf children, with finishing touches by Tchelitchew.

At about three in the morning a delicious supper was served. People were getting more and more drunk. Marius Bewley, impersonating a British magistrate, weaved past me, his wig askew.

At six in the morning I passed out, and when I woke up, I found myself in one of Alice De Lamar's guest cottages. Later that day I asked Parker if he knew who most of the guests were and he told me that many were the same people who attended the jazz concert. "Charles knows all the free-floating, very rich internationals."

Journal, October 1945

Thinking over George Poole's letter on the insubstantiality of Surrealist politics (it cannot be denied that Breton engaged himself in flurries of political polemic from 1930 on, largely directed against the Communist party members who were formerly Surrealist, such as Tzara and Aragon), I still hold to their notions of the sublime, their desire for *le merveilleux*. It is Imagination, man's power to imagine, that makes living in society, any society, possible. I think what Paul Goodman says about doing away with "intolerable biological deprivation and spiritual impoverishment" through what he calls "creative cooperative production" is the right and humane solution to our social woes.

The war brought about no positive good. It is only a negative good that fascism was destroyed, but this is hardly balanced by all of Eastern Europe being taken over by the USSR. Society as we know it is unlikely to improve; the atom bomb gives infinitely greater power to corporate establishments; the United States is richer than ever; there are more billionaires to do mischief.

Perhaps Goodman's utopian schemes for a decent society will not be realized, but at least he is making suggestions for improvement.

Letter to George Poole

I'm afraid your charming idea about the possibility of dreams being "class-determined" simply won't do. Apparently scientists know quite a bit about dreaming and the biological basis for sleep. All human organisms dream and for good physiological reasons. I suppose the question of interpreting these dreams is subject to considerable variation from culture to culture. Purely empirical scientists probably think nightmares are a result of the wires upstairs getting crossed. Being a Freudian myself, I believe dreams *can* be interpreted, and do cast light on our motives as well as our actions. It is in this sense that the Surrealists insist that the daytime and the nighttime (dreaming and wakefulness) should interpenetrate. The irrational aspects of human nature are not to be despised, since the deepest source of creativity resides in the irrational. Man cannot be free until he recognizes this power, the vitality inherent in irrationality.

I'll admit this is a difficult view to uphold, since on a practical level we have seen the rise to power of such maniacs as Hitler, Mussolini and Stalin, to name a few. The Ku Klux Klan, the anti-Semites, the Daughters of the American Revolution, are all quite crazed and destructive, sometimes wildly so.

Of course, Breton and his followers are aware of this and are stringently against fascism and totalitarianism. In fact, I think, politically speaking, Surrealism arose as a protest against the increasingly rigid powers of governments and the suppression of individuality. I am sure a phrase like Benjamin Peret's, "I affirm that a suicide is more beautiful than a peace treaty," sets your teeth on edge and, without a proper context, mine too. But think of the sort of "peace" treaties that were made after World War I, and now the dumb notions of "total victory" after World War II. I can't see how we won't have more wars in the near future (dreadful ones) when Rational, Clear-minded, Prudent politicians throw their weight around. It is always amazing that a handful of people can literally decide the fate of millions upon millions of other people. What in the world did a man like President Truman mean when he said he was taking "full responsibility" for dropping the

A-bomb on Hiroshima? Is it a *rational* statement? One can't help but remember Gertrude Stein's line in *Four Saints*: "If it were possible to kill four million Chinamen by pushing a button, would it be done?" The answer is perfect: "Saint Theresa not interested."

Come what may, I continue to feel close to Breton's ideas. They are an extreme response to the wretched world in which we live.

Best wishes,
John

Journal

Waldemar Hansen and I try not to be glum about not having enough money. We barely get the rent together each month. Some days we sponge meals from Betty Cage; at other times we eat rice and onions. Waldemar has become an excellent cook—when he has the right ingredients.

I am having a bad time with my teeth but am terrified to go to a public clinic. I have gone to a dentist up the street from where I live but stopped going when I realized that the doctor had only partial vision in both eyes. I get bad toothaches that eventually go away.

Both Waldemar and I are underweight, which makes us pleasant to look at but leaves us vulnerable to colds and other minor ailments.

Diary

The problem of eating dinners has been solved by organizing our invitations better. I have made a new friend, a novelist, Charles Yale Harrison (one of his books is called *Seven Red Sundays*), who has been inviting me rather regularly for dinner. Harrison was for many years a publicity director for the American Federation of Labor. He is passionately anti-Stalinist and religious about psychoanalysis. He believes his therapist, a Dr. Edmond Bergler, is a genius who can "cure" anybody of neurosis. Bergler is not a strict Freudian, since he bases his theory of neurosis on breast traumas. (I wonder, of course, about people who were bottle-fed.) Charles Yale Harrison is a nonstop talker and loves a captive audience. When I leave his house I am exhausted by the length and loudness of his monologues—but he and his wife, Eva, are such good cooks!

Two invitations that delighted me were an evening party given by Muriel Draper and a lecture-tea in the drawing room of the very rich Mrs. Murray Crane.

Mrs. Draper is the mother of a well-known tap dancer, Paul Draper. She is an ardent member or possibly "fellow traveler" of the Communist party and lives with high elegance in her town house on lower Lexington Avenue. Before she took up politics, Mrs. Draper was a hostess to musicians, and her musical soirées were famous. She's written a charming book, *Music at Midnight,* about her friendships with artists.

It was to hear the historian Dr. Edgar Windt lecture on Veronese that I went to Mrs. Crane's. The apartment is gigantic; the drawing room, with its splendid French furniture and pictures, must be about sixty feet long. It was an occasion for me, since I have always wondered what a true *salon* would be like. This one seemed very much like the ones described by Proust, although Mrs. Crane is rather more of a blue-stocking than either Madame Verdurin or Oriane de Guermantes. The tea was delicious. Wonderful little thin sandwiches of watercress. (I could have eaten a whole plate of them and tried hard not to.)

Diary

Edouard Roditi, a sometime private dealer, having sold a few pictures as he does from time to time, invited me out for an evening of pub crawling. When we were seated on our bar stools at Red's, a saloon we all go to on Third Avenue at Fiftieth Street, Edouard asked me about my friend Waldemar Hansen. I explained that Waldemar was my protégé, meaning that when he was a student at Technical High School in Buffalo his English teacher was my friend, Reuel Denny, a poet. Denny decided to put Waldemar in touch with me and my group because of his ambition to write verse.

I then told him that Waldemar's mother is an English Jew who was born in London, the daughter of an East End rabbi. She has a pronounced cockney accent. The father was a gentile, a Dane who was a house painter. When the five Hansen children were very young he disappeared. The family was so poor that the mother had to accept charity at one time to keep it together. Waldemar, being a *Wunderkind,* was sent to Technical High School to learn chemistry, a subject in which he was so proficient that when he graduated he knew as much as if he had studied it at college. At the age of nineteen he was excused from military duty to work in a large chemical plant testing liquid viscosities, which somehow or other had to do with research in atomic fission. He did not tell me this until after the end of the war.

"But isn't Waldemar rather a difficult person to live with? It seems to me he's terribly opinionated," said Edouard.

I answered no, that he could be and was quite considerate to me, and except for an occasional depression, he was full of fun, stories, jokes, imitations. "He has a remarkable talent for getting acquainted with unlikely people," I said, "usually as bright and clever as himself. As for his disagreements with me, I like to argue as much as he does; so it makes for a lively home life."

Changing the subject, Edouard launched into funny diatribes against Harold Rosenberg, Nicolas Calas, Lionel Abel and Paul Goodman. Of Paul he said, "I quite believe Paul's boast that he never rewrites. How else can you explain his flat and boring prose style?" Of Lionel Abel he said, "Never, my dear, leave your wallet lying around when *that* one is in the house." Quoting Marianne Moore, he said of Calas that Nico moves his head with "compass-needle nervousness," exactly like Miss Moore's ostrich. And he declared Harold Rosenberg a visual illiterate.

Journal, December 1945

I have become friends with Ernst Beadle and his wife, Gina. They are unbelievably gifted photographers. Charles Ford put Ernst in touch with Mr. Brodovitch, the art director of *Harper's Bazaar*, which has led to work for the fashion magazines. Ernst does photos of jewels and precious stones. Gina is a fantasist.

Communication between *View* and its contacts in Europe seems to have become more voluminous. One outstanding person who has been written to and who has responded is Edith Sitwell. Her portraits by Pavel Tchelitchew are perhaps the finest he has done. They have been very close friends for several years. What will make the January issue particularly glamorous is Miss Sitwell's previously unpublished poem called "A Sleepy Tune" and more of her "Notes on Shakespeare." As a part of the View Editions series, Vanguard will publish her collection called *Green Song*, which has already appeared in England. But the greatest news of all is that she will be coming to New York in the near future. Two of Tchelitchew's other admirers will also be coming over from England, Peter Watson, the publisher of *Horizon* magazine, and Cecil Beaton.

I called on an editor at Schocken Books to see if they would advertise in *View*. Hannah Arendt interviewed me; her seriousness, her courtesy, her sad but lovely smile, are unforgettable. I wasn't surprised when I heard later that she is a philosopher who studied with Karl Jaspers and Martin Heidegger, and is herself a good writer. Two other extraordinary Germans that I have been to see are Helen and Kurt Wolff, who manage a small but distinguished firm called Pantheon Books, which is located on the south side of Washington Square. The books they produce are very handsome. I particularly like their editions of Constantin Guys' *Femmes Parisiennes* and *Fragonard's Drawings for Ariosto's "Orlando Furioso."*

Journal, December 1945

I feel *View* is slowly dropping the Surrealists and changing toward a Neo-Romantic attitude, but it is hard to define. Charles Ford is rather more catholic in his tastes than he would seem to be. He also has a strong bias toward anything "new," or what he thinks of as new. But his moods are mercurial and one cannot predict from day to day what they will be. He can be unspeakably rude on Tuesday, very kind on Wednesday, completely withdrawn on Thursday, full of fresh ideas and enthusiasm on Friday. He is quite capable of snubbing anyone who has fallen out of favor and makes no bones about being a snob. His attitude toward Lincoln Kirstein (who is back from Europe and the war) is one of condescension. I cannot imagine that Kirstein finds this amusing, since he is in his way a far more remarkable person than Charles, and even more complicated.

Peggy Guggenheim complained to me the other day that despite the fact she faithfully takes ads for her gallery in *View*, we never feature any of her contemporary American artists. I relayed this message to Charles.

"It's quite enough that the ads reproduce their pictures," quipped Charles.

"She feels," I continued, "that it's not quite fair."

Charles exploded. "Our editorial policy is not now and never will be influenced by our advertisers. Those artists of hers are simply not up to our standards. Furthermore, you might as well get it through your head that the people she pushes are terrible, especially that Motherwell, with his tinselly Parisian chic, and that crude Clyfford Still and that fraudulent Mark Rothko. And while I'm at it, you better know that I don't want to hear anything about her pet and your pal, Jackson Pollock."

"But how will we solve the problem? I don't want to lose Art of This Century and some of the other galleries that are complaining. You don't have to listen to their complaints. But I do." This was the first time I had ever stood up to Charles, in whose presence I feel invariably uneasy.

Charles gave me one of his Columbus, Mississippi, smiles. "You can solve the problem by featuring anyone you want in your column, which you will begin in the March issue." Turning back to his desk, he added, "Now vamoose, honey! Ah'm real busy."

Diary, December 1945

Christmas Eve produces in me the blackest of depressions. As usual, I went through tears, remorse, my sense of being useless and wicked. I feel abandoned and in a void. Poor Waldemar always wrings his hands in compassionate concern, but this time he said brightly, "John! I wouldn't worry so much about your acedia. Don't forget you told me that when you were a child at Camp Turner in the Alleghenies your spiritual advisor, the red-haired Father Hennessy, *promised* you that if you made a nightly novena at the shrine of Saint James—no matter what happened—you'd go straight to heaven!" This reminder gave me the giggles and off we went to an all-night Christmas party.

Journal, January 1946

I am so used to hearing Tchelitchew spoken of as probably the greatest living painter by Charles and Parker that I've become quite conditioned to believing it. Recently I found myself arguing this opinion rather more exaggeratedly than I should have.

"Do you mean to say," said my opponent, "that you think Tchelitchew is a greater painter than either Picasso or Matisse?"

The argument went on and on and I found myself upholding it simply to be perverse. Of course, I couldn't win such an argument. What I was doing, I daresay, was rationalizing the peculiar editorial policies of *View*, where the unspoken exclusions are quite obvious even to discreet subscribers. I don't feel comfortable about these prejudices, but on the other hand, perhaps this is what makes Charles' editorial oddities so interesting.

I agree that there is no such thing as serious American art except for perhaps Alexander Calder, Georgia O'Keeffe and Joseph Cornell.

I've seen no American abstract painting that can touch Kandinsky or Mondrian, who has lived the last few years of his life in New York. I like abstract art very much, but it seems to me that what Peggy is showing is messy and ugly. It's not as bad at the Betty Parsons gallery, but then there seems to me to be no "line" followed there. Betty seems to show almost anything that pleases her, a lot of it being eccentric and even crazy. As for American "regional" art, the sort of kitsch exposed at the Whitney Museum down on Eighth Street—God preserve us and "I say it's spinach," to quote the *New Yorker* cartoon.

4

*T*HE *VIEW ITALY* FOR JANUARY 1946, WITH SERGEANT PETER LINDAMOOD, AN old friend of Charles Ford, as guest editor, appeared a bit late. Lindamood brought back from Rome a mass of material: stories, poems, catalogues, photographs. He was convinced that postwar Italy had produced a flowering in the arts such as had not been seen in generations, including such people as Alberto Moravia, Carlo Levi and Fabrizio Clerici. He also was enthusiastic about Mario Praz, who, he declared, was Italy's strongest critic-essayist (I shared his admiration for Praz's *Romantic Agony*). But I was not certain that I cared for the painter Leonor Fini as much as both he and Charles Ford did. Fini had done an opulent and highly flattering portrait of Charles, but then she painted many handsome young men. She also did self-portraits very much in the style of the young men. There was an excellent poem by Eugenio Montale called "Ballad Written in a Clinic," perhaps the best thing in the issue.

But for me the January number was thrilling because my column, "Interaction," had at last appeared. I will always stand by one sentence: "We think the time is passed when literary magazines should go their separate ways; the most vital art or literature of our period will continue to show mutual interaction and influence." I suppose the sentence means that I believe artists must inevitably get their "ideas" from poets, writers of science or even philosophers.

Meanwhile, my confidence in Breton was beginning to fade. He was, for instance, very friendly with the high-powered commercial art director Enrico Donati, who was given an exhibition by the prestigious Durand-Ruel gallery, which was soon to close after many generations in New York. Breton wrote an introduction to the show, but when I read this catalogue after seeing the pictures, I had no clue as to what Breton intended or meant. At the same time, he was making powerful propaganda for the painter Arshile Gorky, who, he felt, was the most important discovery of his movement in some time. His enthusiasm was unequivocal.

I thought a sharp change must be occurring. George Keller announced that he was moving his elegant Bignou gallery back to Paris at about the same time that the celebrated Pierre Loeb announced his plans to move his gallery from Paris to New York. Loeb had kept his gallery in Paris closed throughout the German occupation.

A further event occurred that few people noticed, but that I believe was seminal in changing the course of American art criticism. Oddly it began with Paul Goodman. In a short, brilliant article for a catalogue, he criticized his psychoanalyst friends who analyzed paintings on the basis of their "images" or "icons" or "subject matter." He declared them hopelessly mistaken, and said that instead, it was the surface, the strokes made with the brush, the thinness or thickness of the paint itself as applied heavily or lightly by the artist, and the disposition of the forms that disclosed the quality and sincerity of the work. Surface reveals the artist just as handwriting reveals, in some part, any writer's character. Many years later Harold Rosenberg expanded Goodman's basic notion and called it "Action Painting." A stricter formulation of this approach to painting was further organized in the criticism of Clement Greenberg.

During the month of February, while we were preparing an all-French issue, a concert at Town Hall was presented by Arthur Gold and Robert Fizdale, the duo pianists. It seemed to me the most unusual recital I had ever attended. The audience did not resemble others I had seen in concert halls, since most of the people were either artists or members of what I suppose must be called international society, including Perry Empiricos, the son of the Greek shipping magnate; George Bemberg, whose family in Argentina, it was said, had caused three revolutions; the beautiful Peggy O'Brien and her famous debutante daughter Esme; Edelgey Dinshaw and his sister; the wealthy Oliver and Isa Jennings; Arthur Lopez-Wilshaw, another fabulous Argentinian multimillionaire; Alice De Lamar with her entourage; as well as the various princesses and *marquesas* who surrounded Tchelitchew.

Peggy Guggenheim was the patroness of the concert. Two major works were performed, written especially for the occasion by Paul Bowles and John Cage, both of whom Miss Guggenheim admired and encouraged.

There was a party afterward at the apartment of Oliver Smith. It was here that I met Jane Bowles, John Cage and the two pianists. It was a mystery how so many of the women managed to look so smart, since many of them had been cut off from their Parisian dressmakers. I suppose it wasn't so mysterious when one considers that in the middle of the war Marie Mellon had somehow managed to get to Switzerland to visit her mentor, Dr. Jung.

As the party was breaking up, Peter Lindamood accidentally pushed the actress Stella Adler down the stairs. She was wearing a Gainsborough-sized hat, and despite the dramatic tumble, when Stella picked herself up, everything was in place, including the hat!

When I visited Pierre Matisse I was astonished to be shown the newest work by Giacometti. I had been told that Giacometti, whose *Palace at 4 A.M.* and other early works I loved, had stopped making sculpture and was now designing and making furniture and lamps with his brother. Mr. Matisse (looking exactly like the little boy playing the piano in his father's painting) placed a series of tiny statuettes on a table; some of them were not more than three inches high, others a bit taller. They were standing or walking figures needle thin and emaciated looking. I asked what the point was of making miniatures, and learned that Giacometti had returned to sculpture but was seeking to discover a new scale, a new dimension for figures existing in space. "He has become a new artist-hero since the Liberation, particularly for the philosopher Jean-Paul Sartre," said Pierre.

Examining the material that Charles Ford had collected for *View Paris*, March 1946, one sensed a new note, a distinct change in the intellectual climate. Names only vaguely heard before were emerging, and several of them were featured in that issue: Sartre, Jean Genet, Albert Camus, Henri Michaux, Maurice Blanchard, Georges Bataille, Jean Paulhan and the painter Jean Dubuffet. I had been shown Dubuffet's work by Pierre Matisse when I went to pick up photo reproductions. Pierre told me that the Parisians said Dubuffet had invented *art brut*, and indeed it looked primitive and brutal and full of savage energy.

"I think," said Charles one afternoon, "that Surrealism is on its way out."

"And what is on its way in?" I asked.

"Existentialism, honey, Existentialism."

I was very much amused, therefore, to hear that the ever-popular Greenwich Village chanteuse Stella Brooks was singing a song called "Existentialism Blues"!

Charles was secretly pleased that Breton and his followers were beginning to be old hat. But then he was never more than a fellow traveler, especially since he detested politics in any form unless it was directly associated with art. Charles was not without his admirers. Djuna Barnes stopped by one day and asked if "Charlie" was in. It would seem they once lived together and were still close friends. Miss Barnes was as handsome as a polo pony, her cloak floating behind her like a magnificent mane. But Marius Bewley, who visited her regularly, said she was a recluse and had a sign on her door telling people to stay out. I once asked if she was still writing, and Marius said he thought she was writing a long play.

Charles Ford, of course, never made a move without having a purpose. His sudden espousal of Existentialism and the alert attention he was paying to Sartre had to have a reason. I thought I found a clue in an article by Wallace Fowlie called "Existential Theatre." In it Mr. Fowlie described a play called *Huis-Clos*, a three-character (two women and a man) drama by Sartre. Charles was always on the lookout for a good play for his sister Ruthie. Could it prove to be a vehicle for her? She was, after all, making a big reputation for herself in the theater.

I went to a party at Ruth Ford's wittily decorated apartment. Among the guests were E. E. Cummings and his wife, Marian, Peter Watson and Cecil Beaton. I seemed to hit it off with the latter two. "Ruth," said Parker Tyler, "has a gift for making friends with everybody." And indeed the rooms were full of celebrities. She is extraordinarily beautiful, as can be seen in photographs of her, especially the one by Man Ray. I know nothing of her gifts as an actress. Charles says she is a "great tragedienne." One of her best friends is the novelist William Faulkner, who says he will write a play for her. Somebody said he attended the party, but I didn't see him.

February 1946

Lionel Abel, having been a friend of the philosopher Jean Wahl, seems to be more *à la page* with regard to *la vie intellectuelle de Paris* than anyone in New York. He has apparently been reading Sartre's magazine, *Les*

Temps Modernes, has already perused *L'Être et la Néant* (*Being and Nothingness*) as well as texts by Simone de Beauvoir and others in Sartre's group. For the French number of *View* he has written an essay called "Georges Bataille and the Repetition of Nietzsche."

Nico Calas, however, may be just as *au courant* as Abel, since he has contributed an article reviewing *The Stranger* by Albert Camus and *Thomas l'Obscure* by Maurice Blanchot. He is not enthusiastic about any of the Sartre group. In one sentence Calas says, "To rely on Kierkegaard for psychological meaning, as the French Existentialist school of literature is now doing, is like abandoning astronomy for the sake of astrology." He thinks Camus' *The Stranger* is on a lower level than the detective stories of Simenon, and Blanchot is so boring and repetitious that in the end we are "suffocated by so much emptiness." (He must be giving the official Surrealist line.)

Charles Ford daily grows more enthusiastic about the new movement in Paris. At last he confided to me that Jean-Paul Sartre is coming to New York and *View* will present him in a lecture at Carnegie Recital Hall. He will be introduced by the French anthropologist Claude Lévi-Strauss, who is also cultural advisor to the French ambassador.

"Be sure to put it in your column. We've got the hall for March fifth. Sartre will speak on new tendencies in the French theater. Ah just love that play *Huis-Clos*. It's so perfect for Ruthie. And a big feather for Oliver Smith, 'cause he's going to produce it. Ruthie is one of Oliver's biggest admirations." Who would have thought this would all happen so quickly?

My column, "Interaction," has become twice as long as usual, packed with news. Since my first column, my social stock has risen perceptibly. I guess everybody thinks I'm *in* on the latest, and in a way I am. I got invited, for instance, to meet the Corrado Cagli circle, all of whom seem to live in a small area along Second Avenue in the East Sixties. The painter Corrado speaks the G. I. English he learned in the American army, for which he volunteered while, I think, still living in Rome. He is close to the composers Vittorio Rieti and Darius Milhaud and their wives and children. Their sons Fabio Rieti and Daniel Milhaud study painting with him. This means he is also an intimate of Eugene Berman, his brother Leonid, and their cousin, Leon Kochnitsky.

It is difficult for me to organize my thoughts about the Neo-Romantics. Eugene Berman is awful, spoiled, touchy, demanding—a bore. I have never met his brother Leonid because he did not escape from France and has, from what is known, been a slave laborer for the Vichy government on the German-supervised "Atlantic Wall" near La Rochelle. Julien Levy has told me Leonid is quite the opposite of his brother Genia—good-natured, kindly, amusing. Nor have I met Christian Bérard, since he has remained in Paris. George Davis, a close friend of Bébé's, as everyone calls him, explained to me that Bérard now does few paintings because he is heavily drug-addicted, and perhaps this is the reason he gives what energy he has to making designs for couturiers, perfume manufacturers, the theater and ballet. But then, this is true of all the Neo-Romantics: all of them have had to paint things they might have preferred not to—in order to survive. It is strange how these four disparate talents are invariably grouped together in the public mind. In New York this is probably because Julien Levy exhibited them as a group back in 1937. Pavel Tchelitchew has little time for the other three and very little of their art is reproduced in *View*. He has aesthetic reservations about their work. That the Berman brothers came from a rich *haut bourgeois* banking family in St. Petersburg impresses him not at all. And I suspect Tchelitchew, being a Russian aristocrat, remains an anti-Semite in the way only the old *noblesse* and Eastern European grandees can be and usually are. As for Bérard, Tchelitchew is too much of a health enthusiast to have patience with a drug addict. One can imagine him saying, *"Il n'est pas sérieux."*

Cagli, the Bermans, the Rietis, Kochnitsky are all Jewish but none of them seem in the least aware of it. Leon Kochnitsky converted to Roman Catholicism years ago and had been a papal secretary. One evening he confided to me his three passions—"the Vatican, pederasty and good Havana cigars." Alas, Kochnitsky is, as we used to say in Buffalo, "on his uppers." In his heyday Leon was a habitué of the Diaghilev circle, a patron of the arts, an extravagant *boulevardier* as well as a scholar, a critic, an expert on African art and artifacts. He is quite cheerful despite his penury. It is his consolation that at least he has his Picasso, Braque and 1917 de Chirico—all superb—and if worse came to worst, he could sell them for enough money to live on for the rest of his life. But his Belgian fortune has disappeared. He has no money for bus fare to get home after the occasional dinner at my apartment. Fortunately, Leon has enough friends to rotate dining out—and why not? This perennially amusing raconteur and dandy is welcome everywhere.

At one evening gathering in the Rieti flat Corrado slyly hinted that the lady he was about to introduce to me was his inamorata. He was lying, of course, but that is how I came to meet Mrs. Alfred Barr; Corrado called her "Daisy" (I am learning to take almost everything he tells

ur issues of View, *with covers by* (clockwise from top left) *Wilfredo Lam, Marcel Duchamp, Fernand Léger d Alexander Calder.* COURTESY RUTH FORD

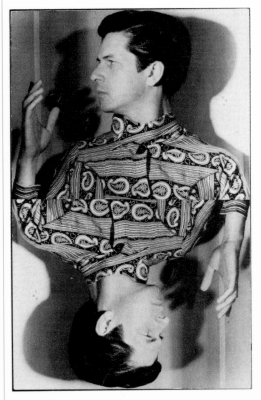

Upper left: *Charles Henry Ford, publisher and editor* View, *photographed by Carl Van Vechten.* COURTESY RUT FORD

Upper right: *Pavel Tchelitchew in his East Fifty-fift Street studio, about 1946.* GEORGE PLATT LYNES

Parker Tyler, poet, critic and co-editor of View, *as po trayed by the film artist Maya Deren.* COLLECTION CHARLES BOULTENHOUSE

A group photo of European artists who lived in America during World War II: From left to right, front row: Mata Echaurren, Ossip Zadkine, Yves Tanguy, Max Ernst, Marc Chagall, Fernand Léger. Second row: André Breton, Piet Mondrian, André Masson, Amadée Ozenfant, Jacques Lipchitz, Eugene Berman. Top row: Pavel Tchelitchew and Kurt Seligmann. GEORGE PLATT LYNES

André Breton's "circle," photographed at Peggy Guggenheim's house in 1943. Left to right, first row: William Stanley Hagter, Leonora Carrington, Frederick Kiesler, and Kurt Seligmann. Second row: Max Ernst, Amadée Ozenfant, Breton, Fernand Léger, Berenice Abbott. Top row: Jimmy Ernst, Peggy Guggenheim, John Ferren, Marcel Duchamp, Piet Mondrian. GEORGE PLATT LYNES

Arshile Gorky and Willem de Kooning pose in front of Gorky's Organization, 1934. COURTESY ELAINE DE KOONING

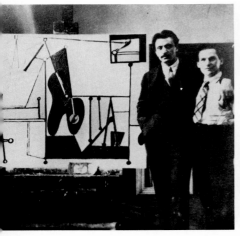

The author manipulating a puppet designed by Kurt Seligmann for Jane Bowles's A Quarreling Pair. ERNST BEADLE

A 1946 snapshot of Max Ernst and his wife, Dorothea Tanning, with two Lhasa apso terriers. COURTESY DOROTHEA TANNING

Max Ernst in Huismes, France, 1957.
DENISE COLOMB; COURTESY DOROTHEA TANNING

Wifredo Lam. COURTESY PIERRE MATISSE GALLERY

al Masqué celebrating the fifth anniversary of View, *October 1945. The décor was by Tchelitchew.*
COURTESY ALICE DE LA MAR

Joan Miró, photographed by Sabine Weiss.
COURTESY PIERRE MATISSE GALLERY

Kurt Seligmann in his West Fortieth Street Studio. PHOTO:
EINSON; COURTESY KURT SELIGMANN

Joseph Cornell "rescues" the celebrated antique doll Bébé-Marie in Central Park. ERNST BEADLE

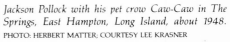
Joseph Cornell in 1971. HANS NAMUTH

Jackson Pollock with his pet crow Caw-Caw in The Springs, East Hampton, Long Island, about 1948.
PHOTO: HERBERT MATTER; COURTESY LEE KRASNER

Meyer Schapiro—a passport photo by Robert Frank.
COURTESY MEYER SCHAPIRO

Lee Krasner with Gyp and Ahab in her East Hampton studio, 1959. PHOTO: HALLEY ERSKINE; COURTESY LEE KRASNER

me as perhaps 5 percent true). The Rietis are wonderfully attractive. In a book about the early Ballets Russes I recall seeing a photograph of Vittorio, at that time a protégé of Diaghilev, looking like a Bronzino. His music is light, charming, well made—as though the composer were the great-great-great-grandchild of Pergolesi. It is little wonder that Maestro and Madame Stravinsky treat the Rietis as if they were blood relatives. Elsie Rieti is the brain of her family—cultivated, funny, *simpática*, but for all that, a woman who holds things together because she is practical. Berman is very dependent upon her. I like the fact that all these former collaborators of the ballet continue to be friends. Madame Stravinsky, for instance, has just had Berman design her new art gallery in Los Angeles, which she calls "La Boutique."

Journal, March 1946

Cecil Beaton is "doing" a suite of rooms in the Plaza Hotel and asked me to come and see them. This is an ingenious method for cutting down expenses, since he will have the "Beaton Suite" to live in when he's in New York. He has found and used all manner of discarded furniture that was down in the cellar—handsome, gingerbready brass beds, for instance. Luckily, he even found elaborate lace curtains that were once *à la mode* and the right size for the tall windows. On the walls are a Léger, a Tchelitchew and a Paul Klee. I asked if the pictures might seem out of place in such a *fin-de-siècle* décor. Cecil replied that pictures had nothing to do with interior decoration. "The better the pictures, the handsomer the room." He added that he had learned this principle from Mrs. Somerset Maugham, whom he called Syrie. I asked Cecil what he had been doing during the war and he replied that he worked with the British army as a photographer, much of the time in Africa, and that he's hoping to have a book of these war photographs in print soon.

How Cecil manages to look so fresh and well-groomed, considering he works harder than anyone I've met, is a mystery to me. He rises at seven o'clock, writes letters, works on his diaries. The bed is covered with papers, watercolor sets, brushes, pencils, notebooks, photographs, newspapers, magazines, whatever he needs for the projects he is pursuing. By midmorning he's off to *Vogue* photography studios, by one he's lunching at the Colony Club or some other smart restaurant. His afternoons are crowded with appointments with clients who want designs, décors, portraits. By seven he is out of his bath and into

his dinner jacket. He loves high society and moves in this watery element like a dolphin. Since he's certain as to who he is, Cecil is without
snobbery; he is as at home with a boxer, an impecunious dancer, a
charwoman, "colored" people, or dressmakers as he is with his duchesses and field marshals. There's another reason for this: he's totally
nonintellectual, and below his crisp surface is a childlike nature. Only a
naïf could believe that the eccentrics and monsters he deals with are
creatures of glamor.

Journal, March 1946

Peter Watson, the publisher of *Horizon*, came to dinner. After the austerity of London, he has fallen in love with New York. Waldemar Hansen made himself very agreeable, cooked a delicious dinner and fell
into a deep conversation with Peter. I was so pleased that they had hit it
off well that I didn't mind simply listening. Around midnight I excused
myself and went to bed while they went on talking into the small hours.

Peter's money seems to come from a large soap fortune, and he has
used his inheritance largely for the support of the arts. He is tall, lean,
with a fine bony face. He has a quick intelligence and a warm heart. No
wonder Peter is so well liked wherever he goes. I have seen a portrait of
him by Tchelitchew in which he is clad in a suit of armor. A corny
symbol, but a true one: he looks like a true knight in shining armor.

Journal, March 1946

For Sartre's lecture, Carnegie Recital Hall was filled to the rafters. He
spoke in French and discussed the kind of theater he envisioned: little
or no scenery, characters engaged in actions that reveal *what* they are,
the facing up to contemporary problems without theatrical claptrap.
His audience seemed split between professors of French literature from
Columbia and people from the Fifty-seventh Street art world. Oliver
Smith was there, of course, and I asked him if it was true he was going
to produce *No Exit*. He said he was; it would be done in the autumn,
would be directed by John Huston, and would star Annabella, Claude
Dauphin and Ruth Ford. "I am the coproducer with Herman Levin."

I think it strange that a movie director like John Huston would be
chosen to interpret so subtle a play. It was Mr. Levin who wanted Huston and Huston who wanted Annabella and Claude Dauphin. Apparently the play was brought to Oliver Smith by Paul Bowles, who has

also translated it. It was Paul's enthusiasm that convinced Oliver to go ahead with the New York production. I am impressed that a designer has the energy to be a producer, but I suppose it is a way to get more work for oneself.

It was Tchelitchew who gave Oliver his first job, which was to paint the drops and flats for the Balanchine–Stravinsky ballet *Balustrade* that he himself had designed. Tchelitchew also inspired in Oliver an interest and enthusiasm for ballet, which apparently goes very deep.

No Exit proved to be a great success. All of us who saw it were very impressed.

Journal, March 1946

Since my first introduction last year to Clement Greenberg by Marius Bewley, I had only chatted with him at various openings. We never had a real tête-à-tête until recently, when we met by chance on Park Avenue at Thirty-fourth Street and went into the bar at the Hotel Vanderbilt for a drink.

Clem is one of the editors of *Commentary* magazine, art critic for the *Nation*, and contributes articles from time to time to *Partisan Review*. I like him because he has a certain big-city élan, a pleasing urbanity that goes well with his understated conservative clothes and plain manner of speech (he drops the *g* from words ending in *ing*). One might possibly guess he was a securities analyst, not a New York intellectual. Yet he is a highly controversial critic and quite far removed from the world I move in. A good deal of his art criticism deals with contemporary American painting and he eschews writing about this subject from a literary or social view. The Surrealists do not generally signify much for him, except possibly Matta. He has no feeling for Tchelitchew or the other Neo-Romantics. He was at one time close to the George L. K. Morris Abstract American Artists group and more recently he has been a supporter of the abstractionists at Betty Parsons', Peggy Guggenheim's gallery and the Jane Street group.

"The last really important movement which changed the history of twentieth-century art was Cubism," he declared at one point. I find it difficult to argue with Clem because my approach to painting comes from poetry and history. But we agree, luckily, on enough things to make for a pleasant friendship. For instance, we agree that Jackson and Lee Pollock are okay, that Bonnard is wonderful and that the

1910–1912 Picassos and Braques are among the great works of European art. We also share a similar fondness for Marius Bewley.

One last thing that Clem said that impressed and saddened me was, "You know, Paris has been limping along as the world center of art since 1936." "But what will replace the School of Paris?" I asked. "The place where the money is," he replied, "New York."

A letter from Germaine Brice, *View*'s Paris correspondent, informs us that Surrealism under the Occupation became moribund. Aragon has deserted to the Communist party, Éluard and Georges Huguet are on the fence. Very few new painters of Surrealist stamp have emerged. Even Julien Gracq has produced nothing as good as *Chateau d'Argol*— and he's now serving in Indochina; his latest novel about the Viet Minh movement would indicate that he, too, has moved to the Communist party.

The important news is that Giacometti has re-emerged as a major sculptor and that Jean Dubuffet is considered a formidable new figure in the international art market.

Secret Diary, Undated

My mother died of a heart attack, and I went to Buffalo to attend the funeral. In the kitchen many people were drinking a lot of whisky—it was an Irish wake. In the parlor where my mother was laid out people came and went, few of whom were known to me. I was told some were my mother's friends in the Democratic party, others were her card-party and horse-racing cronies and still others were simply Irish Catholics she had known for years. I could not and did not cry. When I went to look at her in her coffin I felt nothing, and at the funeral I simply stared. My father went into paroxysms of grief and tried to throw himself into the grave. I asked my sister Evelyn how my mother had died, although I knew she had had a heart attack from which she had recovered some months ago. It seems she went out to play bridge early in the evening, despite a snowfall, and by the time she returned home, over two feet of snow was on the ground. Our house is about fifty yards from the street, and no one had as yet shoveled the path. In trying to get through the snow, she overexerted herself, which caused another bad attack. She collapsed in the snow. A neighbor heard her cries. She was carried into the house, but it was too late.

The night after the funeral, I went to a dancing party given by old Buffalo friends. On the train back to New York, Emily Dickinson's poem went through my head: "After great pain, a formal feeling comes." I have still not shed a tear.

Journal, March 1946

If anyone were to ask me which painter in New York is most talked about I would say it is Matta. A Chilean, formerly a student of architecture, an enthusiastic Surrealist, Matta is high-strung, hyperactive, given to playing cruel jokes (l'humour noir), a womanizer. Although he is married to a lovely, quiet girl named Anne, he does not adhere to the Surrealist ideal of monogamy. The incident that has caused the most gossip is the fact (and it is true) that when he heard his wife had given birth to identical male twins, Matta instantly developed two black eyes and looked as if he had been socked in a boxing match. He was so "struck" by this experience that he packed his bag and abandoned the family. Edouard Roditi says it is the first case of an authentic stigmata since the blessed Saint Teresa of Lisieux ("a bourgeois saint, my dear") received hers. I said I think Matta had been reading too much of the Marquis de Sade.

Tchelitchew doesn't see Matta anymore, since each claims that the other has been "stealing" his colors. The new Tchelitchew heads, through which one sees the veins, capillaries, brain and bone, are the colors of acids, of chemicals. Fairness requires an admission that these colors were Matta's all along. But such a debate is absurd; nobody can claim any hue to be his and his alone—not even the blue of Maxfield Parrish.

Charles Ford has become interested in a discovery of mine, Dmitri Petrov. Petrov is a curious mixture: he is a confirmed Dadaist (his nihilism comes to him quite naturally, since he was raised in a commune in New Jersey by his Russian anarcho-syndicalist parents) and at the same time anxious to make money in the advertising business. He is successful, and at the moment has a big job as art director for Bonwit Teller. He has only one hand; when he was nineteen he lost the right one in an accident with an electric buzz saw. Perhaps it is for this reason that he does little painting but specializes instead in drawing and graphics, to which he brings a passion and a bravura technique that is startling. Charles has accepted a two-page spread of drawings for View that illustrates a child's reader published in Boston in 1893. It is called The Praying Mantis and is wonderfully obscene (or should I say pornographic?). The mantis strongly resembles a stiff penis.

I made a trip to Philadelphia to stay the weekend with Petrov, his wife and several children in their very old house not far from the Rodin Museum. Pete (everyone calls him that) took me to the Philadelphia Museum to see the Johnson Collection; afterward we went to see the Rodins. I had never seen so many all at once. I realized for the first time that Rodin occupied a position in modern sculpture comparable to that of Cézanne in painting.

Despite his handicap, Petrov is full of frenetic energy. He commutes between New York and Philadelphia, does a full day's work, socializes with many old friends, and still manages to be a productive artist. Luckily he has an assistant, Bernard Pfriem, who is equally driven and determined to be a serious painter. Pfriem is obsessed with the work of Arshile Gorky and many of his canvases look like Gorky's.

It is through Bernard Pfriem that I met Babs Simpson, an editor for *Vogue*, a woman both brainy and worldly. It is difficult to imagine that fashion is her business, since she is completely indifferent to its values and regards fashion simply as a way to make a living. I suppose I like her as much as I do because she is full of curiosity about a wide variety of subjects and is, like myself, a compulsive reader. She, too, is enthusiastic about Petrov's drawings and was pleased when I told her he would be exhibiting with the Hugo gallery.

Journal, March 1946

Looking through a file of *Views*, I noticed that Harold Rosenberg, a close friend of Parker Tyler's, has been a regular contributor since its beginning in 1940. Rosenberg is primarily an essayist, although early in his career he wrote verse that reads like William Carlos Williams. The best essays deal with literature, philosophy and politics. Harold believes that the visual arts exist on a lower level of human expression; at any rate, what he has to say about painting doesn't interest me. As a man of letters, Harold's best qualities are obvious and excellent. He has written a long essay on Kierkegaard in relation to identity for the May issue that seems to me as good as any of the essays we have received from the French Existentialists, although it is obvious that these new philosophers (new to us, not to the French) have not been without impact on Rosenberg's thinking.

Harold is a lucky man, since he works only three days a week at the Advertising Council, an organization that has nothing to do with advertising. The Council thinks up ways that Jewish philanthropists can and should best spend their money to improve society and alleviate suffering. There is a strong rabbinical strain running through Harold, although he's not the least bit religious. I daresay he's a powerhouse in a committee room because he is capable of arguing pungently and convincingly. He can also be very funny, which is probably why so many of the artists around town enjoy his company.

Letter to George Poole in Buffalo

Your question about how artists make a living, how they survive, is not an easy one to answer. I don't know many artists who paint nice pictures to hang over the fireplace. I don't know regional artists who paint corn fields and cowboys. I have met a number of skilled designers, photographers and illustrators who work for advertising firms and magazines. They apparently are well paid.

But I suspect what you mean are serious artists who are concerned with a personal vision, an idiosyncratic style. The most famous painters like Picasso, Matisse, Braque and so forth—painters who have achieved international reputations and are associated with that loose conglomerate called the "School of Paris"—do very well financially, I believe. The artists who are in exile in New York do not have an easy time. Mondrian, who died a few years ago, lived in a very modest flat. The Neo-Romantics like Berman and Leonid sell their pictures at prices that seem to me reasonable but not startling. This also applies to artists such as Tanguy, Masson, Calder, Tchelitchew, Seligmann and several of the Surrealists. You can buy Max Ernst for very little. Prints and drawings by quite famous "internationals" are not expensive, even though such prices are beyond people like you and me. (Curt Valentine offered me a beautiful color lithograph by Miró not long ago for $75, but who has $75?)

After you deduct expenses involved with the sale of artworks, the artist does not stand to make much of a profit. Luckily most of them are resourceful, know how to attract personal patronage, and in a curious way are indifferent to getting rich.

To tell the truth, even though I am in and out of the galleries almost daily, I rarely inquire as to what things cost. I seem to have no itch to acquire artworks myself, and the economics of art rather baffle me.

Oh yes, there is one artist who is openly and disgustingly avid for money: the celebrated Salvador Dali. He's struck gold.

As to your final question, what do the really wealthy Americans buy in the way of modern art, my reply is simple. They buy Cézanne, the Impressionists, Post-Impressionists, Picasso and Matisse. In Hollywood it's Renoir and Monet. Americans buy for investment the same way they acquire stocks and bonds. They buy from Knoedler, Durand-Ruel and Wildenstein, but more often they buy in Paris (they like a Paris label). Very few buy good contemporary or "avant-garde" art. The critic Clement Greenberg predicts all this will change, but I'm rather dubious. There is almost no American art worth buying.

Journal, April 1946

Words. Marius Bewley declares that all words popularly used to designate homosexuals—"pansy," "fairy," "faggot," "queen," etc.—are no good. "And what," I asked, "do you propose to use instead?" "Athenian," he said. "What could be more classical?"

I notice that there is a word shift occurring in heavy conversation. "Alienation," "contingency," "dread," "the Absurd," "the Nothingness" seem to pop up in the way people used to use "phobia," "inferiority complex," "primal scream," "self-destructive." The language of Existentialism seems to be pushing out psychoanalytic jargon.

Changes in taste. The Mexicans—Rivera, Orozco, Siqueiros, Tamayo, who for so long kept the Americans bemused—are quite suddenly considered *passé*. There is also a lessening of interest in the New York style of "social conscience" pictures—William Gropper, Adolph Dehn, Robert Gwathmey, the left-wing painters of the A.C.A. gallery. On the other hand, there is an increase in the popularity of "magic" realism—Paul Cadmus, Jared French, George Tooker—a form of pseudo-Surrealism espoused by the Ed Hewitt gallery and enthusiastically endorsed by Lincoln Kirstein.

Parker Tyler has taken umbrage at what he considers my "prejudice" against art by Americans. He agrees with my idea that to speak of "American art" is parochial and imprecise, but he then surprised me by urging me to really *look* at the work of Edward Hopper, a painter who he believes is first rate. I did so shortly afterward by going to the Frank Rehn gallery—a rather obscure gallery that specializes in Americans. I realized I hadn't really *seen* Hopper's work, that I simply had lumped him with "social conscience" artists like Reginald Marsh and Moses Soyer. It gradually dawned on me that Hopper's painting is sophisticated and deeply felt. Parker feels that there is something timid and a little shallow about my much-too-influenced taste. Perhaps this is true. He suggests that I ask myself whether I like or do not like *any* picture or statue I see even if I have never heard of the artist.

I have been asking myself this question and trying to draw up a list of Americans I like. First and foremost I seem to enjoy the work of my friends and tend *not* to ask how good or bad it is. I am trying when I go to a gallery to simply look at the pictures without too much inner jab-ber-jabber. Maybe I like more American artists than I think I do. I like Georgia O'Keeffe, Jerry Kamrowski, Dmitri Petrov, Rico Lebrun, Xenia Cage, Isamu Noguchi, Leon Kelly, Ivan Le Lorraine Albright, Walter Murch, Judith Rothschild, Charles Seliger, Louis Eilshemius. Perhaps the list will grow longer (if Florine Stettheimer were alive, I'd include her).

Paul Goodman believes that inevitably all works of art must be judged in relation to the greatest. At the moment this may not be a good rule for me; I suspect such an exercise in taste is difficult to shake off. I can recognize, too, that fashionable taste is easy to come by. It comes from listening and reading reviews.

Journal, April 1946

Since the day I first met him in Peggy Guggenheim's gallery, I have seen Joseph Cornell several times, but never long enough to form a clear picture of what he is like. I told him I had first seen his work at Julien Levy's in 1939 while visiting New York and that I still had the catalogue for that show. The catalogue by Parker Tyler was entitled *Toys for Adults,* since most of the objects presented in that show were of a play-ful nature. Then, as now, Cornell's work has been inexpensive; the larg-est objects still sell for $75 and $100. I told him I was sorry he no longer wished to appear in *View* (his last contribution was a homage, *A Watch Case for Marcel Duchamp*), but he was firm in deciding not to contribute. My suspicion is that he does not wish to be associated with Surrealism as a movement (exactly why, I am not sure), nor does he wish to appear in *View*, I believe for reasons of moral disapproval (the nature of which I cannot fathom).

How to describe Joseph? He is of average height, his nose rather beaklike, his hair simply combed back without a part. His eyes move about and then occasionally stare straight into one's own, piercingly. He has a firm mouth and a face that remains expressionless unless stirred to mirth or strong interest in an idea or mild anger. The very passivity of Joseph's expression is the giveaway of an exacerbated sen-sibility oddly combined with an almost rigidly disciplined character.

He speaks little, but when he does it is to the point, specific, intelligent. However, the facial impassivity gives an effect of aloofness, a certain iciness; it is the expression of a man who dislikes excess and is intolerant of fools. His friendliness toward me has been a source of satisfaction, and when he invited me to his house for lunch and to look at "work," I felt flattered.

The visit took place on a Sunday. I took the subway out to Flushing and made my way to Utopia Parkway, a street where all the houses look alike: each two stories high with attic, a little lawn in front, small garden and garage in the back. I was met at the door by Mrs. Cornell, Joseph's mother, a woman who resembled the club ladies depicted by Helen Hokinson in *New Yorker* cartoons. One perceives quickly that she is almost completely deaf. I was led into the living room, which would have been quite typical of a conventional middle-class parlor except that a large portion of it was taken up by a platform on which an electric train set was installed in an elaborate toy landscape. At one end of the platform in a high chair was seated a crooked little person who was placed in a position to manipulate levers that regulated the movement of the trains, signal lights, bridges and other special features of the miniature terrain. It was hard to tell how old he might be. I guessed about twenty.

Joseph came into the room and introduced me to his invalid brother, Robert. As he did so, I could not help noticing the difference between Joseph's usual expression and the one he now wore. His whole face radiated sweetness and loving care. Robert said some words, but I had difficulty in understanding what he was saying. Joseph interpreted that Robert would like to show me what a good stationmaster he was. The trains began to move through the landscape—over hills, through tunnels, past a waterfall; villages lit up, green and red signals flashed on and off. Thus I learned that Cornell had been inventing lovely diversions and entertainments for his brother, who was born totally helpless except for a few movements of the hands and arms. This was why he had collected old movies such as Mack Sennett and Charlie Chaplin comedies, and short films made as far back as 1900. Near where Robert sat there was a small screen on which movies could be projected. Joseph has been searching for early films assiduously, and as a result, has a unique collection. He also has a collection of several thousand movie stills.

There were not many constructions in the living room. One object, made for Robert, was a kaleidoscope that had inside it an eight-pointed, three-dimensional star that tumbled about as the kaleidoscope was turned. There were, however, other things in the room lying about casually—old magazines, books, boxes containing postcards at which I could only throw a tantalized glance. Presently we went through the kitchen, where Cornell's mother was sitting reading the Sunday paper. It could have been any kitchen on Utopia Parkway—ruffled curtains on the windows, some plant cuttings on a sill. I glimpsed the pantry, which seemed to be filled with bags of birdseed, for the good reason that Joseph had in his backyard a birdbath, birdhouses, bird feeders. He explained that he enjoyed the visits of sparrows, pigeons, robins or any other bird that came by. There was a wire fence in the rear of the yard. Other backyards stretched to the left and right, all fenced off, each with a garage. It was to the Cornell garage that I was led, and when the doors were swung open, I felt as though I were entering Aladdin's cave. There were shelves and more shelves lining the garage on which were stored objects, constructions, materials for new boxes, dolls. I cannot say which boxes I liked the most. I cannot say if I understood the meaning of them. I only knew that these creations were among the most beautiful and mysterious things I had ever seen, the total embodiments of *le merveilleux*.

After a light lunch of cottage cheese, toast, bologna, jello and milk (Joseph picked at his food as though eating were a nuisance), I was invited to go for a bicycle ride. There were two bikes in the garage and off we went on a tour of the neighborhood. But the sights most memorable were pure Cornell. "Stand here," he said at one spot, "and hold your hands to the right and left of your eyes so that you see only what is in front of you." In the distance was a small old-fashioned brick building, probably a pump house. By cutting off the surrounding environment, it became a Swiss chalet nestling among trees. It looked like the kind of romantic vista one sees in an old engraving. The next spot provided a spectacular view of New York, the whole of it stretched out and illuminated by the silvery gray light of the afternoon. I had never seen New York from such a vantage point. Its skyscrapers became minarets, it seemed to float on a low-lying mist. It was Baghdad. When we got back to the house, I was not shown the attic, where more treasures were stored, or his cellar, which serves as a studio. Instead, we went upstairs to Joseph's room—as austere as a monk's cell—where there was a large collection of Victrola records and a wind-up Victrola. I was shown a portfolio devoted to an early nineteenth-century opera singer called Malibran. In it were programs, engravings, sheet music, reproductions of letters, a host of memorabilia through which Cornell could summon the presence of the celebrated diva. (Cornell had already put his vast collection of this sort of visual material, plus several thousand silent movie stills, to practical use. He conducted an archives service rather like the huge-scale Bettmann Archive; commercial art directors who needed a picture of, let us say, a kitchen stove circa 1846 would call Cornell and invariably he would have the sought-after image.)

While I was looking through this sheaf of material, selections on various recordings were played on the wind-up Victrola. These were not necessarily operatic arias or overtures. Some of the music evoked a Malibran who might have lived in another period—music by Erik Satie and Debussy, for instance. It became clear, however, from glancing at the covers of many of the record albums, that Joseph's passion was for the Romantic composers—Schumann, Schubert, Berlioz, Chopin.

It was time for me to leave, but Mrs. Cornell insisted I have a cup of tea and some Lorna Doone cookies. Her deafness prevented much conversation, and I felt I had stayed too long, although Joseph assured me I hadn't. I said goodbye to his brother, Robert.

Jottings, April 1946

I know that Peggy Guggenheim sells a certain number of paintings and gouaches of Jackson Pollock, but who the buyers are I'm not sure. I was surprised that Princess Zalstem-Zalesky has acquired one, however.

Edouard Roditi, noting that I was looking rather glum, said he had something to tell me that would cheer me up. He said that Breton had spoken well of me, in fact had praised me. "And what," I asked, "did he say?" "I will quote him exactly," said Edouard. *"Myers, il est vraiment un animateur."* "Waldemar Hansen says I'm more like a mountain goat, leaping from crag to crag, never quite on firm footing," said I, only half pleased.

May 1946

In a few weeks Charles Ford and Pavel Tchelitchew will be leaving for Arizona to be near Max Ernst and his wife, Dorothea Tanning. By the end of June I shall once more be faced with the problem of how to get through the summer.

I have become friendly with a writer of lyrics and "special material" whose name is Billy Davis. He says he's on the payroll of the singer Gertrude Niessen. At night he is the cashier at Spivy's Roof, a club in the penthouse building at the corner of Fifty-seventh Street and Lexington Avenue. We meet almost every day at the Oak Room of the Plaza Hotel in the late afternoon. Usually two or three other friends are with him. Billy always pays the bill, even when, after leaving the Plaza's Oak Room, we all go to what he considers a smart restaurant.

I told him I was worried about how to stay alive during the dormant summer period of *View*. He said I should take up my puppets again and would suggest to Miss Spivy, his boss at the club, that I perform there starting perhaps in late June or early July. The idea delighted me and I asked Charles Ford to write a puppet play for me of five to eight minutes' length. Charles then suggested I also ask Jane Bowles for a sketch of similar length and Paul Bowles to write some music for both. "And since you are so friendly with Kurt Seligmann, why not ask him to make the puppets?"

I have approached all four and all have agreed to collaborate. Kurt says he will also paint a folding screen over the top of which the hand puppets will appear.

Since the night of the Fizdale and Gold party given at Oliver Smith's house, I have seen Jane Bowles several times. The first time we met I told her I had read her novel *Two Serious Ladies* when it first came out in 1943. I said that I ranked it as a masterpiece of comedy, a triumph of prose style, that I had reread it at least twice and had lent it to many friends. "Well," said Jane, "I wish there had been a lot more readers like you. It certainly wasn't a best seller." She said this with a rueful smile, but a smile that makes other people smile. In subsequent conversations I found her one of the funniest people I've ever met, but it would be hard to describe her humor or her wit, they are so idiosyncratically her own.

Jane has a bad leg; she cannot bend it, and this forces her to limp noticeably. Apparently in high school she fell off a horse and was so badly injured that she eventually ended up in a hospital in Leysin, Switzerland, where, for two years the leg was kept in traction. It was in Switzerland that she learned French, so well that she wrote a novel in that language—*Le Phaeton Hypocrite*. It was never published; indeed, the typescript had disappeared.

Paul and Jane were married in 1938 and the two of them began their travels in Central America and Mexico. It was in Mexico that *Two Serious Ladies* was completed in 1941. Alfred Knopf published it two years later. And now Jane is engaged in writing, or shall I say the end-less rewriting, of a play called *In the Summer House.* Oliver Smith urged her to write it and it is he who is determined to produce it.

At any rate, Jane was delighted to do the little play for me. I told her I could only manipulate two figures at once, that they shouldn't be required to do things hand puppets cannot do, that each character should have a little song and that it would be amusing if they had a fight.

June 1946

Charles gave me his sketch for three characters. It's called *A Sentimental Playlet* and involves a clown, a sailor and a wild-haired lady. Jane's play is called *A Quarreling Pair* and has two sisters who live in separate rooms, one room very messy and the other room very neat. The sisters don't get along very well. They say things like, "Wouldn't it be won-derful if we could have our milk one day in your room and the next day in mine?"

"That's the sort of thing that *never* happens."

Kurt and his wife, Arlette, have taken to making the puppets, all five of them, with a kind of bouncing glee. I have had a three-section folding screen made, about six feet high. I will stand behind it manipu-lating the puppets above my head while yet remaining invisible. Kurt has painted it with his strange, atmospheric, skeletal figures dancing about as in a fresco by Tiepolo the Younger. The puppets are unlike any I've ever seen: most of them have several faces; one has mirrors covering his blue head and a plume of chartreuse-colored feathers sticking out of his crown. One of Jane's ladies has a wig that soars high above her head in a topknot; she can fling it about in all directions.

Paul's songs, written for a nonsinger like myself, are simple and beautiful. They are not easy to learn, however, and Paul has shown great patience while teaching them to me. The pianist at the nightclub, Ralph Strain, will be my accompanist.

Late June 1946

Since I opened at Spivy's Roof sooner than I thought, Charles, Paul, Jane and the Seligmanns were able to attend the first performance. The room was jammed with friends. Spivy is, of course, the chief attraction, and she sang a medley of songs written for her by John Latouche, who

was also in the audience. The song about the meeting between a tattooed lady and a *Surréaliste* brought down the house. Another favorite
was "I brought culture to Buffalo in the 90s." Latouche came to me after
my performance, full of effusive congratulations, and shortly after that I
was taken to Mary McCarthy's table; she said she had enjoyed the
show. Everybody was very kind. Billy Davis prophesied that the club
would shortly become "more chic than ever." When I went out to the
terrace for some fresh air, a friend beckoned me to a table, where I met
Ned Rorem and his companion Maggie von Maggerstadt. Ned said he
too would like to compose some songs for puppets if I ever did another
show. I felt flattered, since I hear Ned is talented.

Later in the evening Waldemar Hansen remarked, "I don't know
why you waste your time on that art magazine when you would be
much better off doing puppet shows." I had enjoyed my little triumph
too much to argue with him.

From the Summer 1946 Notebook

I don't think it's true about "everything changes, everything remains
the same." I feel life around me is changing rapidly, and that part of remaining responsive to life is to be *aware* of the changes and to react ac-
cordingly.

The phrase "grow old along with me—the best is yet to be" seems
equally stupid. The "best" is what is happening right now; the future is
a blank that no one can foresee. As for getting old, I can think of nothing that makes me feel more uneasy. Being old must be an unpleasant
state, certainly not something to look forward to. "Never tell you age," I
remember my mother saying. She firmly believed that the young punish people for aging.

I approve of Charles Ford maintaining his youthful good looks. He
looks fifteen years younger than he actually is. What is less attractive is
his rampant narcissism; he rarely ceases to think of his appearance and
never allows a day to go by without fulfilling his physical and dietary
regimens.

I have continued entertaining in nightclubs even after I finished my
engagement at Spivy's Roof, and never seem to get to bed until dawn.
But I'm quite bored with breakfast at Longchamps, bored with drunks
and bored with the endless small talk of the night people. Billy Davis
goes on endlessly about actors and actresses, the ups and downs of
"show business," the successes and failures of celebrities. I'm fed up

with sitting in jazz spots on Fifty-second Street, much as I like the jazz. But I did enjoy delivering a poem by Charles Ford called "Chanson pour Billie" to the singer Billie Holiday. How beautiful she was, despite a face ravaged by suffering and drugs.

As the summer drags on I realize I cannot live in two worlds—a serious one and a frivolous one. Listening to the art history lectures at the New School made me realize how little I know, how ignorant I am. It will take me years to learn even a small amount about art. Perhaps Waldemar is right; perhaps I should stick to my one little talent—puppetry—and develop that. As I write this, it is daytime. I feel solemn and anxious. I can't get over the feeling that to stay out all night is somehow wicked. I go to *View* for a few hours each day and make resolutions to lead a better life, but by five o'clock I'm back at the Plaza with my "show-biz" cronies.

At night my outlook is better, more light-hearted perhaps. I have become adept at the clever wisecrack, wounding remarks that make people laugh. I have been frequenting the apartment of John Latouche on East Sixty-seventh Street, where I meet his circle of theatrical and literary friends including his patroness, Alice Bouverie, the sister of Vincent Astor. I seem to fit right into the varnished sophistication of certain evenings; luckily Latouche has a serious side and another group of friends who are gifted and dedicated. But here, too, the socializing and drinking goes on until dawn and each day I face the resulting letdown and depression.

A few times I have managed to get away from the city—one particularly lovely weekend with Lee and Jackson Pollock. I envy them their quiet, almost bucolic life in a white farmhouse with the land in back of it sloping to the sea. Neither of them gives a damn that I don't understand either one's work, a fact I have not hidden from them. On the other hand, I like them so much that being tactful is easy. And they are tactful about the artists I am involved with, although I am quite aware that they have no liking for most of them.

October 1946

Right after Labor Day Waldemar Hansen announced that he would be studying poetry with Kimon Friar at the YMHA. "And since I don't know a word of French, I shall be studying that also—with Madame Chareau, the wife of the architect Pierre Chareau. We seem to have reached some sort of impasse and I don't think it's healthy." I agreed and said I, too, had a plan. Beginning in October on Friday nights I would have open house and invite twenty or thirty people to hear a paper—either an essay or a story—being read aloud, after which discussion would take place. "I want to know as many intellectuals as I can. I already know quite a few, but by bringing them together, I'll be able to learn more about what and how they really think. Besides, it would be fun to have a kind of salon." Waldemar agreed. "I can't," I added, "go on with the night life. It's destroying me."

Full-time work had resumed at the magazine, and as I went about from gallery to gallery I realized the changes I had felt coming had arrived. Marius Bewley was resuming his academic career and would be teaching literature at Fordham University. Several artists who have been with Peggy Guggenheim are leaving her gallery to show with the new Betty Parsons gallery at 15 East Fifty-seventh Street. Among those who will be with Betty are Hans Hofmann, Ad Reinhardt, Mark Rothko, Clyfford Still, Theodoros Stamos, Alfonso Ossorio and Hedda Sterne. She has quite a few other artists lined up, but with the exception of Walter Murch, I don't know them. The Valentine gallery is closing. Most of the dealers complain that business is not good. I gather that Nierendorf is going out of business. This saddens me, since he exhibits extremely fine things and has discovered some excellent new people— Louise Nevelson, for instance, who should have a big future.

On the other hand, there are some exciting new developments. Lincoln Kirstein is back in New York working full swing on the creation of The Ballet Society, which will use designs by good painters. One of the people Kirstein listens to is Tchelitchew; the productions ought to be *première classe*, since money is no problem and the main choreographer will be George Balanchine.

The Museum of Modern Art has put together a highly controversial show called *Fourteen Americans*, but it is important because the selections (I believe Dorothy Miller organized the show) may indicate a shift in taste toward new work by Americans that will no doubt have an impact on the public and the market. According to Parker Tyler, there is only one real "star" in the show, Isamu Noguchi. The others are of little interest to him: Motherwell, Gorky, I. Rice Pereira, Theodore Roszak, Loren MacIver and several nonentities. The inclusion of Saul Steinberg, a *New Yorker* cartoonist, surprised him but, hung on the walls of the museum, Steinberg's pen-and-ink drawings looked "splendid."

The bookseller George Wittenborn has become increasingly influential, not simply because he carries such a wide variety of stock but because he has also been publishing editions that reflect avant-garde attitudes in New York. For instance, a new series will be coming out called "The Documents of Modern Art" and small editions of art pamphlets with a polemical slant.

The gallery that does seem to be making money is Sam Kootz's. They say Mr. Kootz used to be in the advertising business, most successfully, and that as a salesman he is the master of the hard sell. With the artists he shows, he would have to be.

Charles has made *View* into a quarterly again. Our expenses have risen; we will charge $1 a copy (the same price as *Fortune!*), but even with this price rise it has become increasingly more difficult to pay bills. Oh well, to use another of our mottoes: By the imagination we live. The Fall issue, however, is worth every penny. Meyer Schapiro has given us a truly great essay called "On a Painting of Van Gogh." It is a profound analysis of *Crows in the Wheatfield*, the picture Van Gogh painted a few days before his suicide. There is a handsome cover by Noguchi, a disturbing story by Paul Bowles, a review by William Carlos Williams of Breton's new poems, in which he applauds his "pure classicism."

December 1946

My Friday evenings have been launched; people pack themselves into our living room, everybody drinks wine, mostly from jelly glasses, and it is understood that wine is to be brought, as in the old Depression days when there were "bottle parties." Oddly enough, there is very little drinking and there's invariably a half gallon or even a gallon left over, which we save until the next gathering. So far, Paul Goodman, Lionel Abel, Parker Tyler and Harold Rosenberg have read essays. The discussions sometimes get very fierce but never out of hand. Many of the men bring their girlfriends and wives, two of the wittiest being May Rosenberg and Lionel's friend Margery Mason. The general bent of the ideas is philosophic, but different philosophic notions brought to bear on literature, politics, psychoanalysis and ethics—rarely on the visual arts. I am amused that *two* of the regulars were secretaries to Leon Trotsky in Mexico—Bernie Wolfe and Van Heijenoort, the former a novelist, the latter a mathematician.

I steadfastly refer to these Friday evenings as my salon despite the one person who calls them "bull sessions."

Jotting

I revealed to Jackson Pollock that the one museum in New York I couldn't stand was the Museum of Nonobjective Art. It is managed by a Baroness Hilla Rebay, who is the mistress of Peggy Guggenheim's uncle Solomon. The baroness has purchased truckloads of Kandinsky, some of which I think are splendid. But I dislike the geometric-looking ones, full of triangles and circles. However, they are beautiful by comparison with another compass-wielding painter who does big, candy-colored circles, "Bubbles" Bauer, and the execrable junk by the baroness herself. I wonder if the old gentleman knows (a) how much of his money is being spent on Rebays and Bauers and (b) if he realizes that the baroness was an ardent supporter of National Socialism in Germany?

"You needn't tell me anything about Hilla Rebay," said Jackson. "I once worked there, when I was dead broke, as a guard. Between the canned music and the craziness of the director I got myself fired." He agreed with me that it was impossible for a painting to be "nonobjective," since canvas and paint are quite real and touchable. It is surprising, however, how many critics use the word instead of "abstract." In fact, "nonobjective" has gained widespread usage, but since it doesn't refer to a school or a group like the Cubists or Constructivists, no doubt it will be dropped.

Pollock finds it odd that I like the work of Mondrian, Kandinsky and the Russian Constructivists while abstract paintings by Americans remain incomprehensible to me. Maybe I have not seen enough. Probably I don't understand what they "mean," or their "significance," referring to Roger Fry's idea of "significant form."

Journal, December 1946

The December issue devoted to Surrealism in Belgium is essentially a homage to René Magritte, whose paintings have been consistently concerned with fantastical imagery from the beginning of his career in 1915. There was a short period of what Magritte called "abstract and inert images that were, in the last analysis, interesting only to the intelligence of the eye." Magritte sent us a splendid design for the cover: an apple wearing a domino and the word "View" polka-dotted in white— the only other color being apple green. To our delight the collector and close friend of Magritte, Harry Torczyner, gave a reception in his apartment to which we were invited. At first I could not discern which man was the Belgian master, even though I had seen photographs of him. The reason became clear when finally I was introduced. Magritte is tidy, short and totally bourgeois in manner and appearance. It is he who wears the bowler hat, the neat black overcoat, and smokes the little pipe as the night sky is daytime blue and the street lamps are lighted, as houses float off in the sky, as a woman becomes a violin or a pair of shoes possesses toes. Who would have expected such reticence? He has the manner of a shy shopkeeper.

Our host, Harry Torczyner, had many of Magritte's pictures on his walls and their titles recalled a sentence by the artist: "The titles of the pictures were chosen in such a way as to inspire a justifiable mistrust of any tendency the spectator might have to overready self-assurance."

Journal, December 1946

When the war was on, from time to time someone who didn't know me would ask why I wasn't in the army. If the person was very impertinent, I would respond impertinently, but usually I simply answered truthfully that I was rejected because of ear damage caused by mastoids. The 4-F jokes never bothered me, nor did I lose sympathy for conscientious objectors, even so adamant a one as the artist Lowell Naeve. But sometimes *View* has been accused of frivolity, of "fiddling while Rome burned." During a paper shortage there was one patriot who thought we were criminal for using paper, which could be better utilized for fighting the enemy. Yet, we received many letters from soldiers overseas who wrote saying that receiving *View* was their brightest moment. One letter from Eugene Walters, an artist stationed for two years on a remote Aleutian island, declared that if there was any reason why the war should go on, perhaps it was to continue the possibility of free circulation for publications like *View*. Just a few months ago Walters showed up in the *View* office and offered to let us use his archive, an extensive one, of the Memphis Mardi Gras, a much older carnival than the one at New Orleans. Another soldier, Tom Prentiss, stationed in Europe, was inspired by *View* to make a long series of fantastical drawings for the amusement of the editors. In short, our magazine perhaps helped at least some people to retain their sanity, to retain some notions of civilized values in a world that was going to pieces.

View, it is true, had a libertarian stance from its beginning. We do not proclaim we are against capital punishment, rather we publish a poem by Joe Massey, who is in the Ohio State penitentiary for murder.

Slowly and slowly we waste away
Where we go we stay
I haven't seen anyone yet
Come back here sit down and eat

Declaring I shall live
With something to give
Know what he says is true
With no fear of me or you

Lowell Naeve describes what it is like to construct a guitar and a globe of the world with uneaten oatmeal and newspaper in order to pass the time while spending a year and a half in solitary confinement for being a nonreligious conscientious objector who refused to do any other work except "artcraft."

Can personal freedom be maintained even in extreme situations? *View* supports the possibility, knowing full well the horrors of worse prisons, worse tortures. We have published the art of children on our children's page, as well as art by the insane. Shall we not include them in the Surrealist ideal of liberty?

Our "humanism" has steadfastly supported the claims of mind and imagination, the desire of man to be free. We have done this not through pedantry, editorializing or propagandizing, but by presenting the art and ideas of artists and thinkers as *they* choose to delineate them.

5

THE LAST DAYS OF *VIEW* AND THE EXODUS THAT FOLLOWED MUST BE RECON-structed from scraps of memories, letters, conversations and perusal of the avant-garde publications of that time. There can be no question that the tiny art world of the 1940s existed ahead of the general public and was divorced from it. The people who comprised it were aristocratic in point of view, contemptuous of middle-class values, intellectually snobbish—a good combination for the making of any kind of art, since "democracy" is beside the point when it comes to twelve-tone music or classical ballet or direct metal sculpture. There was a rich "bohemia" uptown and a poor one down in Greenwich Village. I loved both of them. For me both spoke the same language—the uptown one liked millionaires and duchesses; the downtown admired Trotsky and Dorothy Day—but the *snobbism* was equal.

The exodus was not merely physical—it was the conclusion of a way of living and thinking that for me could never be the same again. Nor was it. However, I still did not realize this for several months previous to the farewells, and on my own I began a series of pamphlets, limited in number, which were called Prospero Pamphlets. Dmitri Petrov was the designer and Gotham Book Mart agreed to circulate them. The first was a poem by Charles Henri Ford called "The Half Thoughts, The Distance of Pain" and the second an essay by Parker Tyler entitled "Little Boy Lost," which compared Marcel Proust and Charlie Chaplin—look-alikes. There existed a photograph of Proust, leaning on the railing of a hotel porch wistfully gazing into the distance, which resembled Chaplin astonishingly. This photo was Tyler's inspiration for the comparison. For the third pamphlet I had been in correspondence with Wallace Stevens about his writing a puppet play, only to be told that he had many years before written two—but would send us a pamphlet-length poem instead. What I received was the magnificent (perhaps a masterpiece) *A Primitive Like an Orb*. Kurt Seligmann, upon reading it, instantly agreed to provide three drawings. Frances Steloff suggested we print a few more of the Stevens. I believe the price was fifty cents each, but some people thought this too expensive as there were so few pages.

Meanwhile, my apartment mate Waldemar Hansen got a job with Cecil Beaton, serving as his secretary, although all-round amanuensis would be a more precise description. They got along well considering that Waldemar approved of little that Beaton wrote or designed or photographed. "Perennial chi-chi," Waldemar would say, "but of course the world would be a dull place without a little chi-chi." The fact was he liked Cecil's character and so did I, since Cecil would often invite me to go over sketches with him or ideas for ballet décors.

Cecil enjoyed designing for the theater, especially the ballet, and I was flattered when later on he asked me to make suggestions for the ballet *Illuminations*. I suggested he look at the work of Paul Klee for an image to suggest a dour sky and crazy-looking church suitable for the painted backdrop. He had decided to make the costumes like those of the mime Debureau as played by Jean-Louis Barrault in the film *Les Enfants du Paradis*. All of the dancers would wear the white, clownlike costumes of the commedia dell'arte, but a few costumes would be in scarlet, to suggest evil or the world. The results were enchanting. Just before the opening, at a dress rehearsal, Cecil and the choreographer Frederick Ashton got into a screaming quarrel about Karinska's dressmaking. (Cecil was devoted to Karinska.) Somebody asked Lincoln Kirstein what the ruckus was downstairs, and Lincoln replied, "Oh, Cecil and Freddie are once again at needlepoints—" Of course, the two of them were the best of friends, but temperamental when it came to production time.

In 1956 I was a guest for a few days at Beaton's fine English country house near Salisbury. His mother, although of great age, was still vigorous enough to do a little gardening and to enjoy the pugs that scampered underfoot. Cecil had a glass room with a small pool in the center and a wide variety of potted plants on shelves; there we would have tea.

Mrs. Beaton was particularly proud of the tuberoses. Tall, doughty, very proper, the old lady, when Cecil told her he was considering marriage to Greta Garbo, looked at him sternly and asked, "Pray, who may *that* be?"—and became quite frigid when he explained she was an actress.

"You know," Cecil once said to me, "when people get old they should be better groomed than ever." I didn't see Beaton in the last years of his life; he had had a serious and paralyzing stroke. Still, he went on trying to make watercolor sketches and executed a final, grand series of fashion photographs for Paris *Vogue*. But I did see some snapshots of him taken just before he died. There he was with his marvelous white, wide-brimmed hat and twinkling eyes—absolutely immaculate.

Waldemar and I particularly enjoyed going to Beaton's parties, first at the Plaza, later in the penthouse of the Sherry Netherland Hotel, and lastly at the Drake—each a different suite. The décor of the last was inspired by Vermeer's colors, and had completely abstract paintings by Robert Goodnough instead of Mondrian, whose work at the time was unobtainable. It was fun to meet such celebrities as the Duchess of Westmorland, Tilly Losch, Garbo or the plump Elsa Maxwell. Beaton loved to encounter new, unknown people, and at his parties he mixed old and young, rich and poor, the fashionable and the bizarre—many of whom he liked to photograph. He particularly admired the filmmaker Maya Deren and the boxer Sugar Ray Robinson. I used to talk to Cecil about Jackson Pollock, and the world of fashion was stunned when he photographed *Vogue* models against the whirling expanses of Pollock's "poured paintings" at the Parsons gallery. Cecil was a barometer of changes of taste and seemed instantly aware of what was "now."

I, alas, was very slow to catch on to where the wind blew, so I was jarred when Charles Ford came into the office of *View* and announced that the magazine would be closing in a few weeks. We were abandoning the theater issue; all our affairs must be wound up by the end of the month. Betty Cage expressed no surprise, since (having a clearer conception of our account books) she had been aware of the coming demise. The magazine was hopelessly in debt. Charles was selling everything salable in the office, including all the back numbers of the magazine, which the Gotham Book Mart was only too happy to obtain.

Throughout that spring, my Friday evenings had continued. Mary McCarthy read a story about a college girl getting fitted for a diaphragm—or pessary, as it was called then. This was attended by several of her friends—among them Niccola Chiamonte, Dwight and Nancy

MacDonald, Philip Rahv, Harold and May Rosenberg and Peggy Guggenheim—who for a change concentrated on the story and were as amused as everyone else in the room. Waldemar asked me why I liked Mary so much, considering her stories and criticism were so acerbic. "She must be a bitch in real life." But, of course, Mary was nothing like that. Despite her arresting good looks, she was warmhearted, helpful and shed a kind of radiant intelligence; she was learned but never a bluestocking. Perhaps Mary smiled a little too much, quick on-and-off smiles that betrayed a certain nervousness but also a kind of diffidence, which made one like her all the more. She had a marvelous laugh, a delicious sense of humor.

One morning, as we were cleaning out the desks in the *View* office, Betty Cage said, "What shall we do with these drawings by Gorky that were reproduced in Breton's *Young Cherry Trees*? I've sent notes to several people asking they be picked up for months now, but no one has responded." "In that case," I suggested, "let's throw them in the trash can. After all, they were reproduced in the book and are of no value to anyone." And in went the black-and-white drawings.

The future seemed bleak for me; but I was delighted that Tchelitchew had convinced his friend Lincoln Kirstein to hire Betty as an assistant to Francis Hawkins, then the business manager of his ballet company. My own wheel of fortune had not stopped turning, however. A reprieve came through the good offices of Nico Calas, who telephoned me and said he wished to meet me at East Fifty-third Street. He would bring his friend Robert Altman, with whom he was collaborating. We met the next day.

For many years Altman had lived in Cuba, where he had married a mulatto woman and had two *café-au-lait* children. He was desirous of making his residence in New York so that he could educate his children properly. Nico had already told me about Altman's bank account, a reassuringly solid Liechtenstein fortune. Could there be anything more solid than Liechtenstein?

Altman wished to publish portfolios of prints in New York. He had asked Nico to select the first set of seven and to write an introductory essay. The artists were Wifredo Lam, Max Ernst, Kurt Seligmann, Miró, Matta, Yves Tanguy and William Stanley Hayter. Each portfolio would cost $100 and be limited to seventy-five copies. Would I, he asked, care to supervise such a venture? He would take over the *View* office for the remainder of the lease; I would get the same salary as I received from Charles Ford, $35 a week. And so Brunidor Portfolios was launched. "What," people asked me, "does the word 'Brunidor' mean?" And I would explain that a *bruñidor* was a burinlike tool used in engraving.

The pulls of the prints were to be executed at Atelier 17—Hayter's studio on East Eighth Street, which was a center for many European artists. Before the war Hayter had made his headquarters in Paris and had a considerable reputation there. But the artists included in our portfolio were scattered about and the only one who worked at the Atelier was Miró. Seligmann had his own press and the others sent in their plates. Miró came every day at nine, worked until one, went to lunch for two hours and quit at five. Then he would take the Third Avenue El uptown after buying a Spanish newspaper and smoking his little pipe while waiting for the train. Miró's worktable was extremely neat, every instrument in place. His work smock was always immaculate, and when he put his tools down he would wash his hands and remove any discoloration from his fingers with a bit of soapstone. Needless to say, Miró never wasted any time.

I had difficulties selling the portfolios when they were ready. Prints were not popular at this time in America, even though, like drawings, they were inexpensive. The bookseller Weyhe on Lexington Avenue was quite alone in carrying a regular stock of prints. There were few collectors. Julian Goldschmidt, a dealer in fine books, was enthusiastic but even he found the trade not brisk. The curator of prints at the Museum of Modern Art, William Lieberman, was loyal—but it cannot be said that Brunidor Portfolios was a success.

Depression, however, did not set in for me. Another very rich man appeared on the scene—Bill Copley from California. Petrov found him first and brought him around to One East Fifty-third Street. An amiable man, Copley was a short, stocky, round-faced fellow with a speech defect. Apparently he had inherited a large chain of Western newspapers, was interested in art and in buying it. Perhaps one day he would himself paint and open an art gallery in California. The artist I showed him who most caught his attention was Joseph Cornell. Nothing could have pleased me more—since my own feelings for Cornell were this side of idolatry. I telephoned Joseph and arranged for Copley to make a selection. He bought thirteen boxes, all to be shipped to California. Good heavens, I thought, how can such delicate objects be shipped that far and not arrive broken? However, I called the best art movers, Budworth, explained the difficulty of the problem and was told they would most happily accept the job. What I did not know was that Cornell had very specific instructions for such transport. Many of the boxes were opened, stuffed with soft tissue paper and cotton, and their lids screwed back on. It is awesome that not a single object was injured when the shipment arrived at its destination. (Oddly, I have heard of very few of Cornell's constructions, even the most fragile, which have been smashed.) Many years later, when the market for Joseph's boxes had risen precipitously—after his death—I asked Copley what he had done with his boxes, where were they? "Oh," he said, "I gave most of them away as Christmas presents, so I don't know."

Managing Brunidor Portfolios did not keep me sufficiently busy. When the critic and playwright Lionel Abel suggested that another publication be launched, I asked what he had in mind. The painter Matta and he wanted to make a broadsheet, to be called *Instead*. Matta's idea was to print all of it on a single large sheet of paper that could be folded down into a square and printed by offset, making the cost far lower than that of an ordinary magazine. When I saw the design, I became excited. Matta had devised a layout and typography that reminded me of the early publications of the Dadaists. His *mise-en-page* was intended to provoke and amuse, in the same spirit as Picabia's, although the style was pure Matta.

"Does the title suggest something else instead of *View?*" I asked. "Heavens, no!" Lionel declared. "We mean instead of the status quo, instead of mediocrity, instead of 'common man' options, instead of 'noncommitment'—a reference to Kierkegaard's *Either/Or.*" And indeed, Abel was after a publication in which he and his friends could philosophize in New York as similar literary people were doing in Paris. Existentialism was the current intellectual fashion in Paris, the leading avant-garde magazine being Jean-Paul Sartre's *Les Temps Modernes*. But Lionel, fascinated as he was by Sartre and his circle, also wished to be critical of them and remain independent. Francophile to the hilt, most of the material would be by French writers, some of it translations from *Les Temps Modernes* and *Le Combat*, as well as translations of poems by Malcolm de Chazel, Henri Pichette, Henri Michaux, Jacques Prévert. There were exclusive essays by Jean Wahl, Andrea Caffi, and one complete issue was filled by a long rumination on the nature of pleasure and pain by Maurice Blanchot. It was illustrated by a reproduction of one of the Marquis de Sade's manuscript scrolls. Matta's own drawings and drawings by others—Max Ernst was one—were witty and truly in the service of these philosophers and poets.

But in truth, I participated very little in the activities of *Instead*. I had gone at Lionel Abel's request to Bill Copley for the necessary funds to launch this publication and the money had been given. Matta, however, had a new girlfriend, Patricia Kane, who became—in effect—the managing editor, which probably was a good thing, since she was quite rich (macaroni, it was said, was the unmentionable source of income). From her rather grand East Seventy-ninth Street apartment, she was immersed in the making and distribution of Marcel Duchamp's now celebrated *Valise*—a box that contained every scrap, note and reproduction of Duchamp's total *oeuvre*. Miss Kane managed both *Instead* and the *Valise*; my name was dropped from the credits and I was no longer invited to editorial meetings. Matta was later dropped, but by then he was not in good repute in the small circle he inhabited.

I was to know more about Matta's exclusion from favor at lunch one day when I was taken by Miró to the Lafayette Restaurant on University Place. We joined Duchamp, Robert Altman, Nico Calas and Bill Hayter. The chief topic was Calas' polemic *contra*-Matta. Most of the conversation was in French because Miró, like Breton, spoke not a word of English. But then Miró never spoke; he liked to listen, and, of course, he was timid.

Miró's timidity was the cause of many stories, most of them probably apocryphal, but the one most amusing to me concerns an incident that occurred in the mid-1920s, when Max Ernst and Miró both had studios in the same building in Paris. Max was on the fourth floor and Miró on the first. No two people could be more unlike in their habits and personalities. Ernst was flamboyant, a womanizer, a party-giver, highly articulate and cerebral; Miró was quiet, retiring, neat, orderly, a family man. One night Max, having sold a picture, gave a big, noisy party with lots of high-flying girls and other artists. They all got terribly drunk and at one point Max decided that everyone should go downstairs to test Miró's loyalty to Surrealist ideals. They trooped down to quiz Miró, who, upon seeing them weaving about, was terrified.

"We've come to test you," cried Max waving a rope over his head, "and if you give the wrong answers, we're going to hang you from the rafter!" Miró was so disturbed he couldn't speak, and no matter what Surrealist questions were hurled at him—"Do you believe in the systematic destruction of the bourgeoisie? Are dreams more important than reality? Will you participate in the blowing up of the Arc de Triomphe?"—Miró could only sputter. "All right, Miró, if you can't answer, we shall prepare for the hanging."

Of course, Miró was aware of the Surrealists' delight in *l'humour noir* and practical jokes and saved himself by blurting out, *"Je suis peintre! Je ne suis pas philosophe!"* This of course pleased everyone and they all hugged and kissed *le petit* from Catalonia.

Miró would commit himself to no movements. It was not his fault that he was included in so many Surrealist exhibitions. Still, if he were asked which were his favorite poets, he would promptly answer the approved pat names, "Lautréamont, Baudelaire and Rimbaud"—an answer that could always warm Breton's heart.

I discreetly believed that Matta had been excommunicated by Breton because he was getting friendly with the Existentialists around whom Breton detected the odor of Stalinism; Calas had already written that a true Surrealist must necessarily be *contra* Sartre and his magazine. Here was Matta collaborating with Abel, who was sympathetic, even though critical of the new enemy. However, the conversation, when it turned to Matta and Gorky, was concerned with Matta's perfidy. Had he not seduced the beautiful wife of Breton's favorite rising star Arshile Gorky? Gorky had the misfortune of being afflicted with cancer; his neck had also been seriously injured by an accident in a car driven by Julien Levy, and he was disturbed with pain and anxiety. His wife, Magooch (as she was called affectionately), had two children to worry about; her husband had grown increasingly angry and was often hysterical with suspicion. At times he seemed dangerous. Magooch had sometimes fled the house in fear. Gorky's gloom was compounded by a fire that had occurred in his studio, destroying a large part of his work. Little wonder that he was often beside himself.

All the more reason, Breton and Calas argued, for Matta to behave himself. The circumstances were unattractive. Apparently at a dinner party given by Jeanne Reynal, the mosaicist, signs had been made of the cuckold, two fingers spread at the back of the head, after Matta had gone upstairs with Gorky's wife. This had been done without Gorky's being aware that he was being made fun of. The sign of the goat made behind his back! From the strict Surrealist point of view, this was appalling—although I wondered to myself why then the admiration the Surrealists pretended to have for the Marquis de Sade? Further, I wondered how anyone at Jeanne Reynal's dinner table could know precisely what occurred "upstairs"? Perhaps Matta was simply being helpful to a woman who was in terrible trouble.

Calas very much wished to publish his diatribe against Matta, which would be couched in allegory (a retelling of the story of the seduction of Agamemnon's wife, Clytemnestra, by Aegisthus after which

Agamemnon was murdered). Altman, sensible bourgeois, was not at all willing to proceed or lend himself to an opinion that in the end might prove libelous and unfair.

Throughout the discussion, both Duchamp and Miró sipped wine and smoked their pipes. They were uninvolved and unwilling to commit themselves to such an ambiguous moral morass.

Several months later, Gorky, in despair, took a rope, went to his studio and hanged himself by his injured neck. The horror of this suicide was heightened because he had made telephone call after telephone call asking many fellow artists to come and talk with him. They all claimed to be busy because they had become bored by Gorky's cries of pain. There was a meeting of the Artists Club after his death at which one artist after another got up to explain to the assembled members why he had not responded to the call. Those of us there who knew the weight of the sadness were left numb. Not the critic Emily Genauer—who in a feature article in the Sunday *Herald Tribune* attempted to prove the emptiness of the "new" American art by pointing to the example of the bankrupt unhealthiness of phonies like Arshile Gorky.

But I get ahead of my story. After I had sold a paltry thirty-five editions of the portfolio, Altman came to me and said he did not think New York was ready for such a print series. Anyway, said he candidly, his wife detested New York. She did not enjoy being treated like a "Negro," nor did his children. "It is very unpleasant," he said. "They are not used to that. In Cuba it was not that way. The Americans are impolite to people of another color and so we are moving to France, where it will be easier for all of us." Brunidor was over; Altman would take the remaining portfolios with him and begin another series in Paris. (Years later I was astonished to hear that the portfolio was a much-sought-after collector's item, and that one of the prints, the Miró, had sold at auction for $3,500.) What could I say? I had given all of my prints away. Robert Altman had lost money on the venture and none of his dreams had come true.

Instead came to a halt very soon after that. Lionel Abel had decided to move to Paris, where he remained for several years. In Paris he would bring his major talent to the fore: face-to-face discussions in cafés.

Two more art publications appeared. One was *Tiger's Eye*, an emanation from the Betty Parsons gallery, where artists were encouraged to congregate and talk a good deal. Even in the 1940s Mrs. Parsons was unlike any other art dealer, perhaps because she was herself an artist. Widely read and traveled, Betty was open to almost any aesthetic experience, including the most iconoclastic. She was rooted in the avant-garde and "making it new." *Tiger's Eye* attempted to reflect this attitude, and the attitude of the artists who congregated around Betty.

Perhaps the person who talked the most was Barney Newman, a regular at the gallery and a painter who exhibited work rarely—only a few pictures in group shows. Newman had an authentic flair for conversation, argument, polemic. His monologues, like those of Major Hoople (Barney wore a monocle and a tweed Sherlock Holmes hat), were very amusing, Once in a dinner conversation about high style in men's clothing, Barney startled his dining companions by explaining he had one of the best tailors in America, none other than the tailor of Al Capone.

Aesthetic philosophy, however, was Barney's chief interest; the advanced abstract painters in Parsons' group listened to what he had to say with keen interest. It wasn't until 1950 that the first full-scale exhibition of Newman's work was mounted, mostly large color fields of blue with one or two white vertical lines. It was a *succès de scandale*, a scandal that Newman kept alive for the next two decades. No doubt aided by his engaging personality, Barney possessed a genius for publicity when it came to his own work. At the end of his life he became a *monstre sacré*, and even after his death young artists continued to debate the merit or vacuity of Newman's work. The minimal sculptor Donald Judd maintained it was Newman's example that gave him the necessary courage to become a serious artist. It is, perhaps, Larry Rivers' witty, bigger-than-life-size portrait of Barney that will ensure his desired immortality.

The editors of *Tiger's Eye* were Ruth and John Stefan—she a writer of verse, he a painter of sorts. They had sufficient collaborators to put out a rather handsome quarterly with pictures and text—all unsigned (names were given on the back page). It was a vaguely unpleasant magazine because it mixed the very good with the very amateur in equal proportions, and had an atmosphere of piety about it that was unsettling. One editor had no talent for poetry and the other was a bad painter—a rueful combination.

The other publication was more complex because it was both worldly (in the sense of ambition) and sophisticated (in the pattern of intellectual snobbery). The editors were Robert Motherwell, Harold Rosenberg and Pierre Chareau—an intellectual like Frederick Kiesler, a "brain trust" architect who never built buildings. Motherwell's ambitions were global, and he had already launched his *Documents of Modern Art*—a rather badly edited series of paperbacks that the bookseller George Wittenborn patiently supported. Many of these *Documents* were useful, but not altogether trustworthy. Motherwell was at that point inventing what he called the "New York School," to replace "The School of Paris." He remained at the center of the "New York School" of painting for many years and his propaganda strategies were his finest achievement.

The day I came home to tell Waldemar that Brunidor was finished, he announced that he was leaving shortly for London to live with Peter Watson. Naturally, I was pleased for Waldemar. It is difficult to be a poet—especially a poet who is in earnest. And how wonderful it would be for him to live in London and meet the great English world of Cyril Connolly, the contributors to *Horizon* magazine and the artists Peter collected, among them Francis Bacon, John Tunnard and Giacometti. Peter also had a *pied à terre* in the Rue de Bac in Paris and went back and forth from London to Paris. Could there be a nicer, more enlightened rich man than Peter Watson to have as a sponsor?

The return to Europe by most of the artists in exile was by now complete. Breton, Masson, Tchelitchew, Berman, Lévi-Strauss and most of *le gratin* of international society had returned to agreeable Paris. Julien Levy closed his gallery. Peggy Guggenheim had closed hers and retired to Venice. Others had gone to Mexico, to Arizona; many simply disappeared. Atelier 17 continued for a few more years, but it too closed, and Hayter also returned to Paris.

Since I could not afford to maintain the apartment on East Thirty-eighth Street without Waldemar, I was fortunate to find a new friend, the ambitious playwright Randolph Carter, who was willing to share expenses. But the emptiness was not easily discarded. Even my two beautiful Siamese cats, Anthony and Dominic, having in their merry way destroyed much of my wardrobe, had to be given away (one to a cleaning lady with whom he lived happily ever after, the other to Harold Rosenberg—but that cat took off within two days).

It was the beginning of 1949. A murder had occurred in the apartment below mine. I discovered the apartment was being redone to cover the bloodstains left on every wall by the gruesome violence. My own apartment was in need of repainting. "Does it take a murder to force the repainting of rooms in this building?" I shouted at the landlord. What a mistake. Soon after I was told to find a new place to live.

"Why," I would ask the good analyst who was attending me, "why do I feel so happy when I take the Madison Avenue bus past Grand Central Station and down Park Avenue?" I would get off at East Thirty-eighth Street and each time I descended from the bus, and stepped on the curb, I felt this inexpressible happiness. Every time. Was it Murray Hill? The station? The pretty trees on Thirty-eighth Street? Was it the sunset in winter, the skyscrapers in the strange cold air of autumn? Was it the elegant, parcel-laden ladies dashing out of cabs? Was it the light cast into the sky? I would walk across Thirty-eighth Street to Third Avenue, usually stopping at the Italian grocery store. I would climb the stairs to my third-floor apartment, put the food in the Frigidaire, sit down in a chair—and wait. The Third Avenue El rushed by. Silence for a while—and then I would wait again. What, I asked myself, am I waiting for?

"Listen," said the doctor, "if you are lucky enough to feel that happy every day, don't ask why. Just grab it—or as Horace said, *'carpe diem'*—seize the day!"

I didn't wait very long. I was street smart enough to know that soon I would be "beginning to begin."

6

Letter to Art Historian Barbara Rose, November 1961

Your questions about the mid-1940s were naturally of interest to me, especially your suspicions that the art world was at that time much too cerebral and literary. It's taken me so long to understand whatever little I *do* understand that I'd like to give you a "cerebral" answer. It's a quote from the philosopher Alfred North Whitehead and I believe an excellent argument on behalf of the intellect as it relates to the making of art.

> The deliverances of clear and distinct consciousness require criticism by reference to elements in experience which are neither clear nor distinct. On the contrary, they are dim, massive and important. The dim elements provide for art that final background apart from which its effects fade

Artists for many generations believed that the shifting screen of ideas, poetry, religious texts and classical learning was the "background" before which they stood. True, these "elements in experience" are "neither clear nor distinct," but in the end are they not the "background" for the largest part of both Western and Eastern art?

"Painting culture" (to use Clement Greenberg's phrase) is simply a part of a larger culture, and in fruitful periods art and the "background" come together in a unique and productive way. Throughout the 1930s and the 1940s literature and politics were "dim, massive and important" for painters and sculptors. The best artists were influenced and fed by "ideas," perhaps rather vaguely and indirectly. I don't believe anything springs from the forehead of Athena, do you? Thus in New York it was considered perfectly normal that "intellectuals" influenced artists to a greater degree than they do today, even though it would be difficult to prove direct and specific influences. Did Sartre, for instance, influence Giacometti? Did the Existentialists dramatize the Nothingness, man as a "contingency," *without* influencing other artists in the dying School of Paris?

Surrealism has been completely out of fashion for the past several years; in fact, it has been sharply rejected by successful American painters and sculptors who are now triumphing on a worldwide scale, certainly influencing new styles and new attitudes. Sooner or later they will also influence the art market in Europe and elsewhere. Many notions involving politics and philosophy have become old hat. Perhaps this is a good thing, since both politics and philosophy are as prone to fashion (who reads Bergson anymore?) as the arts.

What I fear is the steady growth of anti-intellect. This is something I cannot quite put my finger on; rather, I have an uneasy feeling that it is "in the air" of the New York scene. Let's hope I am wrong about this.

I sat staring into space for a very short time. Chance led me to meeting Tibor Nagy in 1948. He is called by his Hungarian friends Nagyceri Tibor. His acquaintances call him Baron de Nagy. This meeting took place at the New York City Ballet. After the performance we went for coffee and I heard his story—for me, sad and moving. He had recently escaped from Hungary after a period in a German concentration camp in the Carpathian Mountains, one of two survivors. When the Russians moved into Budapest, more people were being sent away to Soviet concentration camps. By means of a false identity card he got to Prague, London and finally New York, where his young daughter, Marianne, lived with his former wife.

Tibor wanted two things: citizenship and a business. He had very little money, only a few thousand dollars to start with. I suggested that it might be a good investment to organize a professional marionette theater that could be booked into schools, summer camps, museums, hospitals or wherever an engagement could be procured. I would supply my technical and artistic experience, Tibor would serve as business manager and the company would be called the Tibor Nagy Marionettes.

Tibor came from the old nobility, the landed squires who lived on estates famous for their Tokay wine, disdaining titles unless they were obtained before the eighteenth century. He was educated abroad at Basel and Edinburgh universities and obtained the degree of doctor of economics. He then joined a bank in Budapest, where his chief duty was to serve as liaison between his bank and banks in other countries dealing in international currencies. His ability to speak German, French and English was an advantage he put to practical use. After Germany occupied Hungary, Tibor, along with other "unreliables," was sent to a concentration camp and escaped during the Russian advance. But the return to his home in Budapest was again made impossible by the Soviet Army's takeover, as they, too, regarded him as "unreliable"—possibly a spy for England or the United States. His former wife had married a Scandinavian and was able to get herself and her daughter to New York.

Tibor seemed eminently suitable to manage the affairs of our company. He had always been interested in the arts; his father, a prominent liberal judge, had collected paintings; the Nagy family had supported the opera and symphony. They were typical of that enlightened bourgeoisie that had made Budapest one of the most delightful of European capitals before the Holocaust. In any case, he did not wish to work in a bank again.

The first production we launched was a Pueblo Indian fairy tale inspired by Max Ernst's enchanting collection of Kachina dolls, many of which I had seen in the home of Jeanne Reynal. Our collaborators were Bernard Pfriem, who designed the production; the playwright Randolph Carter, who wrote much of the dialogue; the poet Charles Boultenhouse, who wrote three lyrics; and Ned Rorem, who set the lyrics to music for voice and tympani. Some of my old puppeteer friends were induced to work with me on the construction and costuming of the stringed figures. The hour-long play was entitled *Fire Boy*.

There are many "quest" fairy tales, particularly among the Indians of the Southwest. Our story had to do with a young hero's quest for a magical piece of turquoise guarded by a powerful dragon. Fire Boy would be ready for initiation into the mysteries of his tribe only if he came back from his dangerous adventure with turquoise in hand. There was a witch to be bypassed (played by me), two very peculiar butterflies (both played by me), and then the awful smoke-breathing dragon (also played by me). Other parts were enacted by Peter Grey and his

talented wife, Ty Grey (Ty played Fire Boy). Tibor served as stage manager and executed the lighting and special effects.

In a sense we were involving ourselves with *le merveilleux*, because
for the several thousand children who watched our marionettes during
the next three years, whether in the poorest settlement house or in the
ballroom of the Sherry Netherland Hotel, it was the marvelous and the
magical that held their attention. Gradually we added other little plays
to our repertoire, but *Fire Boy* continued to be the favorite.

It was a hard and taxing form of employment. In order to be at a
school for a nine-fifteen performance, we sometimes had to be in our
station wagon by six in the morning. If there was a one-fifteen performance at another school on the same day, we barely had time for lunch.
Sometimes we would have to haul our trunks and folding stage up
three flights. Often we had to make do in rooms where there were no
proper lights or even a platform on which to place our puppet stage.
There were weeks when the going was very good. The Parent-Teacher
Association was most cooperative about booking us into the public
schools of New York City and environs. We averaged about $150 per
show. If we did two in one day, which was more often than we had
hoped for, and if we were booked solidly for the week, our income
wasn't bad.

The satisfactions were many. It was particularly interesting to give
performances in poor neighborhoods where the kids had never been
exposed to "live" theater. Many had not seen string puppets in action.
They would shout to the "actors" things like, "Watch out! He's going to
bite you!"—referring to the dragon—or, "Don't go that way! The witch
is there!" I had a hand puppet, a little clown, who appeared in the booth
to the left of the proscenium. Before each act he had a conversation
with the audience, and it was often hilarious.

Sometimes we played for privileged children in private schools.
On weekends, due to the kindness of Cecil Beaton, who introduced me
to Prince Serge Obolensky, we played in the ballroom of the Sherry
Netherland Hotel. Obolensky was the manager of the hotel and his
staff would set up a few hundred little golden chairs, place potted palms
at each side of our stage and in would march bunches of kids with their
mothers or nannies every Saturday morning and afternoon. I guess all
kids are the same, for the well-off ones behaved exactly like the ones on
the Lower East Side.

The editor of *Flair*, George Davis, came one Saturday, and after the
performance we had lunch at the Central Park Zoo. I was an admirer of

his writing and had read George's Harper Prize novel, written back in the 1920s. After this triumph he had moved to Paris, where he became the close friend of Bérard, Cocteau and Colette. Paris was his home for many years, but when he returned to America he became in short order the editor of several magazines, the last being *Flair*, published by Fleur Cowles, wife of the owner of *Look*. Our lunch at the zoo was enchanting because no one else I knew could tell such interesting stories. He would tell me about his "boarding house" in Brooklyn, where W. H. Auden, Carson McCullers, Oliver Smith and other artists lived with him, and about his extraordinary marriage to the stripper Gypsy Rose Lee, or about the vaudeville performer who stayed at his house with trained dogs and chimpanzees!

Best of all, I liked to hear about Colette, whose stories about young girls, cats, demimondaines and her mother, Sido, I often reread. When she was old and completely bedridden, George would visit Colette in her room above the gardens of the Palais-Royal. There she would be surrounded by flowers, her mineral collection, her barometers and thermometers to observe the weather. One day he came in and was delighted by an exquisite odor he couldn't identify. "Look behind you," she said. On a table directly behind him, George saw a large bowl of fresh apples. "I released their perfume by warming each one in my hands," Colette explained.

A few years after our lunch at the zoo, one of George's best friends, the composer Kurt Weill, died. George had assisted him in many ways after Weill and his wife, Lotte Lenya, had moved to New York. Lenya was more than a close friend: she adored George and it was entirely suitable that they were married. I had never met Weill; but since George liked me, Lenya immediately did, too, bringing about a friendship that proved to be an abiding one, even after George's death several years later.

My absorption in puppetry did not preclude a continued interest in painting. I kept in touch with many artists. In Provincetown, for instance, I would visit Adolph and Esther Gottlieb; Adolph, an ardent sailing enthusiast, would take me out in his dinghy. Other times I would visit Stamos, who enjoyed showing me new work. One Friday evening we did a performance of *Fire Boy* on Eighth Street for that casual alliance of painters and sculptors called The Club. I used to go to meetings rather often because it kept me abreast of new developments and I liked the people who gathered there. After the performance I was "taken up" by Elaine and Willem de Kooning. In fact, it was shortly thereafter that Bill invited me to his studio on Third Avenue, near Grace Church, to see his paintings. They astonished me, and I said I didn't understand them because I couldn't tell what was in front and what was in back. "It's my problem, too!" he commented.

The friendship that had begun in late 1944 with Lee Krasner and Jackson Pollock had in no way lessened, either. It was through them that I began to apprehend difficult contemporary art. If the word "epiphany" means a sudden, sharp understanding or insight, or if it means experiencing something for the first time, having missed its significance repeatedly, then what I had on one visit to the Pollocks' was an epiphany.

I was in Jackson's studio. It was a fine sunny day. I was seated on a high stool looking about me. Canvases were tacked to the wall, and spread out on the floor was a large one. Jackson was, as usual, uncommunicative; his attention was on his pictures. As I had in the past, I stared at his work, receiving nothing. Then I said, "That picture on the floor is so big I wonder how you get to the middle part." Then he said, with a little laugh, "That's easy. I throw the paint off a soaked brush or whatever else I have in hand."

"Throw the paint? But where do you throw it from?" Again he laughed. "Wherever I happen to be. Sometimes I'm kneeling on the canvas or bent over it on one side. I dip and I throw or else I dribble it."

Two images came to mind. One was Jackson on a Sunday afternoon coming home with a tub of clams he had dug from a nearby inlet. He had invited about twenty people to the house for clams and beer. As the guests sat around, Jackson knifed open several dozen clams (with what seemed to be superhuman speed) and placed them in fine order on plates. The movement of knife into shell never faltered. He seemed to open each mollusk with a single jab and slice.

The second image was watching Jackson hammer a series of nails into a door he was repairing. The nails, each about two inches long, had to be sunk in a precise row. Each nail was held in place while, with a vigorous blow, it was hammered in to its full depth in a single straight motion, just as with the clams.

As Jackson said "throw," I suddenly had a memory of a knife thrower I had seen in a sideshow. The perfect aim and perfect delivery to the target was like Jackson's throw of the paint. Like the Zen archer, he knows exactly where he wants the drops or pools of paint to fall. The "target" was the harmony of color and movement that he wished to bring about. The piece of canvas on the floor was a "space," whose dimensions would be forever altered by the rhythms created by skeins of pigment hurled forward even as a spider flings his threads to create a beautiful architecture, gossamer-thin yet strong.

Jackson left the studio and I sat alone, looking. A moment came when I was not merely looking; I was *seeing*. I had even stopped associating his forms and colors with fields of waving grass or with rocks in caves or the movement of constellations. There is no form we cannot associate with another form; something is always like something. Pollock was not *like* Nature; he was a part of the natural world; he was his own Nature.

I realized that I would never again see works of art the way I once had.

If anything, my understanding was further enhanced by Pollock's wife, Lee Krasner. When the Pollocks first moved to the Springs in 1946, there was only one small room upstairs, where Jackson worked. But as soon as the studio in the barn was finished, Lee took over the upstairs room. During this time and for a few years afterward she was painting "little image" pictures.

One of the things she and I liked to do together was to invent names for pictures, since Lee was careful about identification, and names are a good way to keep organized. Jackson used numbers for a while, but later took to making up titles, some of them quite fanciful.

One evening, while we were sitting in the kitchen, which at that time was separated from the living room, a large rat came scampering from behind the refrigerator in full view of the three of us. Lee and I let out wild screams and jumped up on the kitchen table, both of us being completely phobic about rats. Jackson grabbed a broom and went after the rat. But in order to keep it from going into another part of the house, he put one of Lee's paintings across the doorway. The rat rushed bang into the painting and down came the broom! Holding the rat by the tail, Jackson threw the carcass into the nearby field.

"Did you know," I said, picking up the conversation, "that I heard a lecture recently by Meyer Schapiro in which he explained the symbolic meaning of a mousetrap in the right-hand corner of one of the panels in Robert Campin's fifteenth-century triptych in the Cloisters. It had something to do with Christ and the trapping of souls."

Lee said, "Well, I guess Meyer has never heard of a painting catching a rat. With Jackson's help, of course."

"Have you named the picture yet?" I asked.

"As a matter of fact, I haven't."

Jackson thought *Deterrence* might make a nice title. Then Lee said, "How about *The Trap* or *The Rat Trap*? That will make the critics buzz."

"No," said I. "Let's be a little classier. Let's call it *The Mouse Trap*, making a subtle, truly subtle reference to the Renaissance." Lee thought it a lovely name for a painting and put it down.

It must be understood that all of this conversation was accompanied by laughter. If someone were to ask me what was the single attribute which most endeared Lee to her friends, I would say it was her wild gaiety, a sense of humor that was irresistible and irrepressible. Her conversation was often peppered by sharp observations or satirical thrusts at fools, whom she could not suffer at all. Her wit could be acid; she detested stupidity; and she never believed it was unwomanly to be intelligent.

Much of Lee's intelligence focused on art, both her own and other people's. It is apocryphal to believe that her husband was jealous of her talent or that he in any way discouraged her from working. A strong argument could be made that as their talents grew and developed, they shared their discoveries; theory was practice, and practice became theory. The Pollocks were together a very long time and had profound respect for each other's work.

Some critics have superficially found Krasner's paintings too influenced by Pollock's. This is a serious mistake—the mistake of looking and not *seeing*. If a careful study of each one's work were undertaken, a study in comparisons of paintings done between the years 1936 and 1956 (the year of Jackson's death), the shallowness of such opinions would be revealed.

However, there are ways in which it could be said that they were alike and in complete agreement. Both enjoyed painting "abstractly," that is, inventing forms and discovering forms as they worked. Both liked to animate, to bring vitality to the whole of any given area, be it paper or canvas—a process that gave rise to the catch phrase "all-over." Both of them saw the surface of a picture as a definitive reality that needed none of the props of illusion. Creating very large pictures gave them deep pleasure, but, equally, they painted small ones, middle-sized and even very tiny ones. Color was integral to their work, although it might be said that for Krasner color was somewhat more important than it was for Pollock—perhaps because Krasner was (and is) inner-directed, given to an idiosyncratic mysticism.

Nature, the outside world in all its variety, was deeply important to the Pollocks, not for the reordering or imitation of it as some critics have imagined, but as an abiding presence.

Jackson's pet crow, Caw-Caw, exquisitely illustrates their love of creatures. Probably Caw-Caw was "imprinted," as Konrad Lorenz would say, when found in the nest, since he followed Jackson around, came when called and adored sitting on Jackson's head.

"That's some bird," Lee would say. "Our neighbor is furious with him because every time she hangs out the laundry, Caw-Caw flies over to her yard and pulls out all the clothes pins!"

Lee, of course, had her jumbo-sized dogs, Gyp and Ahab, padding after her inside the house and out. Gyp was a cross between Newfoundland and Labrador; Ahab, a throwback of a standard poodle. Whatever they were, they were big and full of fun. Both lived to a venerable old age, staying with Lee in the city after Jackson's death.

What I liked best when I arrived in the Springs was to be shown the Pollocks' beautiful collection of rocks, minerals and sea shells. There was always something new, for they loved the fantastic in nature with the same passion that Breton displayed when he, too, collected such objects.

There was one very tall vase in the living room into which Lee put a single gigantic sunflower every summer. In the fall she combed the fields for flowers to dry. In the bay window was her indoor garden of magnificent hanging pots of begonias, ferns (the more exotic the better), Canary Island ivy, fuchsias, spider plants. On the floor below were spread stones picked up along the seashore, and on these were placed more pots of plants.

Much has been written about the Pollocks, from the silly and idealistic to the scurrilous; they have been made myths and they have been slandered. But many writers have not looked at the simple facts of their lives: they do not ask the obvious question of how so much work could have been created had the Pollocks not been essentially quiet, orderly and productive. Considering how little money they had, it was a triumph that both were uncompromising in their determination to earn their living through their art. The world has not been kind to such artists. It is they who, despite their determination to ignore the encroachments of society, are most vulnerable to society's curiosity and exploitation.

Much has been made of Jackson Pollock's tragic malady by half-baked psychoanalysts, untalented novelists and fifth-rate journalists. The myth, for instance, that Pollock was drunk the day of his accident was disproved many years later when it came out that Jackson had exchanged two drawings with Geoffrey Potter, a neighbor, for a piece of heavy machinery. This machinery was in the back of the car and when the car hit the soft shoulder of a curve in the road, the machinery was flung to the other side of the car trunk. It was heavy enough to cause the car to go out of control. Jackson was thrown from the car and killed instantly. In all the years I knew him, I saw Pollock drunk perhaps twice. I prefer to think of him simply as a serious artist.

One day, after Jackson had seen my marionettes, he called me into the studio and said, "Look! I've made a puppet for you!" It was a figure about eighteen inches high, cut out of wood, on each side of which canvas was glued. Both sides were gaily painted and the figure seemed to dance as it hung from a string and turned. I don't think any other gift ever made me so happy. Unfortunately, a few years later the puppet was accidentally destroyed by Larry Rivers' children. Some time after Jackson had died, I was at a retrospective showing of his work and came upon a good-sized canvas from the middle of which was cut the figure that Jackson had pasted onto the wooden puppet. I suppose anyone looking at me must have wondered why I was so melancholy.

It was easy to remain in connection with the art world during this period. In 1949 I moved to Ninth Street, near First Avenue. It was a two-bedroom apartment with a garden and a decent-sized living room. The area was new to me, but I soon discovered I had friends in the neighborhood. I began to attend meetings regularly at The Club and to go to the Cedar Bar. My former social life with my intellectual companions no longer existed. My natural gregariousness found satisfaction by finding new people and a new life.

I think many artists who went to The Club preferred it to meeting in the Waldorf Cafeteria on Sixth Avenue, and the owners of the Cedar Bar liked artists, which made the bar another sympathetic gathering place. It was a way to stave off loneliness. The weekly meetings on Friday nights were immensely stimulating. Someone would give a talk, the floor would be thrown open to discussion, and, on occasion, the arguments could be explosive. People could throw a donation into a "kitty" to help pay the rent and to buy beer and booze for the end of the meeting. On New Year's Eve there was a big, noisy party. At one such shindig I found myself suddenly grabbed by a big polar bear. It was Alexander Calder. "Come on, Johnny! Let's give it a whirl!" And around and around the room we one-one twoed, one-one twoed,

everybody jumping out of the way. What can come to mind but Edith
Sitwell's lively refrain in *Façade*:

> ". . . See me dance the polka,"
> Said Mr. Wagg like a bear,
> "With my top hat
> And my whiskers that—
> (Tra la la) trap the Fair, . . ."

There were no officers or rules or membership requirements. A
few volunteers did what little organizing needed to be done—the most
active of these was the sculptor Philip Pavia, whose geniality and patience kept The Club going.

Often three or four painters would hold a symposium, each
speaking in turn. The subject would often disappear in the exchanges
that took place. When Ad Reinhardt proposed an art that should have
no connection with anything, not God, Morals, Politics, Movements,
Aesthetics, Philosophy, Science, an Art pure and of, from, and in the
studio, unsullied by the world, especially the art world, tempers would
start fraying. At other times the meeting would be highly decorous, as
when Sir Harold Acton held forth on Vasari or when Buckminster
Fuller explained his geodestic principles with egg containers and Ping-
Pong balls. Occasionally the meeting would take the form of entertainment, such as the music of John Cage with Pierre Boulez playing the
piano.

As time went by and the attendance grew larger and larger, a
change began to be noticeable: The Club was being used by certain artists as a sounding board to promote their careers. No one could make a
critical remark, favorable or unfavorable, without self-promoting
shouts of "Name names!" Some of the older artists whose careers were
better established began to feel exploited, and one by one they began
dropping away. How often the untalented believe that if they hobnob
with the genuinely talented, some of it will rub off on them! However,
new and younger people flocked to The Club and it managed to continue well into the 1950s.

The Cedar Bar went on much longer. It remained a rendezvous for
the Abstract Expressionists and the so-called Second Generation for
many years.

But the marionette theater did not. Much as I enjoyed the fun of
being with young audiences, the work was backbreaking, the income
got smaller and smaller, the problem of obtaining bookings became

ever more difficult. The day arrived when both Tibor and I realized it was impossible to hold the company together and pay their salaries. He had decided, now that he had obtained the papers he needed to apply for naturalization, that he would go back into banking, the business he had been trained for. I had been harboring some ideas of my own, much encouraged by Clement Greenberg and the Pollocks. I wished to open an art gallery that would represent the new, up-and-coming talents to whose studios I had begun to go. And so I became an art dealer.

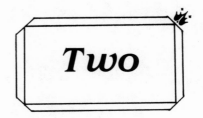

Two

The secret of being a bore
is to tell everything

—VOLTAIRE

7

"**Y**OU KNOW," I SAID TO MY FRIEND ROBERT ISAACSON, WHO LIVED ON West Fifty-eighth Street, near the Plaza Hotel, "you ought to start an art gallery." It was early in 1951. He had just turned eighteen and already had the elegant, bony face and heavy-lidded eyes of one who knows the world. Robert had played a set of pieces by Couperin on his harpsichord for me, and one knew, watching him play, that culture, not higher education, was his forte. "Why not?" he mumbled. Like many who are more sensitive than they should be, Robert was not given to clear or loud enunciation, but one got used to it. "It would be unique," I said. He looked thoughtful. "I'm sure of that, but what would I exhibit? There's not much available unless you have pots of money and can buy the best in Paris."

"Couldn't you," I suggested, "put on shows that nobody else would do? For instance—a show of useless objects." I said this glancing around at the objects that decorated the room, some of whose use or meaning I couldn't fathom. "Or maybe you could get Cornell to give a show." Robert loved Joseph Cornell's work.

After a while the conversation lagged. We both lost interest and I had to go to dinner. Robert wasn't prepared to be an art dealer—yet. But a week or so later I thought about our conversation and I made the decision to do myself what I had suggested for him. I realized I didn't have the necessary money, but I knew I had the gall.

It was shortly after this that Waldemar Hansen and I were invited to a party given by a poet of Waldemar's acquaintance, Harold Norse. It was to be a big splurge of a party paid for by an admirer of Harold's, the rich, Anglo-American collector Dwight Ripley, a friend of Peggy Guggenheim's. Both Waldemar and I were in the best of moods, ready as always to sing for our supper, and determined to be as agreeable as possible to Dwight Ripley. He immediately caught our attention, and was fascinating. More fortunately still, he found us amusing. "Strange," said Waldemar, "the way the rich always turn us on." Not quite true, of course. The brilliant, the beautiful, the talented rich, turn *all* of us on.

Harold Norse was a poet of sorts. He was short, hefty and remarkably hirsute, with an engaging New York accent (which borough one couldn't quite tell; maybe it was simply Hunter College). At any rate, Harold Norse was Ripley's obsession that season, and Norse was richly rewarded by him with the gift of an expensive Picasso that made it possible for him to move to Italy. It must be said to Norse's credit that while in Rome he cleverly translated the marvelous street poetry of Giacomo Belli, a nineteenth-century Italian Villon. Fidelity was not a Norse characteristic; as Rupert Barnaby, Dwight's closest friend and colleague, later said, "Dwight is not a griever or a whiner. Gone are the snows of yesteryear."

Not too long after the Norse splurge Waldemar and I were invited to Ripley and Barnaby's country house in Dutchess County, just outside of Wappingers Falls. It was a large property of a hundred and five acres. A simple farmhouse had been adapted into a comfortable rural retreat with a rock garden, lawns and a fine greenhouse surrounded by beautiful woods. The fields extended into the distance with only one dairy farm's gleaming silver roof to spoil the vista. Both Dwight and Rupert were serious scientists: the rockery and greenhouse contained a wide variety of specimens from various parts of the world—copper-striped miniature tulips from behind the casino at Monte Carlo; a tiny lilac from Siberia sent by their fellow botanist Justice William O. Douglas; small, exquisite iris from Turkey. The greenhouse featured conical-shaped flycatchers, as well as tables of seedlings and cuttings.

Rupert spent most of his day peering through his microscope, a taxonomist of the first order, who had made field trips in the Western mountains and deserts, as well as in Mexico. Before he turned to exploring American flora, the countries bordering the Mediterranean and its islands had been his hunting grounds for many years. Now, in Dutchess County, Rupert was preparing his magnum opus on high-altitude species for the U.S. Department of the Interior.

Dwight had interests beyond botany. He was an accomplished linguist and both spoke and wrote a dozen languages, including one as archaic as Catalan. Dwight surprised Miró when he sent the artist some verses in the master's native tongue. "How could anyone write such poetry who wasn't a Catalonian?" Miró wrote back, delighted of course with Dwight's homage. Both Rupert and Dwight, having been educated at Eton and Oxford, were classicists and quite at home in Italian, French, Portuguese and Spanish. But Dwight's capacity for languages embraced several of the Slavic dialects, as well as Turkish and the fiendishly difficult Magyar. I sometimes wondered to what end all this linguistic talent would lead. I didn't learn until many years later he was writing a botanical dictionary giving the names of flora in sixteen languages other than Latin.

Rupert always looked and acted what he was by vocation—a dedicated scientist—but being the youngest son of an old county family, he wore his learning lightly and never showed off. Dwight, on the other hand, looked and acted like a handsome international playboy. He loved to show off and was terribly funny. Nothing and no one was sacred to Dwight—including himself. His sense of parody was precise: pretentiousness, folly, hypocrisy were the ever-favorite targets of his exquisitely barbed wit. He was as funny as S. J. Perelman, as sardonic as Groucho Marx, as fantastical as Ronald Firbank.

Waldemar and I had never spent a more enchanting weekend in the country. Inside the house there was a wonderful library containing everything from novels, poetry and travel books to a superb collection of botanical volumes, as well as a host of dictionaries, atlases, encyclopedias. What pleased me, of course, were the artworks—many Mirós, several Cornell boxes, a wide variety of abstract paintings, some fine nineteenth-century prints and watercolors, Edward Lear landscapes and a collection of nineteenth-century, highly fanciful birdcages. The furniture, the china, the carpets, even the bibelots, denoted a certain kind of highly sophisticated European taste; Dwight and Rupert were thoroughly English in their style. How they managed to keep everything looking so well, to live so comfortably, surpassed my understanding, since they could not abide any servants in the house. They compromised with a groundsman to help with the outside gardens and woods. Rupert was a skillful cook; his meals were no-nonsense elegant—simple but delicious.

We went for walks and were taught the names of the plants, flowers, trees. The rockery was so fascinating one went back to it over and over again, often discovering tiny specimens one had missed. Just before dinner we placed records on the turntable—sometimes classical, sometimes jazz. After dinner we all went to the parlor, where Dwight, sitting at the Steinway baby grand, would play *his* outrageous repertoire of pop tunes. Sometimes we would look at Dwight's amusing color drawings, most of them parodies of contemporary art, or read Dwight's satirical poems and limericks saturated with puns, spoonerisms, conceits. The word polymath took on new meaning.

Alas, Dwight was also polymorphously perverse and dearly loved to descend on the city, take a suite at the Plaza and have a bit of fun. This would have been okay with the management except that its guest had a Falstaffian appetite for alcohol. When at last the mischief went too far, Dwight was banished forever from the Plaza. I don't think he cared in the least. During these periods of riding the wagon high, Dwight would become madly generous. I suspect he was in that condition when he gave the Picasso to Harold Norse. I shall never know whether he was drunk or sober when, one day at lunch at the Chambord, Dwight suggested I go ahead with my plan to open a gallery; he would give me $500 to start with and $300 a month to keep me going.

"You will, of course, let me show some of your pictures after we open?" I asked.

"I doubt it. I'm not a serious artist. I do what I do for fun. Another thing: I don't wish to be consulted about what you decide to exhibit. I'm *not* that interested. Follow your own taste." That was that; Dwight never interfered with the gallery schedule, and only after much cajoling did he let me show his color drawings.

Once I realized I had the backing to open a bona fide noncommercial, no-strings-attached art gallery, my nerve began to fail me. In secondary school I had been declared subnormal when it came to adding, subtracting, dividing. Fractions were beyond me. I could not pass algebra. I could not comprehend geometry or trigonometry. Faced with a row of figures, my mind went blank. How then would I take care of accounts, the banking, the insurance, and most terrifying, the departments of taxation—city, state, federal? Someone would have to do this for me. But whom could I trust? Whom but Tibor de Nagy—a banker by profession, a worrywart by temperament—the perfect keeper of the exchequer. He would take care of the books, I would do everything else. Happily, Tibor agreed to join forces with me, using his name as the name of the gallery. It would help get him his naturalization papers.

I began to formulate plans for an art gallery. The year was 1951. Dwight Ripley handed me his first check. I needed only to find artists and a place to show them. I needed advice.

One thing I knew for certain: even if I had had the capital to purchase good work in Paris, I didn't have the kind of expertise necessary to buy and sell expensive art by celebrated artists. I did not have the experience nor the panache to merchandise "blue chips"; I had never *worked* in a gallery and had no concept of its inner structure. The only artists I knew were already well along with their careers. The way to begin then must be with unknown people. But it took me awhile to learn this. My first thought was to turn the gallery space over to Joseph Cornell, but he was not interested. I then appealed to Isamu Noguchi, who said he would lend us objects he had collected in the Orient. What a perfect beginning, I thought.

During the summer I went often to East Hampton to visit with Lee and Jackson Pollock and while there I met Tino Nivola, who was part of a Milanese circle of architects and designers—Steinberg, Rudolphsky, Ponti and others. Le Corbusier had been a guest of the Nivolas for several weeks and left behind a painted wall. Tino had remodeled an old farmhouse with a solarium in the garden; Le Corbusier had been helpful. Another architect friend was Roberto Mango, who was having a hard time getting anywhere in New York. Tino suggested that Mango might design a gallery for me once I found a space. In September I found a first-floor, cold-water flat in a tenement at 219 East Fifty-third Street—a few steps from the El. Roberto came and told us what he wanted done, which boiled down to removing unnecessary walls and tailoring those that remained by stripping all gingerbread—cornices, boiserie, curlicues. Everything was painted eggshell white, and a smart, flat door was installed at the entrance. A spider web of black wires with sockets was hung at intervals about eight inches from the ceiling to provide spotlights. The ceiling itself was painted sky blue.

A few weeks before the gallery opened, Noguchi informed me he was not interested in exhibiting anything in a brand-new gallery. I immediately appealed to Tino Nivola to show his sand sculptures. He agreed, with the proviso that the floor be painted the same blue as the ceiling. This was done. The gallery looked beautiful, although the painted floor was still a bit sticky when the opening-day crowd walked in in November 1951. I sat behind my Hans Knoll desk, waiting for sales. But few there were, and at the end of the show Nivola was annoyed and refused to help in any way to remove his work and bring it back to his studio. He made it plain that he was no longer affiliated with the Tibor de Nagy gallery. (The "de" had emerged with the gallery.) The blue floor was a wreck, and before we could open the next show we had to put down heavy, practical black vinyl. Just before Nivola's show closed, a friend brought me a book about the ancient bas-reliefs of Sardinia, the island on which Tino was born and raised. Tino's sand sculptures were made by scooping out forms on the beach and pouring plaster into the concavities. They resembled rather uncomfortably re-markably the antique models. I was sad also to say goodbye to the gifted, elegant, kindly Roberto Mango, who found New York too diffi-cult, too tough to live and work in; he returned to Italy. This was a loss.

Luckily, for months before the gallery opening I was listening to sound advice from three knowledgeable people: Jackson and Lee Pol-lock, and the critic Clement Greenberg. All three urged me to identify with, and work for, the artists of my own generation. But who were they? How would I find them? They gave me lists of names of artists whose work I must go see. Happily, all of them lived in Manhattan.

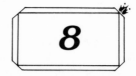

8

*A*S I SAT BEHIND MY DESK IN THE REAR OF THE GALLERY, PLACED SO THAT I could always see who came in and who was leaving, it became apparent that I needed time to gather a group that represented the new. And if Dwight Ripley was to continue to be my patron, I must make efforts to do at least a little something that would please him. Like any mendicant I was frightened to fall into disfavor before I could accomplish what I wished. Two people seemed at that time very close to Dwight, and if they were to denigrate me and the gallery, I might very well stop receiving my monthly check. Ergo: I must cultivate Willard Maas and his wife, Marie Menken. (I need not have, I later discovered; but such is the nature of paranoia.)

Willard Maas was perhaps five foot six and plump; Marie was enormous, about six foot two. It is no exaggeration to say their frequent appearances at parties or openings created instant attention. No doubt they would have been noticed even had their physical appearance been less extraordinary. Everything about them was larger than life and for many years they were popular figures, invited everywhere at least once. Toward the end of their lives both became grotesque, vastly overweight and unhinged—Marie was one of the fantastics in Andy Warhol's movie *Chelsea Girls.*

But when I first knew them they were relatively benign. Willard taught college English and had a reputation as a witty poet whose verses resembled those of George Barker or Ruthven Todd. He was friendly with most of the poets writing then and was often anthologized.

Marie, a Roman Catholic of Polish extraction, was Willard's second wife. She painted small, lime-colored fantasies, which were sometimes shown in the back room of the Betty Parsons gallery. But her art was necessarily an avocation, as Marie worked full time, checking the teletype in the newsroom of *Time* magazine. Since both of them worked, the Maases were able to live comfortably in the unusual penthouse of an apartment building in Brooklyn Heights. They proudly possessed two little structures on the roof with a terrace garden in between. Their view of the river, the harbor and all of Manhattan stretched out like Baghdad, was the most spectacular I have ever seen in New York. There they gave parties, one after the other, which were lavish and often scandalous. (I learned early to skedaddle before the fun got out of hand.) The guests drank jeroboams of wine, quarts of booze. Very few had the capacity of the Maases, who were the last to go under the table. People jammed into the little rooms full of Victorian furniture, feathers in vases, wax flowers under bell jars, pictures and objects covering every inch of wall space. "Bohemian opulence," said my friend Waldemar after our first visit. "Talk about generous to a *fault*."

The Maases applauded Dwight for the support he was giving the gallery. "So much better," they would tell me, "that *you* get a bit of all that money than *some* of the people who gouge poor Dwight." It was none of their business how Ripley's money was spent, but hearing them say so made me a little less uneasy. But one never knew when they would do a *volte-face*.

"I must," I told Tibor, "give Marie Menken an exhibition. She has been painting pictures with regular pigment and phosphorescent paint. Betty Parsons won't be showing them because they present difficulties. They are, however, unusual."

The difficulty was that every window and cranny of the gallery had to be secured against light with heavy black paper and tape. The show was called *Pictures for Daytime and Pictures for Nighttime*. With the lights on, one image was visible; with the lights turned off, an entirely different image glowed in the darkness. The paintings were abstract and vaguely biomorphic.

For the opening Marie brought a gigantic punch bowl, which she filled with champagne and lots of fresh violets. (Willard occasionally laced the bubbly with brandy as the evening went on.) Marie herself was an apparition. She was dressed in a long black evening gown covered with jet beads from top to bottom. In her hair were violets. So reminiscent was she of Margaret Dumont of Marx Brothers' fame that one looked to see if Groucho was behind her.

The Maases were in their glory. They had sent out twelve hundred invitations and about two thirds of the people showed up. The jam in our small rooms was truly like the stateroom scene in *A Night at the Opera*. There was a crowd in the hall and on the sidewalk out front. Violets were getting into everything, the noise rose to a deafening pitch. "Are you ready?" shouted Marie. I was stationed at the light switch. Off went the lights. There was instant silence. Gradually the phosphorescent paint began to glow in the Stygian darkness. There were muffled oohs and aahs. "On with the lights," commanded Marie. "Luminosity must be gathered up to get the proper glow."

The next time the lights went out there were squeals, ouches, comments like, "Don't do that," "If you ever do that again, I'll kick you," and mounting giggles. The uproar was continuous from then on, with or without lights. People outside the gallery were getting angry. The noise became so great that a neighbor called the police and told them a riot was in progress downstairs. The police arrived, declared we were breaking the law by going beyond "reasonable occupancy." "Okay," shouted the sergeant, "break it up, all out." It was my first *succès de scandale!* (It wasn't the last.) The Maases remained benign for a few years. The show was all they could have wished for.

The story doesn't end there. Four years later, while sitting in the Café de Flore in the Boulevard St. Germain, an art dealer whom I didn't know came up to me and asked if I was John Myers. "Yes," I said. "Is it true you opened an exhibition in New York with a gang bang?" "Well," I replied as modestly as I could, "it was not exactly a gang bang; it was more like a bacchanal." Alas, word had gone out that the entire gay community had converged on my gallery for a spirited rally at the Marie Menken *vernissage*. During the weeks that followed the closing I became dimly aware that the Maases, who were both as odd as Dick's hatband, wished to be helpful by encouraging such an ambience. Common sense told me that the sort of financial, social and critical support I needed was never going to come from that quarter. Since 50 percent of the population were female and at least 70 percent were both straight and square, I had best turn on the cold water. It took a lot of effort to do this tactfully—but there are ways of getting what you want without raising a fuss. I succeeded in large part.

9

I HAD BEEN GOING ABOUT LOOKING AT WORK IN ARTISTS' STUDIOS FOR months before the gallery opened. The list Clement Greenberg gave me turned out to be extremely helpful. Unfortunately, I had not seen a show presented by Sam Kootz called *Talent 1950*, selected by Meyer Schapiro and Greenberg. It was a coincidence that almost all the people in that show were subsequently invited by me to join my gallery. My delight and enthusiasm grew as each artist agreed to exhibit. What was even more gratifying, the group stuck with me for several years and the Tibor de Nagy gallery became identified with their exuberant talents.

My first two choices were Larry Rivers and Grace Hartigan. At that time I still lived on East Ninth Street, and Larry had a studio in a loft around the corner on Second Avenue, a big top-floor space that he occasionally shared with other artists. Grace had a loft on Essex Street below Canal; she shared the space with her live-in friend, Alfred Leslie. Since Larry was so close by, I saw him almost daily. Much has been written about Larry Rivers; he has received, since that time, so much publicity that his existence now seems apocryphal. This was no accident, since Rivers firmly believes that even notoriety is better than being ignored.

When first we met, however, Larry was quite unknown, a hard-working artist with more than his just share of problems and responsibilities. He was married, and had two children and their grandmother to support. His wife, Augusta, had left him and lived elsewhere, but from time to time she would reappear, stay for a few days and be off again. Joseph, the older son, was eleven; Stevie, the younger, was six. Birdie Berger, Larry's mother-in-law, took care of them all as well as possible. She was an amiable elderly woman, but very fragile. She did whatever she could to hold the home together, but she never had the physical strength to win a prize from *Good Housekeeping*. Their home was a mess, but always a cozy one.

Larry (*né* Yitzroch Loiza Grossberg) was born to a Jewish immigrant family in the Bronx. Yitzroch Loiza was changed rather early on to Irving. He didn't become Larry Rivers until he applied for his first job with a professional jazz band. The manager didn't like his saxophonist to be called Irving Grossberg. "You better change it," he said. Instantly his *real* name came to him, and from the age of nineteen on he was Larry Rivers. Mr. Grossberg, a plumber, was a cordial, easygoing man, but Mrs. Grossberg was—to put it mildly—a shrew. Larry "cut out" after high school and made his living with his saxophone. By nineteen he was married. His wife was almost as young as he; she already had a child, whom Larry adopted. Birdie Berger became The Mother of Them All.

Larry had always done drawings for pleasure, but perhaps it was while he was doing time on a drug charge at the infamous Lexington poky that he began to draw in earnest. He showed his work to Nellie Blaine, who was at that time a drummer in an all-girl band as well as a professional painter. Nellie was enthusiastic and took Larry to Hans Hofmann, with whom he studied for the next few years. Hofmann thought Larry a wunderkind, and he was just that—a born talent. He was painting in no time. One day he brought Mr. Hofmann an oil on canvas; it was abstract. "Larry," he said, "who told you to paint that? You'll never be an abstract artist; stick to what you do best." And that was Larry's last effort in that direction.

The painter Larry most loved at that time was Bonnard, and all of his work reflected this powerful influence. That was the way he was painting when he first showed in 1949 with an artists' co-op called the Jane Street group. Clement Greenberg wrote a review in the *Nation* full of praise for Rivers' debut; in 1950 he was included in the Sam Kootz *New Talent* show. When Larry and I became friends he was still full of Bonnard, but shortly thereafter he came under a new influence: Soutine. His colors became dark, the pigment thick, the themes of the pictures often dour. Since none of us had the money to afford models, I would often pose for Larry as some biblical character or other, often wrapped in a dirty old blanket. The largest and gloomiest canvas was *The Agony in the Garden*. I was all of the disciples—smothering in the filthy studio *shmatta*. Somewhere along the line Larry painted a full-length, reclining nude, with me as the model, in which he switched back to the cheery colors and lighter brushwork of Bonnard. But a suite of drawings with me posing as a depressed schizophrenic called *The Disturbed* was a reversion to doom and gloom. Then came another canvas even larger than *The Agony*; Larry decided to paint a Jewish funeral, modeling it upon Courbet's *Burial at Ornans*. Someone in his family had died and he did sketches of the mourners at the graveside. I wasn't one of them and didn't pose again until later, in 1935, when he painted me as myself. In the same year he also did my bust in bronze. By this time he had many other models—the most important being the poet Frank O'Hara, who became Larry's closest friend and advisor. At first I was extremely jealous of Frank's presence but gradually I got over my anger and learned to like and admire Frank as much as anyone in the O'Hara circle.

There was much to admire. In 1952 I published Frank's first group of poems, *A City Winter*, and in 1965 *Love Poems (Tentative Title)*. A year later he was dead, killed in a freak accident at Fire Island. O'Hara worked hard—helping to support an invalid mother, a young sister. The Museum of Modern Art was his employer; he began there at the front desk selling gifts and finally became a curator under the warm eyes of René d'Harnoncourt. Among the exhibitions O'Hara put together were large-scale showings of Motherwell, de Kooning and Franz Kline, as well as various traveling group shows. His essay on Pollock was one of the first of its kind; other essays were devoted to a wide variety of New York avant-garde painters. Frank was not a formal critic; his essays were structured by his enthusiasm and bright, particular insights, which made one want to see and enjoy what was being shown. How he managed to write and publish as much poetry as he did was a cause for wonder. He wrote plays, satires, made translations. *The Collected Poems* reveal a wide scope of feeling and interest that would without doubt have developed further had he lived longer. O'Hara's death was a terrible shock to the art community, since everyone regarded Frank as his or her closest friend. Oddly, he was that full of affection— he *was* their closest friend.

I had now begun to develop rather conceited notions about myself as a latter-day Ambroise Vollard or Diaghilev. It is a weakness of many dealers, who conceive of themselves as impresarios without whom artists would be helpless, lost, uninspired. It took several years before I shook off this illusion, a *folie des grandeurs*, similar to the belief that artists love their dealers.

There is no way to explain why, from the day Larry Rivers opened in the Fifty-third Street gallery until today, thirty years later, the public, the museums and the collectors have continued to follow his career faithfully. Larry has remained a perennial favorite. One of the reasons was that he demonstrated an inborn canniness about pricing. "Keep the prices down," he would say. "If necessary sell for pennies. It is better to move work than let it gather dust." From the beginnimg the pictures did indeed move into the world. One day a very young designer who did windows for Delman's and Bonwit Teller, Andy Warhol, came in and saw a drawing he liked. "I can pay twenty-five dollars for it," he said. I telephoned Larry to ask what to do. "Sell it," he said. When I told Warhol that Larry agreed, he was delighted. "Here's my first five dollars. I'll pay five a month for the next four months." Over the years Warhol was one of my nicest clients. When he asked me one day if it was true I was friendly with the playwright William Inge, I replied that I was. Andy then inquired if I would ask Inge to pose for him. "I am doing portraits of people's feet. I've given up shoes." "Let me telephone Inge right now," I suggested. Bill was pleasant about granting the request and only wanted to know if Andy was going to portray his feet "in the nude."

During Larry's show I was surprised to see Pavel Tchelitchew come in. He said he was curious to see the work of a young artist he had heard about, and also wanted to wish me good luck. "How is that Rivers doing?" he asked. I said very well. "He is star. If you have star in gallery, push that one. Only way for gallery *succès*." Alfred Barr, Dorothy Miller, William Lieberman, Betsy Jones and many others who worked at the Museum of Modern Art visited my gallery during that time. It was a satisfaction that, for the next twenty years, all of them kept coming to see almost every show. But it was not only our shows the museum staff visited. Mr. Barr encouraged as much looking and finding out what was current as he and his devoted staff had time for. Meyer Schapiro came and purchased a still life by Rivers of a rubber plant. He expressed belief in Rivers' future. But most important of all, artists of many directions and persuasions came to see what we were up to. I quite knew that a gallery that doesn't attract the serious artists of the community regularly is not a gallery of any consequence. It is also in trouble if the poets and intellectuals don't come. The Tibor de Nagy gallery had many ups and downs; the New York "art world" never failed it.

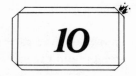

"**D**ID GRACE HARTIGAN REALLY LOOK LIKE THE PHOTOGRAPH CECIL BEA-ton took of her?" I was asked recently. Yes, she did. I was cross the day I first climbed the stairs to her studio on Essex Street. Oh God, I was saying to myself, another female painter whose talent will belie her appearance. There Grace was at the top of the stairs, waiting for me: tall, as "fresh as is the month of May," with what people used to call clean-cut, American good looks. She smiled and put out her hand to pull me up the last step. The studio occupied the top floor of a three-storied building. On the ground floor was a shop that sold pickles and other delicatessen foods; there were barrels of pickles both outside and inside the store and the smell of vinegar, dill and spices permeated the building pleasantly. It was the heart of the Lower East Side; Orchard Street ran parallel two blocks to the west. The streets below the studio were full of pushcarts, trucks, hucksters, merchants of every sort shouting their myriad wares.

"Isn't it a heavenly spot to live in!" cried Grace. "Have a dill pickle." The studio was divided in two—the rear half was the work space of her friend Alfred Leslie, who soon made his appearance. He was six years younger than Grace, about twenty then; they were very fond of each other. Since he was also on my Greenberg list, I was able to see the work of both. I liked them and they liked me and I knew I had two more recruits for my gallery before the visit was over. Their pictures entered my brain so immediately and I felt such enthusiasm for who they were as people that I was certain their art would arouse other people in the same way.

Grace painted large canvases in big, strong patches and swerves of color. The paint strokes were relaxed and swift, wide and narrow, since brushes of varying widths had been utilized. Like others of her generation, Hartigan believed in flat surfaces and "all-over" filling out. She eschewed any basic "grid" compositions, but built the structure of her images in diagonal thrusts, each upholding the other; they seemed to come from the corners toward the center, rather than the other way around. When I knew her better, Grace analyzed the work of Rubens for me, explaining how *his* diagonals worked. One day at the Metropolitan Museum we studied *The Wolf Hunt and the Fox Hunt* by Rubens. This was before I had been to Europe and before I had seen Rubens' magnificent Medici series in the Louvre. Grace explained her theory of holding a picture together so simply and clearly as we went over *The Hunt*, with its distortions, elongations, movement and sheer painterly bravura, that for the first time I was able to appreciate and love Rubens, an admiration that has remained with me to this day. Oddly, we both lost interest in most of Renoir's paintings at about the same time.

Although she had once studied painting with an artist in New Jersey named Isaac Lane Muse, Grace had for the most part educated herself. Her way of doing so, after she had left Elizabeth, New Jersey, was to get a job as a model at the Art Students League and learn what she could as she unrobed for various classes. "I was," she told me proudly, "Eugene Speicher's favorite model; I can't tell you how many times he painted me. A very nice man but nothing of what he was doing rubbed off on me." "Thank God," said I. "He was no favorite of mine, either," said Grace. Grace picked up as much technique and know-how as she could in the ambience of the League. Then she would go back to her studio and paint the way she preferred. What she preferred was the art of the older generation—the so-called Abstract Expressionists, Pollock, de Kooning, Kline, Clyfford Still, Stamos, Baziotes. She admired them and had already become friendly with them. I daresay being so handsome and amiable made it very easy for Grace to get to know other artists. She was popular at the Cedar Bar and The Club, and she loved to give parties. Her domestic life in New Jersey had been unhappy: she was out of sympathy with her own family ("My mother took a bit too much pride in being a Daughter of the American Revolution"); she married the boy next door at eighteen, but the marriage had been a disaster; her child was taken over by her ex-husband and his mother, a further disaster. Gloom and doom was not Grace's style, however. She would spend the rest of her life being a dedicated painter, she declared. And she did.

But like other young female artists of her generation she had her bourgeois holdovers. Work clothes—overalls, army tans, men's shirts —she regarded as the necessary garb for work, only to be worn in the studio. "When I go out," she would say with a giggle, "I'm all woman." She played up her Junoesque figure; her chic was personal rather than fashionable. Men's nostrils seemed to flare when Grace was at a gathering. But at the moment we met, Grace was devoted exclusively to Alfred Leslie, movie magazines and cooking. Most of her waking hours were spent painting large, dashing canvases. Not painting bored her to distraction.

Alfred Leslie had been born Alfred Lipitz in the Bronx. During his high school days he was a body builder, and by the time he was eighteen he was crowned Mr. Bronx in the annual body-building competition. He and two friends decided that they didn't like their names and should go as a threesome to have them legally changed at City Hall. Alfred was furious when the other two didn't turn up and defiantly went ahead and changed his without his friends. He had already decided that he would become a Great Artist. Indeed, his drawings done during his adolescence indicated a large natural talent. He could draw like an old master—a fact I would not have believed if Alfred hadn't shown me his earliest efforts. It was easy for him to enroll in the art school of New York University, where the architect and theoretician Tony Smith became his teacher.

Fame has perhaps obscured what Tony Smith was like in the 1940s and 1950s, for he was not at that time the sculptor he later became. In those early days Smith was a kind of guru for the young art intelligentsia. Born in the Oranges of a highly cultivated Irish Catholic New Jersey family, Smith was throughout his childhood and most of his adolescence an invalid, a victim of the then-dreaded tuberculosis. He was kept at home, isolated from the rest of the family, and educated by a mother who was both intelligent and learned. When he was at last free to move into the world Tony chose to study architecture and went to Frank Lloyd Wright at Taliesin West to do so. He did not pursue a normal architectural career, but he did design and build one house in Connecticut for Dr. Fred Olsen, one for Betty Parsons and another for Theodoros Stamos near Greenport, Long Island.

Tony seems to have read everything and seen an astonishing

amount of art—especially the new, advanced art of the emerging New York School. He did what he could to proselytize for many gifted painters and sculptors. His students were fascinated by Tony, and something of his tone and attitude rubbed off on Alfred Leslie as well as others who partook of the Smith ambience. He held meetings and a symposium of several days' duration called "The Subject of the Artist," at which Smith, Rothko, Motherwell and others urged the dissolution of worn-out work habits, and the breaking of ground with fresh themes, untried techniques.

Alfred Leslie absorbed what was going on with gleeful enthusiasm. Making it new was attention-getting; Alfred's narcissism shifted from the muscle-building Mr. Bronx to where the action was: Abstract Expressionism. He was particularly affected by the authority and sweep of de Kooning, and for several years his work reflected the influence of de Kooning's middle period. Alfred was not alone in doing this— Michael Goldberg, Milton Resnick, Grace Hartigan, Paul Brach and many other young artists were equally dazzled. The new painters were not in revolt against their elders—many of the Second Generation were enchanted by Jackson Pollock and argued continuously as to which, Pollock or de Kooning, was the greater master.

11

*I*N EARLY 1950 WHILE BROWSING IN GEORGE WITTENBORN'S FIFTY-SEVENTH
Street bookstore I came across an extended essay by Henri Focillon
presenting a theory of forms in art. It caused me to wonder if such
forms began as folk expressions among the lower classes, and if they
then move upward to the aristocracy and the privileged classes? Or was
it the other way around? Does, for instance, a simple Scottish reel
eventually become a formal saraband in the Spanish court? I began to
wonder where designs originate, how aesthetic forms evolve. Focillon's
theory fascinated me. Quite arbitrarily, I decided that forms probably
began with an elite and gradually worked their way down the various
social strata. It wasn't until I organized my *Four Hundred Years of Lace*
show the next year that I learned the process of "up" and "down" could
be occurring at the same or different times.

Peter Grey, who had been a puppeteer in our marionette theater,
brought the question up again several months after I had read Focillon.
He suggested that many of the finest artifacts were anonymous: cathe-
dral carvings, for instance, or lace. "My mother," Peter informed me,
"is a connoisseur and collector of lace—the curator, in fact, of the Met-
ropolitan Museum's collection." Since I knew nothing at all about lace,
I said it would be instructive to see his mother's collection. I went with
Peter and his wife, Ty, to Sneden's Landing, which overlooks what Paul
Goodman always called the "Lordly Hudson" and met Marian Powys
Grey.

She lived in a ramshackle eighteenth-century house that looked so beaten by wind and weather that it seemed on the verge of falling over. But not Mrs. Grey. Although she was on in years, and in retirement from her celebrated Madison Avenue Devonshire Lace Shop, she was still a vortex of energy and enthusiasm. A few years later, in 1953, when her *Lace and Lace Making* was published, it was obvious that there was nothing that Marian Grey did not know about her subject. After all, she was a Powys, sister of the writers John Cowper, Theodore Francis and Llewelyn Powys, and brilliantly articulate. Immediately after we arrived she began to haul out boxes and bundles of exquisitely made stuff, which she then flung and unfurled about the room with glorious abandon. "You know," she cried, "lace is strong and durable, but unless it is worn and handled it gets dim and lifeless—like black pearls that lie in drawers, never touching human skin." At one point, to prove what she was saying, she bunched up some royal lace, the wedding point d'Alençon of Empress Eugénie and the apron of Queen Elizabeth I and threw it across the room at the wall opposite (another example, I thought to myself, of *le merveilleux*). More and more lace was held out: pillow and needle laces of Brussels and Bruges, of Venice and Milan. There were varieties of lace from Switzerland, France, Germany. I could not have been more delighted. Would Mrs. Grey consider an exhibition of her lace in my gallery? "Yes," said she. Might I have carte blanche as to the manner in which it would be exhibited? She agreed and added, "Let the show be a lot of fun. Lace was made for pleasure."

I knew exactly who to ask to design an installation that would be deliciously outrageous: the multitalented Alfred Leslie. And Parker Tyler should write a filmy bit of poetic prose to introduce the show. Both agreed to do so; both loved the idea. When in March 1951 Mrs. Grey entered the gallery for our opening, I could only guess what her thoughts might be.

Near the door hung a sign that read PLEASE TOUCH. The entire gallery had been transformed into a fantastic whirl of gossamer—as though hundreds of gifted spiders had been let loose to create another dimension. In one corner were some very coarse weavings—crude fishnets over which fishermen had woven designs in the sixteenth century, the beginning of lace making, primitive and beautiful. It was quickly evident that lace making had developed very rapidly; thousands of women across Europe kept refining the craft with more complex techniques.

But Alfred Leslie was not interested in art history. It was his purpose to make every item an aesthetic experience in itself. Near the ceiling were hung black and sometimes white Spanish fans that seemed like hovering butterflies or moths. Elsewhere, floating through the air, were lace parasols. The magnificent Empress Eugénie bridal veil tumbled down in cascades near the window. On thin dowels sticking diagonally out of the wall were priests' cinctures. Handkerchiefs hung over balloons, chasubles protruded from corners and bishops' aprons invited running one's hands through their foaminess. Visitors took our sign seriously and did touch and handle these luxurious fabrics. But nothing was damaged, nor was I worried when a beautiful young man took up a mantilla to try it on for effect.

Stuffy highbrows whose names I won't mention shook their heads and prophesied doom for the gallery. But many artists were delighted with the show. Jackson Pollock came twice and took great pleasure in the notion of *art anonyme*; the rhythms of swirl and crosshatch, even the highly conventionalized images of French eighteenth-century lace, with its peacocks, pheasants, roses, waterfalls, grottoes, pagodas, ruins and costumed personages, delighted him. I told this to Mrs. Grey, who nodded her head amiably and said she admired the lovely skein pictures of Mr. Pollock and had already recommended that new lace makers find inspiration in his splendid conceptions. She was amused by Alfred Leslie's installation and thought it would encourage another generation to take an interest in lace.

But, of course, sales were nonexistent. One young woman bought a black, machine-made fan (Alfred had thrown in some manufactured material to confuse the cognoscenti) for $75. Few people could afford what was in the show. The three weeks of exhibition went by and that last day came, a rather dreary Saturday afternoon. I was feeling melancholy when the door opened and a drab-looking older woman came in. It was four o'clock.

"May I see your price list?" she asked in a soft, pleasant voice. From the look of her, I thought, What a waste of time. But I did glance down at her shoes. "Always look at the *shoes*," Bill de Kooning had once advised me. "When the shoes are good ones, it means the people are reliable." Mrs. Grey had provided me with a careful and detailed list of every item in the show, and the prices. Taking a pencil from her purse, my visitor went about examining the lace—and making check marks. This took her about forty-five minutes. She seemed to know precisely what each piece was and its name. I sat at my desk, mute.

"There are three point de Venise I don't have, some Burano needle-point berthas, a Duchesse tablecloth, a bit of needlepoint-appliquéd pelerine." Her selections went on through the price list as she showed me indications of what she wanted. "The car will come on Tuesday to pick up my purchases." I accompanied the lady to the door and as she left I looked out the front window to see her enter her Rolls Royce, the door held open by a liveried chauffeur. The lady was Mrs. Satterfield, a relative of Mr. J. P. Morgan. But then, I should have known that Mrs. Satterfield was one of Marian Powys Grey's regular clients—along with other Morgans, and Fricks, Flaglers, Rockefellers, Morrows, Whitneys, Schiffs and both Sara Delano and Eleanor Roosevelt, all faithful lace collectors.

I had learned a lesson about old New York society and the very rich. They "walk," as Marianne Moore suggested, "quietly like the ele-phant" and are not like tapirs. Mrs. Satterfield had purchased $15,000 worth of lace.

But *had* I learned a lesson about the origin or the proliferation of forms in art? Alfred Leslie had turned lace, a venerable old craft, into a fantasia of his own imaginings. It was as though his teacher, Tony Smith, had been behind him urging him to "make it new" and, for Alfred, the lace had become theater, a production on East Fifty-third Street. For Parker Tyler the lace was a vindication of his spidery prose, baroque and infinitely prolix. It would be years before I learned that forms had a "genealogy" that had gone on for centuries, but that only inspired artists could create images both original and meaningful.

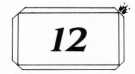

12

*T*HE FIRST YEAR OF THE GALLERY, FROM JANUARY TO DECEMBER 1951, included the end of one season and the beginning of another; seasons in the art world resemble the school year, from September to early June. Summer was always hopelessly inactive. Not only did the collectors depart for Europe, the seashore or mountains, but the artists took off to Long Island, Maine or Provincetown. Dealers did the same. I was already aware that the pace was such that the three-month vacation was a necessity if sanity was to be preserved. That first summer I spent in East Hampton with my friend Waldemar Hansen, in a gatehouse graciously given to us, rent free, by the widow of the architect Pierre Chareau.

Dolly Chareau was Waldemar's French teacher. She was English but had lived most of her adult life in Paris, having married a brilliant but not very successful architect. They had come to America in the late 1940s, about the same time as the other artists-in-exile, and were close to the avant-garde surrounding Breton and Duchamp. But even back in Paris Mme. Chareau and her husband were the intimates of such poets as Guillaume Apollinaire, Max Jacob and Jean Cocteau, as well as many of the Cubist painters, the Surrealists and Neo-Romantics. They had always spent what they could buying the work of their friends; as a result, although they were always rather poor, Dolly had a fine little collection of first-class art. After her husband died, she could survive on the occasional sale of a picture.

Waldemar Hansen was devoted to Madame Chareau and her *cercle français*. The meeting of the group took place one evening a week and no English could be spoken. The tone was lofty; literature, art, philosophy and occasionally politics were discussed. Waldemar served as Dolly's aide-de-camp in organizing the gatherings and setting the tone. Since everyone in the group was as earnest as he was, Dolly's pleasure knew no bounds. The summer of 1951 was sad for her; she was still grieving for her husband and couldn't bear to go back to their little gatehouse, which had been given to her in perpetuity by Robert Motherwell, who had commissioned M. Chareau to build his summer home and studio in the most fashionable area of East Hampton.

Dolly Chareau's admiration for Motherwell bordered on idolatry; she considered herself a kind of foster mother. Indeed, she had taken care of Motherwell in periods of bad health or *crises de nerfs* as only a mother might. She had been particularly attentive after Motherwell's first wife, Maria, an excessively pretty Mexican-Californian girl, got in the car and drove away, never to return. He had fallen into a profound melancholy. Luckily he met another girl. This one, called Betty, was from Connecticut, wholesome and no-nonsense, the soul of suburban cleancut living. Motherwell bought a huge Quonset hut and a few acres of land from army surplus and Pierre Chareau recycled the Quonset, designed an interior, landscaped the grounds and at the entrance built a little gatehouse for himself and his wife. It was a handsome piece of work. The gatehouse could have been lived in happily by Trappist monks; it was like living in an abstract painting by Mondrian. When the weather was lovely, one could be quite comfortable; however, when the damp, the fogs, the rain of Eastern Long Island descended, one joined the weather in its depression. Since the gallery had made no profit—nor would it for the next four years—I was quite broke. Waldemar, returned from England after a two-year visit, was equally out of pocket, as poets usually are. The house was several miles from the shopping district and although we had a bicycle, bringing in food or supplies was a problem.

Motherwell made it quickly clear after we moved in that we were not to depend on him for anything, including rides into town, or invitations to meals. Betty Motherwell, however, was pregnant and had to spend much time in bed or on the chaise longue with knees raised to prevent another miscarriage. She had had one or two previously. Thus, we got to play cards of an evening—Betty loved cards—and this included sandwiches and beer.

Luckily for us we had two guardian angels, Leo and Ileana Castelli, who had purchased a vast house nearby and who were extremely hospitable. Bill and Elaine de Kooning each had a studio there and the house was always filled with guests. Lunch was the big meal and there were seldom less than fifteen or eighteen people at table. Whenever our larder was bare, Waldemar and I would go to the Castellis', where we were always petted and indulged, especially by Ileana.

Elaine de Kooning had decided to paint my portrait with me seated in an armchair. But in order to enter Elaine's studio I had to go through Bill's. Luckily for me he didn't mind the interruption and would often invite me to have a chat. That summer he had begun to paint *Woman I.* I can't remember the size but I believe it was four feet wide and about six high. But every time I went through, the picture was different. De Kooning had pasted pieces of masking paper of different shapes to various parts of the canvas and he would move these pieces about to discover which area he was looking for—rather the way Mondrian used to move his colored squares when doing *Broadway Boogie-Woogie.* One day I said, "Bill, why do you keep changing your picture so much?" His forehead became furrowed. He was silent for a moment and then he answered, "I want to know *where* she is." I mumbled I didn't understand what he meant. "Look there," he said pointing to a doorknob. "Now hold your hands to either side of your eyes so that all you can see is the doorknob without the rest of the room to locate it." I did so and, of course, without reference to distance or relationship to other factors, but only the door, where indeed was it? "Here I am painting a woman on a flat surface trying to make her believable with no reference to anything. It is for me a problem to solve."

Another day we were talking about the beautiful potato fields that surrounded East Hampton. He agreed that they would make a wonderful subject. "But," said Bill, "it would take me another lifetime to learn how to do them." At the end of the summer I asked Elaine how *Woman I* had turned out. "Oh," she said, "Bill wanted to destroy it. But I hid it." When a few years later de Kooning unveiled the *Woman* series at the Sidney Janis gallery, Huntington Hartford took a full-page ad in the New York *Times* denouncing art such as de Kooning's and Tennessee Williams' as degenerate, immoral and ugly. The public rushed to see the show. Everything was sold. It was *un succès fou.* "I never had it so good," commented Bill, delighted with the free publicity.

The Castelli household was full of young people; some were friends of Nina Castelli and her close school chum, Suzi Bloch, others were young painters who were in the neighborhood. Leo commissioned

Larry Rivers to make a statue—a female nude—for the circle of lawn in the middle of the driveway in front of the house. Michel Sonnabend, who eventually married Ileana Castelli, was the house intellectual with whom Waldemar and I could discuss poetry, especially the *Divine Comedy* of Dante, which Sonnabend knew almost by heart. The Castelli long-haired dachshund named Ecco added to the general excitement. It is sad that no one did Ecco's portrait.

Elaine's painting of me went on for days. I never thought it looked very much like me, but perhaps it served as practice for the baseball players that Elaine began to paint a few years later. These, in turn, may have led to her doing the celebrated portrait of John F. Kennedy.

A part of the summer of 1952 was relieved by the presence of Jane Freilicher, Kenneth Koch, Frank O'Hara and John Ashbery, who had rented a tiny cottage for a month. John Latouche was partly responsible for their arrival since he had come to make a "home movie" starring Jane Freilicher in which she would be given the power to walk on water. Latouche had taken a house on Georgica Pond, where the film was shot. Poor Jane was constantly up to her ankles in slimy mud. The movie became a part of a play written by James Schuyler called *Presenting Jane*, which was given by the Artists Theater several months later.

I asked Elaine one morning if I could introduce some friends who wrote poetry to her and Bill de Kooning. I was aware that Bill did not like to be disturbed while he was working. After a short consultation with Bill, Elaine gave the green light. I then went to the door of the studio and shouted "Poets!" Immediately O'Hara, Koch and Ashbery emerged from the bushes where they were hiding and walked through the door. Their sudden appearance hit Bill as very funny; from then on they all became good friends, especially O'Hara, on whom de Kooning doted.

All this family-style intimacy should have made Waldemar and me happy, but it didn't. By the end of the summer we both came to detest the Hamptons as a place that encouraged the most outrageous snobbery and pretension. Robert Motherwell, never one to isolate himself, joined the Maidstone Club, perhaps to please his wife, Betty, and to keep in touch with his own White-Anglo-Saxon-Protestant roots. When other denizens of this fashionable community discovered that Waldemar and I were penniless and "nobodies," the frost was immediate and thorough. We were shocked by the social climbing, the exclusions, the vulgarity of a world that seemed dedicated to outward display, money, tacky behavior and conspicuous consumption.

The return to Manhattan in September was somewhat disheartening. I had sublet my Ninth Street apartment to Larry Rivers and he had moved his mother-in-law, Birdie Berger, and his two children into it. Meanwhile, Larry had made a bid for an apartment back to back with mine on St. Mark's Place, which he could take possession of in a few months. Stevie and Joseph were extremely active little boys given to lots of horseplay. When I entered the apartment I let out a groan. Many things were broken, including my Jackson Pollock "puppet" on a string (it had been tossed away), a couple of pre-Columbian ceramics, a chair or two. Larry's wife, Augusta, had come home for a month or so. The toilet wasn't working, holes had been gouged in the living-room wall from leaning bicycles, the garbage in the kitchen was piled high. Luckily the apartment around the corner suddenly became available and the Rivers family moved in. Order was restored. But no sooner did this happen than one of our friends, Richard Fisher, who shared the apartment when he was in New York, called to say he needed all his furniture back. About half of what was in the apartment was his. Then Waldemar told me he was moving up to Second Avenue with a new friend. Added to all this I was once again in a state of depression because of a few emotional snarls of my own.

Shortly after opening the gallery with paintings by Pennerton West, I was invited to a big party in the town house of Jack and Grace Borgenicht, the art dealer who became prominent a few years later. At this party I met the person with whom I would be living for the next twenty-five years—Herbert Machiz. It took me about three months to realize that Herbert was one of the most remarkable human beings I had ever met. My melancholy was quickly melting away in the face of the gallery bustle and the excitement of making a new friend.

Larry Rivers made his debut on Fifty-third Street on October 1, 1952. I was still modeling for him during that month, this time in the nude for a standing figure posed exactly like Rodin's *Balzac*, except it didn't look like me, as Balzac did in the Rodin bronze. Further, Larry gave me a bulging belly that wasn't mine. Modeled in clay, the figure was about two feet high. It was necessary to pose many times—a memorable experience because the weather had turned cold and so was Larry's front room. One pouring wet night at about nine-thirty we heard noises in the street below. Next door on the ground floor was a bar. We looked out the window and there on the sidewalk outside the bar we saw four felt-hatted men murderously kicking someone. "My God," cried Larry, "they're killing him!" I rushed to the telephone, called the police, then threw a blanket over myself. I was by now chilled to the bone. The police arrived momentarily and instead of going to the bar they ran upstairs and started banging on Larry's door. The first thing one of the cops said, at seeing us and the messy living room, was, "What are *you* two doing up here?" We were both so nervous and frightened that we could only splutter our account of what we had seen, whereupon the cops reluctantly went downstairs to the bar. Soon after that we saw the police car drive way. Apparently the bartender said he wasn't aware that anything had happened.

A few days later I was on the sidewalk going toward Larry's place when a dark-haired man in a gray fedora walked up to me and said, "Hey you, you some kind of smartass? Big mouth, huh? You and that other smartass upstairs. You better learn to keep that trap shut. We got our eyes on both of you." I was so terrified I turned, flew back to my own apartment and began packing a suitcase. I telephoned Herbert Machiz, explained the situation, and he suggested I get out, move in with him. "You can't," he said, "afford that apartment by yourself. So disappear." Larry thought my reaction was exaggerated and absurd. But I had moved to West Fifty-sixth Street by that afternoon.

Herbert's apartment was, as far as I was concerned, paradisiacal. It consisted of one very large room with a twelve-foot ceiling—the former ballroom of a mansion once lived in by the Wanamaker family on Fifty-sixth Street between Fifth and Sixth avenues. There was a tiny kitchen; the bathroom had to be shared with the tenants in the next apartment. The rent was $49.50 a month, paid to the owners of the building, a former vaudeville team, the Dooley Sisters, who lived on the floor above in rococo splendor. The sisters looked and dressed like ancient kewpie dolls. Their age was hard to define, since they both affected blond, bouffant hairdos and theatrical makeup. They conducted an after-hours bar on the floor below us, to which almost no one came except a few wildly intoxicated out-of-towners. They seemed never to have much liquor on the shelves and if someone looked to be a big spender, one of the sisters would run out and buy a bottle of Scotch or gin from a neighboring bar. "The Dooleys," said Herbert, "ought to call their little hideaway The Pits." But his apartment was neat, simple and very elegant. He had not been living in Europe for four years for nothing.

13

*I*N FEBRUARY 1952, OUR WUNDERKIND ALFRED LESLIE HAD HIS FIRST EXHIBItion. It lived up to my expectations. He had picked up the whole vocabulary of his older contemporaries, the Abstract Expressionists, and given it a new precocious twist. "Art," Alfred would explain, "begins with me." The jealous young complained that Leslie was turning out parodies, but the older painters, like de Kooning and Gottlieb, thought he was talented. Franz Kline was sympathetic, but then, Kline tended to have a warm heart for almost all young painters. A few were sold. Soon after the show Alfred and Grace Hartigan parted company, but remained friendly. Grace's second exhibition took place in March and attracted the serious attention of Dorothy Miller, curator of painting at the Museum of Modern Art. The reviews were full of praise; Grace was launched, and very happy because she also had a new special friend, the photographer Walter Silver, to share her studio.

The weather was improving and Grace invited about twenty people, all the gallery artists and her friends, to a kite-making party. The kites were constructed in her Essex Street loft, but the following day they were carried up to Sheep Meadow in Central Park to be sent aloft. The kites, some big and lengthy, others small, were colorful, goofy and beautiful. But when we got to the park the wind began to blow at what seemed hurricane speed. Simply hanging onto the kites became difficult. Still determined to get them into the air, we did our best, only to have them dashed to the ground or blown to bits. All of the kites were ruined. "A real fiasco is what we've got!" yelled Grace. "Let's get out of here." How I wish someone had taken pictures of the mess!

Just before I met Grace she had a short second marriage to a painter named Harry Jackson. Lee and Jackson Pollock thought he was unusually gifted, and when the young couple decided on marriage they went out to the Springs on Long Island, where the Pollocks sponsored the ritual and a little send-off celebration, as the happy pair was driving to Mexico for a honeymoon. The marriage lasted less than a year.

"What I didn't know," Grace explained later, "was that Harry was epileptic, grand mal; he didn't say a word about it and there we were in Mexico driving along, when all of a sudden Harry had a fit. We could have been killed! By the time he came to, I was so mad at being *deceived* that I grabbed my bag and beat it right back to New York. I had no trouble whatsoever getting the marriage annulled. New York State was very nice about it. I guess I was attracted to Harry because he seemed so *butch.*"

That wasn't all that was wrong with Harry. His show opened right after Grace's, and by the time it was over, I realized what I was dealing with. Harry's real last name is Schapiro (not Jackson), and he reputedly came from Cody, Wyoming. He wore cowboy hats, cowboy shirts and Levi's. He assured me that aside from having been a cowboy he was also a radio announcer; his cattle roundup accent was better than John Wayne's—his hero. Each time Harry came to the gallery I had to decide which Harry he was, for there were a couple of others: the well-born young man (he actually came from a decent Chicago family) and the serious highbrow painter. As Lee Krasner commented, "You have to admit he's a damn good painter." There was no question about it. The style was in no way tentative; his images were clearly realized, his color was alluring, each picture had presence. Nothing sold. Harry became depressed and angry. I was relieved when I heard he had moved to Europe. Although I never saw him again, it was amusing to read about him in the newspapers. Harry became a celebrity.

In Italy, Harry set himself up as a portrait artist specializing in American officers and their wives. It was a society that doted on cowboy genius. When this phase was over, a new persona emerged, Harry the literary sculptor. He had the good taste to make a statue of the great early nineteenth-century poet Giacomo Belli, who wrote some two thousand sonnets in a salty, often obscene Roman dialect about the foibles and miseries of the local citizenry. Since Belli was a denizen of the

Trastevere, an old Roman quarter, Harry decided to erect his statue in the middle of one of its piazzas. The commission of *belles artes*, the zoning board and the local *ristorante padrones* had not been consulted. One can imagine the hue, let alone howls, that arose. The statue was promptly removed; Harry had made headlines. The final and fabulous phase was now reached. Cattlemen in Texas and elsewhere found Harry's bronze sculptures of steer and cowhands irresistible, and commissions began to roll in. Then Harry's hero, John Wayne, discovered and bought Jackson bronzes by the dozens. What was comforting about these works was their pleasant resemblance to that other great American artist, Frederic Remington. Harry opened offices in four cities to take care of the huge volume of business and became a multimillionaire. According to another article in the New York *Times*, by Hilton Kramer, Harry Jackson is ecstatically happy.

In May 1952 peace returned to the gallery with Jane Freilicher's straightforward, understated landscapes and still lifes. The work was unabashedly within the traditon of French harmony and restraint, with the difference that Jane's canvases contained touches of idiosyncratic awkwardness so peculiarly honest that one could see an emerging, particular style. It was her choice of colors, delicate yet bold, that stamped Jane's pictures with authority.

Jane, *née* Needlehoffer, had been married to a jazz musician, Jack Freilicher, but was living in austerity in the Village when we met. To make a living she was teaching art in a primary school. How she hated it! And the austerity. I was delighted when a few years later she married a dear old acquaintance of mine, Joseph Hazen, a clothing manufacturer. Joe and I had known each other from attending class in modern dance taught by the Mary Wigmanite Barbara Mettler. Joe had also studied Indian dance, and seemed to me a dead ringer for Uday Shankar. But he had entered the family business after he had married a painter, Sylvia Braverman, whom I disliked. Then they split up and Sylvia went to Paris. I couldn't conceive of a more felicitous marriage than Joe and Jane's. When he retired from Seventh Avenue, Joe took up the brush and became a good painter himself.

Jane was more than a painter, although in what ways it is hard to explain. Let us say it was her intellect, a kind of braininess, her acutely sensitive personality that gave her another dimension. Few painters I've known seem to have read so widely or have had such discriminating taste in literature. Perhaps it was her wittiness that made her as attractive as she was considered by all the new young poets. The summer

Jane and Nellie Blaine shared a country house, people took to calling Jane the "Sybil of Nyack." It is astonishing the number of poems in which she is referred to or which are dedicated to her. John Ashbery and James Schuyler were particularly devoted. In Frank O'Hara's first pamphlet of poems she is mentioned repeatedly.

In October of 1952 Fairfield Porter had his first show at the Tibor de Nagy. It was curious how this event came about. Bill de Kooning had visited the gallery a few months previously, and after lecturing me on why I should always wear a suit and dress like a gentleman while I was working in the gallery because otherwise "collectors won't have confidence," Bill suddenly said, "I've got a terrific painter for you to show, someone whose work I'm really crazy for." "Who is that?" I asked. When he told me I said, "Oh, Bill, maybe Porter is just a friend of yours who hasn't got a gallery. I might not like him." "No!" cried Bill, "I mean what I'm saying. Fairfield is terrific." There was a long pause while I stared straight into Bill's eyes. "Very well," I said, "if you say he's *that* good, I'll show him sight unseen."

When Fairfield arrived with his paintings, I was taken aback, having believed that the work would be in the Abstract Expressionist mode. They were representational, however, and looked like Vuillards, rather dark in color, very low-key. I felt dismayed, but I had given my word and the show went on. Then a curious thing began to happen. Each day during the three weeks the show was up I found myself studying the paintings carefully, and bit by bit, I could discern the quality, the seriousness that went into them. Several of my friends and my partner, Tibor, disliked the show and thought my commitment ridiculous. Perversely, this made me increasingly more interested and certain that Porter was on the way to doing excellent work. What he was trying to do was not obvious. His use of Maroger's solution—a boiled solution of pigment and linseed oil—as his favorite pigment did not sit well with many of the artists; the critics were indifferent. To top it all there were very few sales.

Oddly, Clement Greenberg rather liked Fairfield Porter. Clem was disposed, of course, to a certain kind of representational art, since he himself had been a landscapist (I showed three of them in a group show—mountain and meadow scenes). Clem, through all the years he came to the gallery, would, if I showed him new work without telling him who did it, invariably be more sympathetic to representational painters than to the abstract ones.

Born in Winnetka, Illinois, son of an architect, a graduate of Harvard, Fairfield had studied art in Munich and was extremely well read. He liked to write art criticism, which he later did regularly for the *Nation*. He lived with his wife and five children in Southampton in a big house on Main Street. The barn in the back was his studio. Whenever I visited, I felt as though I were a character in a novel by Louisa May Alcott. Anne Porter was as remarkable as Fairfield. Descended from a long line of New England Unitarian ministers, Anne had converted to Roman Catholicism, but was the only convert I'd ever met who never acted like one. (I say this having been reared in the Church.) She had read the great mystics and had subsumed such Catholic Existentialists as Gabriel Marcel and Léon Bloy. Jacques Maritain was a favorite, too. But for all that devotional reading, Anne's sense of the life immediately around her was surprisingly intense. Her charity was real; she was incapable of censorious attitudes. I read some of Anne's poetry. "My goodness," I remember saying, "she's the real thing!" But Anne was too occupied with children and household to sit at a desk scribbling poems. Her first child, John, was autistic; perhaps her primary concern was that the next two boys and two girls grow up reasonably healthy. Poor John had to be placed in the keeping of a family that cared for disturbed children. Now and then when I was visiting, John would have been home for a few weeks. He was sweet and very unconnected. It was hard for the family, since Fairfield would not put John in an institution and the expense of private care was a burden. Anne's patience with John was not feigned or provoked by guilt. People as selfish as I am are always astonished by real love; few of us are capable of it. "It's embarrassing to say it," Jane Freilicher once remarked, "but there's something saintly about Anne Porter."

Problems or not, going to Fairfield's house was invariably a lot of fun. I sat for my portrait in a chair in the garden wearing a red shirt. I hated my portrait. We ate lunches that were sparked with delightful conversations with the children. Sometimes in the evening we would turn the Victrola on loud and improvise ballets. Anne was particularly vivacious flinging herself about in *Firebird*.

Fairfield, being very cerebral, was an unreconstructed atheist like myself. When Katey Porter was six she went to Fairfield and asked him if he would feel hurt if she took First Communion. This rather annoyed him and he said, "Really, Katey, it's none of my business what you decide are your personal beliefs." Later I asked Anne what happened when Katey was undergoing catechism. "What does one say to a child about eternal damnation?" It would seem a Miss Murphy, a *Common-*

weal-type Roman Catholic, was Katey's instructor. When the question of hell came up Miss Murphy said, "Of course there's a hell. But God's infinite love and mercy is so great He's never put anyone *in* it." Which was a nice way of saying we make our own hells. Both girls became good Catholics.

After Jane Freilicher and Joe Hazen moved to Water Mill, adjacent to Southampton, Fairfield was often in their company. As the dour colors in Fairfield's paintings began to lighten and move to a higher key, I asked him how this had come about. "Looking at Jane's work," he said. "Her use of color has influenced my work a lot."

Despite his rationality and keen mind, Porter had a somewhat morbid preoccupation with modern science and technology, which he regarded as the scourge of mankind. Year in and year out he labored over articles attempting to prove the absolute truth of his convictions. When he wasn't rewriting this polemic, he would sometimes present it in lectures. (At the Chicago Art Institute, his views precipitated boos and a fierce quarrel with technologically oriented students.) *Art News* published several of these articles dealing with Porter's objections to scientific methods as a deterrent to immediate experience. He was opposed to generalized knowledge, scientific schemata, crystallized planning.

One could not deny the originality and passion of Porter's thinking. But the ideas kept changing and became increasingly labyrinthine. For those of us who listened to his cerebrations over the years, both the good and the questionable, it was perhaps best to listen and not get into frantic arguments. In my mind Porter had a big streak of the crank in him.

One day Fairfield came into my gallery and announced that a reliable cure for cancer had been discovered. "What is it," I asked, "and for what kind of cancer?" "All kinds, and the medicine can be produced very cheaply from apricot pits." What, I wanted further to know, is the name of this miracle drug?

"Laetrile," he answered enthusiastically. Among other panaceas Fairfield would recommend to friends suffering from arthritis was a daily dosage of vinegar and honey. He was increasingly attracted to nostrums and solutions that were not far removed from old-fashioned magic. Of course there was complete truth in his objections to atomic weaponry and energy plants and to his complaints about the destruction of the environment, but he seemed not to see the larger and good side of science.

Miraculously, his quirkiness prevented Porter from wasting time cogitating and theorizing about painting. Eakins had done this to the detriment of his art. But Fairfield had learned from Vuillard's paintings not to "think about doing anything else when it is so natural to do this." It did not matter that now and then Porter would have extreme doubts as to whether or not his painting had any significance. During the last ten years of his life he painted with triumphant lack of restraint, and these later works, especially the seascapes, are, to quote the critic-artist Rackstraw Downes, "more and more beautiful and wild, even visionary."

It is easy to overlook Porter's eccentric notions, just as we pay no attention to those of Tolstoy or George Bernard Shaw. The recent retrospective in Boston indicated clearly Porter's progressive development as a painter of the first rank. If he were there to see it, Fairfield might exclaim, as D. H. Lawrence once did, "Look! I've come through!"

14

WERE THOSE THE HALCYON DAYS IN NEW YORK OF ART-MAKING AND ART activities? I think they were for me. I am not given to nostalgia, a sloppy emotion that often blurs the truth and induces self-congratulation. But I cannot help remembering with pleasure the sheer vigor that was endemic to the New York School of artists and their followers. "I define the 'avant-garde,' " said Fairfield Porter, "as those artists with the most energy." The art scene had begun to command widespread attention. New galleries showing contemporary American art were opening: Sidney Janis, Eleanor Ward's the Stable, Leo Castelli, Robert Schoelkopf, Virginia Zabriskie, Grace Borgenicht and many others. In 1951 there were perhaps half a dozen such galleries; suddenly by 1956 there were twenty. Paris was no longer the world art center. However, the beginnings were slow. When Sam Kootz took a group of American abstract paintings to Paris the response from the French was thumbs down. The Museum of Modern Art was attempting to show new work abroad through its International Council (amusingly denounced later by an English Marxist critic as the use of art to spread the influence of American capitalism: cultural imperialism, if you please). The effort remained tentative, since the State Department was none too happy with what looked to them like visual gibberish.

The artists in the circle in which I moved were not concerned with any world but the one they were creating. Their enthusiasm approached euphoria with the arrival of poets. "Isn't it interesting," said

Virgil Thomson to me in a discussion about French painting, "how every artist likes to have a house poet? Think of the services rendered to artists by Apollinaire, Gertrude Stein, Éluard, Max Jacob, André Breton, to name a few." The new poets moved to New York and in no time were in the studios being petted and adored. Frank O'Hara, John Ashbery, Barbara Guest, James Schuyler and Kenneth Koch were the chief objects of devotion. No one was more euphoric about this than I. For me it was like being back at *View* magazine, when poets and painters were invariably making collaborations. I remembered the *éditions de luxe* of Nierendorf, Curt Valentine, Pierre Matisse, the special publication of portfolios of prints, little pamphlets and broadsides, which seemed to me the height of glamor. They were not as grand as the wonderful ones from Paris, but they were good of their kind.

Grace Hartigan and Jane Freilicher divided O'Hara and Ashbery between them. Nellie Blaine latched onto Koch. Helen Frankenthaler and Mary Abbot took up with Barbara Guest, as did Robert Goodnough. *Art News*, edited by Thomas Hess, absorbed all of the poets, including Schuyler. Rivers' claims on O'Hara were increasingly more possessive. O'Hara in turn took a shine to Pollock, Kline, Norman Bluhm and de Kooning, glorifying them in prose and verse. No gathering was complete without poets. Worried that I would not somehow be in the very center of this literary gold mine, I decided to publish a four-page house organ devoted to short prose and poems. It was called *Semicolon*. ("John constantly worries about being the hostess with the mostest," bitched one of my dearest friends.) It would combine seriousness with frivolity.

I invited the critic Harold Rosenberg to write the opening paragraph and this is what he contributed (a flag with a semicolon in it was printed over the type):

> Now that the existence of the highbrow has become a political issue in the United States and in fact the most bitter one in the last Presidential election, with eggs from one side and apologies from the other, the formation of a sentence that exceeds in complexity the capacity of the typewriter to impart in spurts of its mechanical brain the rhythms by which the fingers of reporters, experts and magazine fictioneers excogitate the zeitgeist involves the possibility of lese majesty, particularly if the thought it begins with encompasses the energy to pick itself up at the end of a pause and move on: this situation revealing once for all that the synthesis of literature and politics, not to be achieved in our time by subjecting the first to the force rhetoric of the second, nor, contrariwise, through spraying the vast events and hero-demons of this century with the PRiticism of English-department mysticism

and journalistic mythocracy, simply is, because, since what happens in literature is politics for politicians, and what happens in the world is drama or
dream for poets, literature and politics were inseparable from the start for
anyone whose mind has not been blasted by !! nor so short-winded it can
only sprint from . to

Harold Rosenberg

Our theme of irreverence could not have been stated more boldly.
Let all eggheads unite and roar; let us, like Mozart, be "heartless as the
birds." Actually the first issue was not very cheerful. Frank O'Hara's
"Olive Garden," a prose poem, describes terrifying pain and loss.
Edwin Denby's poem "The Prison" said things like "Therefore I hope
the human species is wiped out." A translation by John Ashbery of
Max Jacob from *Literature and Poetry* said things like, "Sir, your son is a
poet." "That's all right, but if he is I will wring his neck." Meyer Liben
had a tiny short story called "Disappointment" (this one was comical).
James Merrill translated some maxims of Chamfort, which included a
few acidic pieces of advice:

Weakness of character, paucity of ideas—in a word, whatever prevents
us from living with ourselves, saved many a man from misanthropy.

False modesty is the most decent of all truths.

It's unbelievable how alert one must be in order never to appear ridiculous.

Parker Tyler wrote on the problem of "commerce" with the Devil,
Faust's bargain with Mephistopheles. Nicolas Calas, contemplating
Hermes, said, "All art is useless. Style is art's law of parsimony." Paul
Goodman confessed how he wrote: "My way of composition is like a
beast or fish over which is cast a net." Stevie Rivers, son of Larry, aged
eight, contributed a short tale called "The Adventures of Ivanhoe"—ac-
tion-packed.

We printed about 300 copies, a dollar for six, twenty cents each.
Circulation was managed by me: I sold copies in the gallery, at the Artists Club, and in the Cedar Bar. Since no one got paid, contributors received five copies if they wanted them. Someone remarked I had a real
talent for ephemera. Considering the lugubriousness, the heaviness, the
vacuity of the accepted literature of the day, I accepted that as a com-
pliment.

For my second issue Saul Bellow sent me a piece called "Pains and Gains." In it the narrator tries to be helpful to an old woman who has fallen and hurt her knee. Upon being asked what was the matter, the woman grabbed her purse and tucked it securely under her arm. She was already thinking about how to collect damages. The story amused Wallace Stevens and he sent me a brief footnote for the following issue:

> Some years ago a cable car in San Francisco let go and by the time it arrived at the foot of California Street the passengers were all over the place. A man who had not seen what happened came out of a side street and went to the nearest victim and asked him what it was all about. The man who was lying in the street said to him, "Well, there has been an accident and we are waiting for the adjuster from the street car company to turn up." "Do you mind," said the newcomer, "if I lie down with you?"

Mr. Stevens, of course, worked for the Hartford Indemnity Insurance Company.

Chester Kallman gave me a poem called "Epigrams and Epitaphs" and W. H. Auden a little obituary for his cat, "In Memoriam L. K.-A. (1950–1952)":

At peace under this mandarin, sleep, Lucina,
Blue-eyed Queen of white cats: for you the Ischian wave shall weep,
When we who now miss you are American dust, and steep
Epomeo in peace and war augustly a grave-watch keep.

The Beverly Boys' Summer Vacation, an extremely short novel in twenty-one chapters covering three typewritten pages, was sent in by Kenneth Koch. The phrase "deadpan simplicity" took on new meaning.

My third issue contained a longish poem by John Ashbery called "Hoboken," which was a collage made from Roget's *Thesaurus*. Theodore Hoffman translated "Scene 21" from *Woyzeck* by Georg Büchner. There were highly condensed stories by Meyer Liben and David Jackson, some aphorisms by Francis Golffing and an essay by Edwin Kinnebeck on survival through decorum. I later published another tale by Meyer Liben (whom Paul Goodman called the Kafka of the Upper West Side). The new one was concerned with Moon McGonigle being disturbed with a notion that had been planted in his head by his alcoholic pal Mr. Morley, who contended that "Central Park was a waste of space. On this area can be erected enough apartment buildings to house well over a million people." There was a poem called "Prospice" by

Marius Bewley, another by James Merrill, "Three Sketches for Europa," and a prose poem by Frank O'Hara.

Semicolon was never dated and only appeared when there was enough good material to fill an issue. All but about three of the contributors were close friends and acquaintances. I didn't publish anything I didn't like with the exception of a much too long, rather maudlin poem by Tennessee Williams, "Those Who Ignore the Appropriate Time of Their Going." Tennessee had become famous since the time I first knew him, when he was living out of suitcases. (Sentimentality is always the cause of my worst regrets.) Except for Auden, none of the other contributors were well known then. James Merrill, for instance, had not published very much, but I had known him since 1949, when he had come down from Amherst College. He was a protégé of Kimon Friar. It was Waldemar Hansen who introduced me to Jimmy, since Waldemar, too, studied with Kimon Friar, a gassy professor of literature. The introduction took place at Merrill's apartment on East Thirty-sixth Street. Kimon was an enthusiast for poetry and was particularly windy about W. B. Yeats' *A Vision*. Exegesis was his number, as they say in show biz, and he never stopped talking, either at that party or any other gathering. Luckily for all of us he moved to Greece and stayed there.

The reason I knew so many writers was that I went out a lot, sometimes to three parties in an evening. I rarely slept more than four or five hours a night, since I was also a compulsive reader. Going to parties and giving them was a ruling passion, with time out only to go to the theater, the opera, the ballet, movies and art openings. Needless to say, such frenetic activity would cause occasional *crises de nerfs* or a bad cold. All of us drank lots of booze, which is much nicer and more sociable than the later fashion for drugs. Even then I couldn't tolerate the smell of marijuana, and even aspirin gives me heartburn. In crude and inexpensive lofts, studios and living rooms of cheap apartments there was a good deal of dancing. In the mid-1950s the best dance was the Madison, in which everyone shook all over.

Ashbery, Koch and O'Hara were considered very "far out." In Vol. II, No. 1 of *Semicolon* the whole issue was given over to them. The opening poem, by Koch and O'Hara, was called "Poem," and read:

> Sky
> woof woof!
> harp

This stanza was repeated twelve times without variations.

In a group of forty verses, most of them one line in length, Koch and O'Hara each produced what they called their *Collected Poems* and *Collected Proses, An Answer*. The titles for each group of forty were identical. There was a chain-poem written by both called "The Mirror Naturally Slipped."

Serious writers reading this issue shook their heads and thought *Semicolon* was a borderline case, but the artists at the Cedar Bar and The Club were now certain that genius stalked in our midst.

To counterbalance the gaiety of this issue, David Jackson contributed a beautiful story that took up the next whole number. This tale about an event occurring the day after Franklin D. Roosevelt died was called "The Soldiers at the Barbizon."

No. 4 was again an issue devoted to one writer, V. R. (Bunny) Lang—a brilliant artist who died four years later, in 1956, at the age of twenty-six. Bunny was a gifted actress, playwright and one of the founders of the Poets Theater in Cambridge, Massachusetts. The novelist Alison Lurie has written a touching monograph on Bunny Lang. A few years after she died, a volume of her poems appeared and I was gratified that it contained the group included in *Semicolon*. I cannot now be unmoved by such lines as:

> Where were we, what did we
> before we were critical
> between the time of innocence and grief
> when all our gestures froze polemical
> into attitudes
> and we forever wondering what they were

Small though the public was for *Semicolon*, and seemingly unrelated to the making of paintings and sculpture, my belief was fortified that interaction between diverse members of the artistic community could be beneficial in staving off vulgar commercialism and maintaining the climate of fun and seriousness necessary for genuine creativity. Who can imagine a life without laughter? Or a life without the luxury of artworks? The barbarians are always at the gates.

15

*T*HE NEXT FEW YEARS WERE PLEASANT EXCEPT FOR THE SPECTER OF NEVER having enough money. None of us thought of ourselves as poor—we were too conceited, too arrogant and too busy to have a "poverty psychology." In April 1953 I had had a fiasco with an exhibition of abstract paintings by a celebrated *Vogue* illustrator, René Bouché. What possessed Bouché to paint them, or me to show them, remains a mystery. Perhaps Bouché was attempting to prove himself more serious than his rivals, Erik and Vertes, both impressive in the world of fashion and at *Vogue*. Probably I thought such a famous illustrator would bring a new and prosperous public to the gallery, which, of course, he did not. A closing show in May and June set the tone for what would be characteristic of the gallery's real direction. All of my new discoveries were hung together in a delightful group show, a hint of what was to come next season.

Pennerton West's show in September 1953 was one of them. Four months later, in January, we presented the sculptor Frances Weiss. Both women were married to highly successful psychiatrists and were adored and indulged by them. Penny, a former student of Hans Hofmann's, was talented in a heavy, meticulous, skillful manner. Why she was in such constant agony about her work I could not understand. Certainly it wasn't for lack of ideal conditions in which to live and paint. She had a grand house with a large studio not many miles outside New York. She drove back and forth in her Mercedes roadster, and wore a leopardskin coat. Her husband never interfered with what Penny was doing because, besides attending to patients, he was writing a vast study of the psychology of work ("It isn't the kind of work, but the attitude towards it which makes a good worker happy at his tasks. . . ."). The doctor was strictly in the Viennese tradition, and perennially cheerful, in contrast to his wife's constant gloom.

The show was not well received and this made Penny West gloomier than ever. Most of her work had been done months before it was hung—and by then the groaning was in full force. Eventually I became very impatient, since other artists in my group were having difficult problems paying rent, buying canvas and paint, often being forced to do boring jobs such as carpentry or teaching to make ends meet. "I am totally blocked," Penny would say. "What do you mean, 'blocked'?" I would ask. "I go into my studio. I stare at the empty canvas. Pick up a brush, lay it down, and nothing happens." After a few months of listening to this dreary rigmarole, on a day when everything was at sixes and sevens, I burst out angrily, "Penny, do you know that nobody cares whether or not you paint another picture —not your friends, not your husband, not your mother, not even God!" Penny burst into tears and I felt remorseful for losing my temper. Two years later, in January 1953, she had her second show, after which she never did get back to painting, only talking about it. She died in 1958.

Frances Weiss was quite a different cup of tea. She was a chic, pretty woman with big, fine, mascara-laden eyelashes and an alluring personality. Frances had worked for months at her sculptures, which were created entirely for a children's playground. Her material was steel pipe which she shaped into animals: a kangaroo whose pocket was a small swing; a camel with two humps from which trapezes hung; an elephant, down whose trunk a child could slide; and other such fantasies. The constructions were finely wrought, with no seams, no sharp edges. Aesthetically Frances had made real sculpture, without a trace of Disney-cute. Frances was too talented to be "artsy-craftsy." Everyone who saw the show was pleased. Many brought their children, who were even more pleased. But no one offered to buy. I appealed to a shop then in vogue called Creative Playthings. The owner came, looked, and said the whole thing was unsalable because no school recreation department would buy such "dangerous equipment."

At the same time Isamu Noguchi was making a playground for the United Nations garden—one hundred percent safe, since it was a series of earth-made bumps and mounds and hollows guaranteed to prevent skinned knees, cracked heads or broken arms. Frances Weiss was saddened by her failure; her dream was to go on making wonderful objects for playgrounds. But she was too shy, too reticent to push herself or her work, and beyond this she was more devoted to her children than to sculpture. It cannot be said that Dr. Weiss or the children did not encourage Frances; they did, especially one delightful little girl called Muffin. In later years I was always charmed when I encountered Frances at parties or galleries. I would say, "Are you doing anything new these days?" And Frances would always answer sadly, "I'm working on a few ideas that I may finish . . ."

Helen Frankenthaler's first exhibition was on November 12, 1952. She was as young as Alfred Leslie, fresh from Bennington College, a tall, comely young woman, upper class to the nines. I had heard about Helen from Clement Greenberg, whose special friend she was. She had already set up a studio for herself in New York and for all the irrepressible sense of fun and despite her background, which would not seem to encourage a vocation dedicated to art, she was completely serious about a career as a painter. Helen's parents were of the old New York Jewish *haute bourgeoisie.* Her father, the well-known judge in New York State's highest court, adored his three daughters, Helen, Gloria and Marjorie, and encouraged their ambitions. A wunderkind, Helen began art lessons at the age of twelve at the Dalton School with Rufino Tamayo. At Bennington she came into an ambience created by a faculty dedicated to the avant-garde, abetted by lectures and criticism from Clem Greenberg. She seemed to have been born in the middle of the New York School of Painting, a paradigm of what came to be called the Second Generation.

Helen, from the beginning, and even in this, her first show, was an original. She was developing her own technique of soaking pigment into unsized canvas using rags, sponges, sticks or her own hands to create filaments or cascades of color. This same technique was soon picked up by other artists, including Morris Louis, Ken Noland, Friedl Dzubas, and later Sam Francis; but as far as I know, Frankenthaler seems to have done it before all of them, and carried on the technique in increasingly daring, large-scale canvases. It is in this sense that she was an original. Originality in art is often merely eccentric or unnecessarily obscure and becomes rapidly *passé* as the surprise wears off. The only question that might have been asked (as did Bill de Kooning about Barney Newman after his 1950 show) was: Could she keep it up?

There seemed no reason to believe that Helen would not. She was well born, had a secure private income and no personal responsibilities. Although she was considerably shaken by her mother's suicide, Helen's essential seriousness was fortified by a strong will and huge ambition. One autumn Sunday afternoon Helen and I sat drinking beer in a Village café talking about the subjective difficulties that faced many artists, in particular the nuisance of melancholia. "I have the strong feeling," she said, "that it is unlikely that I'll live past thirty-five." I was surprised by this remark. Helen was only twenty-two and already had a sad view of life. But like all melancholics, including myself, Helen was also very funny and had a wild sense of humor. During the seven years she was connected with my gallery we were often hilarious, what with my wicked gossip and Helen's repertoire of jokes and stories. At that time many of us used to gather at her West End Avenue apartment. One of the regulars was Stamos, another was her best friend, the actress Gaby Rodgers (daughter of the distinguished old master art dealer Seamy Rosenberg). Sometimes we would be joined by the playwright Howard Sackler or the journalist Clay Felker. One night as I was leaving I went to the closet and noticed next to my coat a sumptuous fur. "Whose fur is this?" I inquired. "Mine," said Helen. "It was my mother's, and now I have it." "But you never wear it. At least I've never seen you in a fur." Helen was silent for a moment. "I don't think it would be appropriate for me as an artist to go around in a fur coat." All this was changed soon afterward because the furrier and art collector Jacques Kaplan appeared on the scene. He was happy to exchange furs for paintings. Grace Hartigan got a mink in exchange for a five-by-five-foot canvas. Stamos got a big raccoon coat, which made him look like the Sixth Avenue doorway singer Moon Dog. I got a silver fox throw that fell to pieces in two years. And, of course, Helen soon got over her reticence and, like Grace, decided sloppy clothes *in* the studio, smartness outside.

Helen's work was considered beyond the pale by many collectors, and during the seven years she was with my gallery not much work was sold. This is not to say that her public was not growing; it was, and by the end of the 1950s there was an enthusiastic group of Frankenthaler fans. But at the first show loyal friends and relatives showed up, looked baffled, said kind things and probably went home worried about Helen's future. One elderly gentleman bought a nice but smallish picture. He had never bought an "advanced" painting in his life, since he preferred Rembrandt and other cozy old masters. I couldn't imagine why he would make such a purchase, although he did mumble something about his great friend Judge Frankenthaler. No doubt people were puzzled when, years later, the picture was found in his estate. The buyer was the celebrated French banker and financier André Meyer.

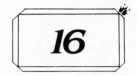

_16_

*E*VERY DEALER TELLS HIMSELF THAT HE LOVES THE WORK OF ALL THE ART-
ists in his group, but of course it is impossible not to like one of them
better than the others. The artist I considered the best—and I continue
to believe it to this day—was Robert Goodnough. He responded to this
belief by sticking to the gallery for twenty years. Yet his career has
been a strange one. He is always serious, his paintings are sophisticated
and well turned out; he is never at a loss for fresh themes. There are
perhaps seven painters of the New York School as talented as Goodnough. His peers are Pollock, Krasner, Rothko, de Kooning, Kline, Still,
Reinhardt, not the painters of the Second Generation with whom he has
always been identified. Goodnough, who was born in 1917, is the same
age as Motherwell, slightly older than Stamos, far more prolific than
Baziotes or Newman, far more inventive than Guston or Gottlieb, and
he is possessed of a painterly intelligence rivaled by no one.

Does anyone know why some artists are popular and financially
successful? I do not have a clue why Larry Rivers and Jasper Johns, for
instance, received instant recognition and continuous monetary re-
wards while other painters and sculptors of greater stature did not. I am
reminded, for instance, of Raoul Hague and Anne Ryan, and there are
many others. Perhaps the answer lies deep within the characters of the
less triumphant. Such people do not learn how to play the game of
being an artist. They are more or less indifferent to critics and museum
curators; a bit hostile to collectors; and not good at socializing in that

amorphic plasma called the art world. Often they are people who need to be alone, undisturbed by the pull and push of groups.

Robert Goodnough was reared in upstate New York, near Cortland, where his father was a farmer. His was a close-knit, loving family and it is to the Goodnoughs that his first loyalty has remained and to whom he has continually returned. Educated at the University of Syracuse, Goodnough took his postgraduate degree at New York University—but not before doing time in the U.S. Army, where he was assigned to the camouflage corps and the painting of officers' portraits. It has always amused me that Goodnough adhered to the conservative Republican party politics of his family; he was a totally unreconstructed, old-fashioned individualist. When in the early days of the gallery he had an opening, all the Goodnoughs would show up. Goodnough *père* would warmly embrace and kiss Robert. Once the father said to me, "I don't understand what Bob's pictures are about, but I'm certain if he does them, they must be good." And so they were.

But how to prove this to the public and above all to the critics? My files show that no other artist in my group was more worried about, more touted, more pushed. In one year, for instance, five shows were arranged outside New York, two of them in Europe. I constantly attempted to get Goodnough into large-scale museum shows and succeeded more often than not. How to pass him through what my Italian friends called *"il portale d'oro"*—the golden door? My main hope for this recognition was the critic Clement Greenberg. Down Greenberg would go to Bob's studio, look, make suggestions ("Cut off six inches on the left side, about four from the top . . .")—to which suggestions Bob might or might not respond—but Greenberg's praise was not forthcoming in any committed way. It was always, "Bob is very good, but . . ."

Was it shyness? Was it boredom that made Bob stay away from his own openings? He would arrive just as the door was about to be locked and everyone had gone home. One year there was an exhibition of his work presented in Washington, D.C. An art hostess of great style arranged a dinner party in Goodnough's honor—but at the last moment he got cold feet and didn't go down to Washington. Cecil Beaton, when he was decorating his beautiful "Vermeer" suite at the Drake Hotel, took my suggestion that four Goodnough geometric canvases be hung in the rooms instead of cheap Vermeer reproductions. The effect was elegant and surprising. Cecil, to show his appreciation, gave a large cocktail party to honor Goodnough and invited all his most celebrated

t: Clement Greenberg, painter and art critic, 1950. **Right:** *Grace Hartigan, in a 1952 photo by Cecil Beaton.*
NS NAMUTH

painters Franz Kline **(left)** *and Alfred Leslie in 1931 Model A Ford pickup named "Rosebud."* PHOTOGRAPH BY
CLYDE; COLLECTION OF ALFRED LESLIE.

Above: *Frank O'Hara with a portrait of
him by Larry Rivers.* Right: *Helen Frankenthaler.* Below: *Tennessee Williams
(left) and Herbert Machiz in the author's
Seventy-third Street garden.*
COLLECTION OF GRACE HARTIGAN

ove left: *A group pose for Hartigan paint-*
Masquerade, *1954, Collection of the*
icago Art Institute. PHOTO: WALTER SILVER;
.LECTION OF GRACE HARTIGAN

ove right: *The author in his Venice*
artment.

ert Goodnough at his Christopher Street
efront studio. ERIC POLLITZER

Jane Freilicher. RALPH BURKHARDT

Frank O'Hara (seated) *and Larry Rivers engraving* Stones, *1960.* HANS NAMUTH

John Ashbery (left) *and James Schuyler reading for* Folder *magazine.* PHOTO: WALTER SILVER; COLLECTION OF GRACE HARTIGAN

The Beat Generation takes a break during the making of Robert Frank and Alfred Leslie's film, Pull My Daisy, *in 1960.* **From left:** *Larry Rivers, Jack Kerouac, David Amram and Allen Ginsberg. The back of the head belongs to the poet Gregory Corso.* PHOTO: ROBERT FRANK; COURTESY LARRY RIVERS

Barbara Rose and Frank Stella. COURTESY BARBARA ROSE

The author (right) *at an opening in his 29 West Fifty-seventh Street gallery,*
1970. PHOTO: ELLEN AUERBACH

Below left: *The Ruckus group at rest.* From left: *Rusty Morgan, Mimi*
Gross and Red Grooms during the construction of the City of Chicago, *1967.*
COURTESY RED GROOMS, MIMI GROSS AND THE RUCKUS CONSTRUCTION CO. PHOTOGRAPHS
COURTESY OF MARLBOROUGH GALLERY, NEW YORK

Below right: The Discount Store, *by Red Grooms.* PHOTO: PETE PETERS;
COURTESY RED GROOMS

Right: *A production of the Artist's Theatre, with décor and costumes by*
Kendall Shaw. COURTESY KENDALL SHAW

el and Mark Rothko, 1964. HANS NAMUTH

te Rothko with her brother Christopher. HANS NAMUTH

A lunch in Bernard Reis's garden. **From left:** *Reis, Theodore Stamos, Rebecca Reis and Mark Rothko. This photograph was taken in 1969, the year before Rothko's suicide.* COURTESY MRS. BERNARD REIS

Mark Rothko. HANS NAMUTH

and glamorous acquaintances. Once again, after the departure of Tilly Losch, the Duchess of Westmorland, Philip Johnson, Dorothy Miller, Michael Duff and a crew of other fashionable and possibly helpful people, Bob arrived in sweatshirt and sneakers. The party was over and Cecil was slightly annoyed, but as usual, understanding. The hotel did not buy the pictures and they were returned a month later.

But then, was Goodnough any more antisocial than Clyfford Still, for instance? No, but Bob didn't have Still's flair for creating intense drama around his work. Still was once much talked about because he had rushed in a flurry of annoyance into Alfonso Ossorio's big house in East Hampton and with a razor cut one of his jumbo-sized paintings out of its frame. Amid yelling and dogs barking he rolled up the canvas, threw it into his station wagon and, as he left, was reported as saying, "Don't worry, I've got another one just like it!" Bob was too quiet, too reclusive for highjinks or making scandal.

During the early 1950s almost nobody could live on what they earned from their work. Goodnough tried the moving business and freelance carpentry—but then luckily got a steady job teaching manual training in Riverdale at the Fieldston School. The first visit I made to Goodnough's studio rather shocked me. He lived and worked in a Village cellar that had no windows and was lit by naked overhead electric bulbs. "What do you do for decent light?" I asked. "I don't need any," was the reply. "It's all bullshit about northern light and a glass roof. People see pictures by artificial light anyway, and I have all I need." When Goodnough could afford a better place, his studio was still downstairs below the street. Later on he got his "ideal" studio, an empty store on the ground floor across the street from the Theater de Lys. Here he would keep the door open and passersby could drift in and chat as he painted. Daytime was not for Goodnough; he liked to work at night ("It's more restful") and when no one dropped in, he liked to paint while watching Westerns on television. "How in the world can you paint and watch TV?" I inquired. "Easy," he replied. "There's so much tedious laying on of paint when I'm doing a ten-footer that I need only glance at where the brush is going and then glance at the TV screen, enough to follow the story." Before he took to the TV, Bob found relaxation by building an eight-foot harpsichord, a very beautiful one, which he never played.

"What in the world do you talk about when you are with Goodnough?" I was once asked. It was a good question, since Bob tended to be taciturn. When we were alone, however, he was articulate and knowledgeable. I would ask questions or drop remarks that would let loose a spate of words. "People have been saying you've been too much influenced by Mondrian and Picasso." "Really!" he would explode. "And would they prefer me to be influenced by Pollock and de Kooning like most of the painters you approve?" "But some days you paint representationally and on others abstractly." "Drivel. There's no such thing. Either you paint good pictures or bad ones." "But what about that painting you showed me of a black girl? It was so realistic, it even had a green highlight on her upper lip that came from the traffic signal on Christopher Street." "Oh well—that. The girl didn't believe I could paint a likeness and when she challenged me to do so, I showed her I easily could."

But there was for him a dichotomy between the world as we seem to perceive it and the shapes that make for formal structure. Goodnough knew this very well. It was his ambition to bring this imaginary dualism together in a statement that would be convincing. After he finished his academic training, he had studied simultaneously with Amédée Ozenfant and Hans Hofmann. He had also joined, soon after, a group called the "Subject of the Artist"—serving as recording secretary to the sessions organized by Tony Smith, Motherwell and Mark Rothko. He was fascinated by Mondrian's *Tree, Church, Chrysanthemums*, as well as the later De Stijl style of syncopated squares. He saw no contradiction between Picasso's Cubist years and his continuous need for "storytelling" pictures of people and scenes. "I haven't," he confided, "the slightest interest in sticking to one thing." Nor did he.

From season to season one never knew what Goodnough would choose as themes or images: allegories, figures, landscapes, formal compositions, sparked his imagination. Many of his pictures referred back to his own former pictures but so removed that only their titles could give a viewer the clues. This used to upset me a little, but what convinced me that he hadn't jumped on a horse and was riding in all directions was his unmistakable way of painting, his style, always there and recognizable. One painting, eight feet wide by four high, depicting a band of maidens in flowing robes dancing, as in a Botticelli or on a Greek marble frieze, completely unnerved me. After Bob had hung it, I said, "I don't see how you can possibly show that offspring of Isadora Duncan. It has nothing to do with the rest of the show, which looks to me totally unrepresentational." "I like it," said Bob. "It has lots of nice Cézannish dabs of blue and gray. Anyway, who knows what it will lead to?" Seeing his point, I swallowed my slight embarrassment, but it was exactly the sort of picture that kept his public puzzled and worried.

There were several mostly black-and-white canvases in that show. To get a little revenge I remarked that Tony Smith had been in and had seen the new work. "Tony says the reason you use so much black is that you're very cheap and don't want to spend money on good Windsor pigments the way de Kooning does." Bob was infuriated. "Nobody could be as cheap as Tony Smith. That's why he cuts everything out of laundry cardboards, and also paints them black!" My bitchery worked, however; from then on Bob used a wide range of beautiful primary or mixed colors. Most artists tend to be skinflints but not when it comes to their own work. Bob was no exception.

At about that time Goodnough began to make vast numbers of collages. He seemed to prefer composing images with kindergarten paper, paste and scissors to drawing with ink or pencil. Like most of the Abstract Expressionists of the period, he was obsessed with "space." Everyone spoke of "positive space" and "negative space." What was emptiness? How did one make it vibrant, living, present? Perhaps Goodnough had initiated his contemplation of spatial concepts after interviewing and writing his much-admired article on Jackson Pollock for *Art News*. On the other hand, he had long studied and analyzed the same question through Mondrian and the Cubist Picassos. At the Ozenfant school, students were required to draw with a hard pencil, no erasures, depicting a bottle or some eggs without lifting pencil from paper until the image was complete. The issue there was form, not space. At the Hofmann studio, painting was uninhibited: the brushwork was freer, forms emerged from the logic of color relations, scale, the total surface under consideration. Hofmann encouraged a dialectic of "push and pull," thick or thin pigment, activation of a one-dimensional plane. All of his students painted from the model. Once this was mastered, you could do whatever you pleased.

I gradually became accustomed to Goodnough's changing themes. *The Battle of Anghiari*, Da Vinci's lost picture known only through an engraving, inspired a series of battle scenes dissolving into frenetic flurries of opposing forms. President Kennedy's ill-fated misadventure at the Bay of Pigs was the basis of the series called *The Ship of Fools* (one of the best is in the Richard Brown Baker collection). Scraps of leftover wood on the floor of the Fieldston manual-training shop produced a four-and-a-half-foot dinosaur (in the Lawrence Bloedel collection), as well as a set of peculiar-looking standing figures that seemed more like robots than organisms. The dinosaur gradually dissolved into a long suite of *papier collage* constructions, which again dissolved into a brilliant portfolio of silkscreen prints, twelve in each portfolio, entitled *One Two*

Three because four were one color, four were in two colors, and four were in three colors. Goodnough's forms began to float and hover, and by 1970 they were like scraps of paper or kites flying through space. Living as I have for twenty-five years with almost every aspect of Goodnough's development, it is a satisfaction to declare he never succeeded in boring me.

In the late 1960s I had a discussion with William Rubin, the distinguished curator of the Museum of Modern Art's painting and sculpture collection, in which I offered my opinion that Goodnough was a major American abstract painter. "He's very talented," said Mr. Rubin, "but hardly major." "But how can you tell?" I wanted to know. "Consensus of opinion, and I see no sign of such a consensus." I daresay Rubin had a point, except I still wonder how we can know what future generations are going to like or dislike. But back in the early 1950s it didn't occur to us that art would become a field for large-scale financial speculation.

*H*ANS HOFMANN AND HIS WIFE WERE REGULAR FOLLOWERS OF OUR GAL-
lery exhibitions, since they were friends of most of the artists. When
Hofmann asked me how the work was selling I admitted that sales were
slow except for Larry Rivers. "Some days I wonder if anything will ever
sell." A warm smile came over Hofmann's face and he said, "But,
Johnny, no one you show has any fame. It takes time for a gallery to
become known." "How long does it take?" I asked. "Seven years," was
the reply. "It always takes seven years." I was taken aback. It seemed a
very long time. But Hofmann was right. That's exactly how long it took.

Few people open galleries without capital or stock. We had neither. Further, I had no position socially; I knew very few rich members
of the art-collecting classes. The rich of the Midwest and California still
bought art in Paris or elsewhere in Europe; few took chances on unknown artists. I had learned there isn't one public for art but many different ones, and many different tastes. It never occurred to me to exhibit a single direction of art, since it was obvious that there were
different kinds of artists and aesthetic experiences. Already people
were saying one couldn't be sure what would be shown next in my gallery.

But how would we reach out to the world, how could we become
known? Even then advertising and announcements were expensive.
Rent, electricity, stamps, photographs, all cost money. Dealers were
given one third percent of a sale, and in the course of a fiscal year a
dealer was lucky if he made 10-percent profit. There were few founda-

tions passing out grants. Individual initiative, much energy and talent constituted our capital; perseverance our guardian angel. Hofmann was telling us to persist, to be patient, that it takes time for good art to develop and longer for it to be appreciated.

Still, one had to cut a figure or be ignored in New York City or anywhere else. More interaction within all of the arts might speed us on our way. Collaboration was the key to open doors. This point was driven home to me by Herbert Machiz. In Paris he had found employment as a stage manager with Orson Welles, Louis Jouvet, Jean Cocteau. He had operated his own theater-in-the-round, the American Theater in Paris. I listened spellbound to Herbert's descriptions of the performances he had attended that had décors by great artists, splendid music, plays by poets. To improve his French, he went to the theater every night during his first year of residence. "Wouldn't it be marvelous if we had such a theater in New York?" My ears pricked up when Herbert said the word "marvelous." Conversations with Frank O'Hara and Jimmy Merrill soon after encouraged Herbert and me to organize the Artists Theater, which, in spite of its at times nerve-destroying vicissitudes, continued until 1969. No one kept a logbook of this theater; if one had been kept it, would be lengthy.

Herbert Machiz's childhood might have been invented by Charles Dickens. It was dreadful. He was the youngest of three children. His mother died soon after his birth. His father, a Russian Sephardic Jew, was tall, handsome, brutal and stupid; he ran a newspaper concession in the Bronx, where the family lived, or rather survived, since the father was often not at home and the children brought themselves up. There was an older brother and sister; often there was no food to eat; Herbert was beaten regularly, and almost went blind for lack of glasses. As in Dickens, the children were rescued by a kindly, very affectionate aunt, Herbert's mother's sister, Mrs. Ray Nicoll. They needed rescuing because their father was caught embezzling and was clapped into Sing Sing prison for several years. The older brother and sister escaped, got married and went their separate ways. None of the three ever again had much contact with one another. Mrs. Nicoll recognized in Herbert a child of great imagination and intelligence and did what she could to help him get educated. At the age of fifteen Herbert left home and never saw his father again until he was laid out in a coffin. Herbert was on his own. His uncle got him a job at the New York *Times* advertising department, he attended classes at New York University, and later attached himself to Erwin Piscator of the New School Drama Workshop.

In no time he was directing a play for Piscator—*Emil and the Detectives,* an exciting children's story translated from the German. He studied acting with the great Russian actress Dayakaronova; he learned the mysteries of stage lighting; he studied speech and rid himself of any New York accent, a discipline that was helpful in later years, since he could always get a job as a speech teacher—and sometimes did. Herbert loved the theater passionately. It was his vocation, his calling.

When the war came he was drafted into the Army Air Corps, but his behavior in training camp was so eccentric that he was shifted to a special assignment, in this case putting on plays and entertainments with disabled soldiers. One production of *The Man Who Came to Dinner* with a talented legless soldier in the Monty Woolley role was performed widely and raised over a million dollars for veterans' hospitals. This brought Herbert to the attention of Dr. Howard Rusk. When demobilization came, with the help of Dr. Rusk, Herbert was given the first Fulbright grant for theater. With it Herbert embarked for France, where he was able to live quite nicely on his monthly stipend. "I don't know why I ever came back to New York," he would say to me. "Paris—Europe—is much nicer." He learned a lot. He traveled during these years, but in the end an American who has to earn his living abroad and doesn't have a private income has a rough time, and so Herbert was forced to come home. It was at that point we threw in our lot together.

If Herbert couldn't have Europe, he was determined to make his daily life some sort of facsimile of it. Since he had never had a proper home, he would make one. He had already developed his obsession with real estate—studying the For Rent/ For Sale ads in the *Times.* He was buying useful objects in junk shops along Second Avenue—chairs, sideboards, tables, kitchen utensils, glasses, dishes—the "comforts of home." I will never understand where Herbert's exquisite taste came from, but he could look at refuse on the street and espy a delightful object, or walk into a thrift shop and discover a piece of furniture that would turn out to be valuable when restored. After a year or so of occupying the "ballroom" on West Fifty-sixth Street, he discovered a fine apartment for $85 a month on East Sixty-fourth Street between Madison and Park. "You see what you find in the *Times?*" he said.

Herbert believed in "maintaining credit." His friend Elia Kazan, a fellow director, had explained that it's possible to survive in New York as long as you had "credit." Charge accounts must therefore be opened everywhere. Bloomingdale's, Lord & Taylor, Brooks Brothers, Bergdorf

Goodman, Bonwit Teller and so forth. He had charge accounts anywhere he could open one. "The trick is, never pay until you absolutely
have to—but never lose your credit rating," was Herbert's abiding belief. "A person without debts is simply on the downward path." It took
me years to get used to Herbert's economic views. On the other hand,
creature comforts made daily life a bit easier.

I don't think I've ever met a person who worked as hard as Herbert. He was incapable of sitting still. Up in the morning at seven,
cleaning, dusting, cooking, shopping, rushing to whatever job was
going—teaching assignments, coaching and, above all, directing plays.
Aside from the Artists Theater, I have calculated Herbert must have
directed, during his lifetime, well over two hundred productions, many
of which took him away from New York to other cities, to Europe and
South America, to universities, summer theaters, festivals, Off-Broad-
way, on Broadway and charities.

Entertaining at home was also a form of theater and Herbert, in his
desire to aid the gallery, believed that I should regularly give lunches,
cocktails, dinners, and evening parties—which we did, often as many as
four a week, large ones and small. During the winter we would give
several Sunday afternoon musicales, always organized by my old friend
Ned Rorem. Baked Virginia ham, pumpernickel and white wine, Mozart, Schönberg, Ben Weber and Ned Rorem were the bill of fare on a
few such occasions.

When we began the Artists Theater in 1953 there was no Off-
Broadway in the sense there is today. The Artists Theater sold memberships in imitation of the London theater clubs. Some tickets, also called
memberships, were sold at the door. Herbert, being a staunch supporter of Actors Equity, insisted that all participants be paid the going
union rate whether they were actors or stagehands—and signed contracts to effect this. Our program that first year consisted of four one-
act plays written for us: Tennessee Williams' *Auto-da-Fé*, with décor by
Robert Soule; *Try! Try!* by Frank O'Hara, décor by Larry Rivers; *Presenting Jane* by James Schuyler, film sequence by John Latouche, décor by
Elaine de Kooning; and *Red Riding Hood* by Kenneth Koch, set by Grace
Hartigan.

We moved to the Comedy Club for our next presentation in early
1953. It was a tiny theater in Sniffin Court off Lexington Avenue. We
used for this program a play by John Ashbery, *The Heros*, décor by Nellie Blaine; *The Lady's Choice* by Barbara Guest, décor by Jane Freilicher;
and *The Bait* by James Merrill, décor by Albert Kresch. (Dylan Thomas,

drunk as a skunk, made a scene and staggered out in the middle of the evening, luckily between plays.)

During the following years most of the plays produced were new but there were some revivals. Among the writers were V. R. Lang with *Fire Exit*; three full-length plays by Lionel Abel; *The Screen* by Parker Tyler; another play by James Merrill (*The Immortal Husband*); *The Ticklish Acrobat* by Robert Hivnor; two plays by Claude Frederick. Rarely seen works were also done: Ibsen's *Little Eyolf*; Cocteau's *Knights of the Round Table*, translated by W. H. Auden with the author's helpful suggestions; *The Waltz Invention* by Vladimir Nabokov; *Victor* by the Surrealist poet Roger Vitrac; *In the Summer House* by Jane Bowles. Fine stage sets were provided by Alex Katz, Kendall Shaw, Kyle Morris, Robert Cato, Alfred Leslie, Julian Beck. Herbert was able to enlist wonderful actors, many of whom became well known later on.

We rarely received reviews in the newspapers, but Harold Clurman and Richard Hennessy were enthusiastic in the *New Republic* and *Commonweal*. As far as the press went, the Artists Theater was "poetic," "hermetic" and "diarrhetic." The slice-of-life theater that was the going "entertainment" seemed to us, to use John Cage's phrase, "slices of baloney." Nor have I changed my mind.

Of necessity Herbert Machiz took jobs in the commercial theater. Some were quite wonderful—for instance, such plays as *Suddenly, Last Summer* by Tennessee Williams and *Street Scene* by Elmer Rice and Kurt Weill for the City Center Opera. He did Brecht's *Mother Courage* in California, with Lotte Lenya in the leading role. Yukio Mishima, whom we met through Tennessee Williams, gave two plays to Herbert, both of which were fascinating.

My partner, Tibor de Nagy, was convinced that all the money-raising and running around that I did for the Artists Theater was not for the good of the gallery but merely to advance Herbert's career. It was the cause of one of the many quarrels we had. My concern, however, was to create an ambience in New York for unconventional or, as we used to say, "avant-garde" art. As far as I can see, the poetry and plays helped to enhance the climate in which we could breathe.

18

BUT WHAT WAS GOING ON IN OTHER PARTS OF THE ART WORLD DURING
the early and mid-1950s? The most important thing was that the new
art, sometimes called "American-type" art (a poor phrase, vaguely
chauvinistic and provincial), was getting more exposure. Sam Kootz
and Sidney Janis offered both native and foreign work in stylish, sleek
surroundings—Kootz with rather more daring than Janis. Betty Parsons, perennially innovative, had many of the important first-genera-
tion Abstract Expressionists in her fold—Pollock, Hofmann, Still,
Reinhardt. Charles Egan had de Kooning, Kline, Jack Tworkov, Reuben
Nakian, Cornell, and conducted exhibitions in a completely unorthodox manner. For instance, one show of de Kooning's lasted six months.
Charlie would often get bored and tell the elevator operator to keep an
eye on things while he went downstairs for a beverage or two. I was
tempted once, upon not finding Charlie on the premises, to walk off
with a Cornell box, keep it a few days—and send him a note demanding ransom. It might have taught Charlie to mend his ways.

In those days the chic galleries were almost all located between
Fifth Avenue and Park on Fifty-seventh Street. This included
Knoedler's and Durand-Ruel, but these international cartels are a history unto themselves, as are Wildenstein and Rosenberg farther uptown, and are of little relevance to our story. The two great galleries in
New York remained Pierre Matisse and Curt Valentine, both for elegance and superb quality. Through the years Matisse faithfully showed

Miró, Giacometti, Dubuffet, Balthus and a few Americans, such as Roszak and Loren MacIver. Only Curt Valentine's catalogues were as fine as those coming from Pierre Matisse. It was at Valentine's one found the German Expressionists and Calder, as well as the School of Paris, particularly Masson.

Alexander Iolas held forth on East Fifty-fifth Street and happily claimed Magritte, Max Ernst, Delvaux and Brauner as his chief attractions. His most important American was Fritz Bultman. Increasingly, however, Iolas spent most of his time in Europe, and Brooks Jackson managed his New York gallery. "It is such a bore," Iolas would say, "to make exhibitions. All I need is one good client to buy good pictures. *Expensive* pictures." Luckily he had just such a client in the de Menil family of Texas (Schlumberger oil drills), who were particularly fond of Magritte and other Surrealists. Iolas loved to buy jewelry for himself and to decorate his ever-expanding house in Athens with baroque antiques. He also loved to make scenes and tell stories. My favorite story, which he told me himself, described the night he was yelling about money. "Bah!" he is supposed to have cried. "What do I care about money!" To prove it he began to throw bracelets and diamond rings out the window. (He had a little hammock below to catch them.)

My Saturday mornings were a great delight to me. By eleven I had started my rounds, going from gallery to gallery. There is no other way of appreciating art than by constant looking. The habit was deeply ingrained; it had begun in 1944 as a daily responsibility while working for *View*. As the years went by, it became a "vocation" rather like compulsive reading. I couldn't bear to miss a show that was of interest, whether I knew the artist or whether it was by a painter I hadn't heard of. I was also fortunate in being invited by the museums to special previews. On Friday nights we all went to The Club on Eighth Street. It should be stressed that the New York art world was small; almost everyone knew everyone else and the general tone was amiable rather than hostile or angry. The breakup and the bitterness came several years later. One of the reasons, perhaps, was that there was little obsession with big money, and art politics was not as yet power-ridden.

The Whitney Museum was still in Greenwich Village and only a few galleries existed below Fourteenth Street. The best was the Peridot gallery, managed by Lou Pollack. It was he who showed Philip Guston before he moved to Egan. In order to keep going, Pollack had a fine frame shop in the rear of the gallery. The Whitney was then a stronghold of regional and "social realist" art. The cleavage between such art and the New York School was as wide as the Hudson River, from beyond which came the corn—Benton, Curry, Joe Jones, Gropper, Gwathmey, Wood.

Nothing bored me so much as the connection that existed in the 1920s and 1930s, even through the 1940s, between left-wing politics and the arts—all of them. It was boring then, it is boring now. I never saw an exhibition at the old A.C.A. gallery, formerly a left-wing stronghold, that didn't make me yawn. (An exception was the touching pictures of Raphael Soyer of working girls, for me reminiscent of Manet and Degas.) The very notion of a Marxist art subservient to a political party has always seemed to me suet-brained. A later visit to the Soviet Union clinched my opinion. (Oddly, there have been some interesting Marxist critics such as John Berger and Georg Lukacs.) Needless to say, Goya, Courbet or Grosz, all touched by revolutionary ideas, were independent of such commitments.

The ambience of the rising avant-garde was nonpolitical when it came to painting and sculpture. One's political or religious opinions were considered private. One was not considered a "bourgeois lickspittle" if one did not care to demonstrate at peace rallies. Some did and some didn't; it was nobody's business either way. And the attitude remained this way until the mid-1960s, at which time large-scale protest again became the fashion with the same lack of result. To this day I don't know what Black Art, Gay Art, Women's Art, Catholic Art, *are.* There is good art and bad.

Journal, 1953

Alfred Barr visits the gallery about once a month, as do other Museum of Modern Art staff people, like Dorothy Miller, Renée Neu, Betsy Jones, Porter MacCray, Bill Lieberman. Barr has been most interested in Larry Rivers' *George Washington Crossing the Delaware.* Gloria Vanderbilt has set up a museum purchase fund for pictures which, selected by a good committee, may be acquired by any museum that applies for a painting. The Rivers canvas was available and Mr. Barr wanted it, and got it. There were a dozen or so studies in charcoal and pencil of foot soldiers and horses done from early engravings that Bill Lieberman wanted for the museum's drawing collection; a nice deal has been worked out. I can't imagine a better way for Rivers to gain recognition, since he is quite unknown.

I told Mr. Barr that the painter Paul Brach insists Larry can't paint horses. This accusation annoys Larry very much. We both agreed, however, as far as the whole canvas was concerned that it didn't matter—there's George Washington with his exhausted men. Barr seems bemused by a young New York artist painting a history picture. There hasn't been a good one of the same subject since Emanuel Leutze's painting. The oddest part of the effort was that Larry had finished reading *War and Peace* and wanted to make a big "machine," but felt that Tolstoy's depiction of Napoleon's invasion of Russia was too alien a subject for him to handle. Why not the American Revolution instead? In the end Rivers employed none of the devices of Leutze. He is too much of his own time and place.

Our conversation veered away from painting. Mr. Barr wanted to know how the Artists Theater was coming along. I told him about some of the new plays we were doing by O'Hara, Ashbery and others. And then I said, "But you know, Alfred, what I would really like to see produced? *The Knights of the Round Table* by Jean Cocteau." He looked at me rather sternly and said, "John, that would be a waste of time. The art of the past is something that takes care of itself. What is much more important for people like yourself is to do new—really new—things." "But we don't know this Cocteau play over here," I argued. "All the more reason for an established theater to produce it." "Cocteau is from another world. Stick to what your group is doing," he said.

I thought about this for several days and discussed what Barr had said with Herbert Machiz. "I think Mr. Barr was right," he commented, "but maybe someday when the time is right we will do Cocteau."

Journal, 1953

It is terribly hard to go on with the adage "make it new." I'm torn between that and liking the old and traditional better. There are so many mistakes and wrong turnings with the new. Even the awful doubt: *Is this new?* An impresario can at best go along with hunches as to *who* is talented. He has to have a lot of conceit about his own taste in an area where there is no right and no wrong.

Alfred Barr fills me with admiration as he carefully builds the permanent collection of the Museum of Modern Art. The problems of money and maintaining harmony with his board of trustees seem to me soul-destroyingly difficult. He speaks in a soft voice, his manners are those of a polite country vicar, or one's favorite professor—yet there he is in the very center of a tough, worldly, expanding organization. I guess he is blessed with nerves of steel as well as much learning and remarkable discipline.

In 1953 the Museum of Modern Art was less than twenty-five years old, yet its effect on the reception and understanding of art from Cézanne onward was felt throughout both the civilized world and in many parts that weren't. Its uniqueness lay in the breadth of its interests; painting and sculpture occupied one point of attention; architecture, film, theater, industrial and book design, were included as equally important. Despite the fact that the museum's salaries were unusually low, it gathered a staff of curators and scholars who were as dedicated as cloistered priests and nuns. None of them seemed to live for anything outside the museum. The museum's coordinating director, René d'Harnoncourt, inspired as much devotion as Alfred Barr. D'Harnoncourt, an Austrian aristocrat of immense height, could charm the tail off a donkey and was instrumental in smoothing over internecine feuds involving space and precedence among the overworked staff. No museum, it seemed to me, ever put on so many shows or offered so many programs—including those of the museum school run by Victor D'Amico. I was particularly fond of Iris Barry, the film curator whose film performances in the auditorium developed a whole public of what used to be called cineastes. The most amusing member of the staff was Allan Porter, who took special pleasure in showing Great Garbo—known as "Miss Brown"—around the museum or projecting privately some of "Miss Brown's" old movies. I was a little scared of Edgar Kauffman, who had commissioned Frank Lloyd Wright to build the Bear Run Creek house. Scared but enchanted, because he ran the design department as though it were a science laboratory. He seemed to be aware of everything that was going on anywhere from Tokyo to Milan—be it dishware or cash registers. Monroe Wheeler was another charmer, sleek and handsome as a seal, who managed to prepare and publish one fine art book after another. I can't think of anyone at the museum I didn't like. But still, I wouldn't have enjoyed working there. The hours were indefinite, deadlines hung like swords over everyone's head, and worst of all, nobody seemed to have more than eight square feet in which to work. The food in the cafeteria was terrible. "Great Art," as the tattooed lady in Robert Hivnor's *The Ticklish Acrobat* declared, "makes everybody suffer."

Without the Museum of Modern Art, the New York School would never have gotten off the ground when it did. It was through such exhibitions as Dorothy Miller's *Twelve Americans* and *Fifteen Americans* that the general public learned what was outstanding and fascinating. The peculiarly refined taste that was her trademark defined the older and newer generation of painters and sculptors, and made them visible. Without her, the artists might have waited many years before receiving the recognition due them.

19

*D*URING THE REST OF 1953 NELL BLAINE, AL KRESCH, JOHN GRILLO AND MI-chael Goldberg all presented exhibitions at the gallery, then left to go elsewhere. All four shows were impressive, but I suspect that the artists did not care to compete with some of their colleagues in the de Nagy group. Kresch withdrew from exhibiting; Blaine, Grillo and Goldberg found other galleries they preferred. A painter whose work I much admired and still do, Robert de Niro, *almost* exhibited with us, but before the show opened Bob and I had a falling out. The disparity between de Niro's big talent and his character was too great for me to handle. As I've already related, more galleries were opening. Other art dealers had their ears to the ground and knew where the talent was located. I made some mistakes in not showing a few of the most remarkable new-comers—the worst error being my hesitancy in latching on to Cy Twombly, a painter of the highest imagination. I hadn't quite understood his work.

It embarrasses me to say that I am a slow learner. I was eight years old before I began to read, but learning to "read" works of art took me years, and even today I worry about apprehending new works to their fullest extent. One person who helped me speed up my capacity to "read" pictures was Meyer Schapiro. It was through his lectures at the New School that I came to realize the sheer number of telling and important details that exist throughout Western and Eastern art, and how many I was missing. Schapiro's lectures were lessons in iconology—but this did not impede the aesthetic impact of any given work; rather it enhanced it.

One day Schapiro was in my gallery looking at a dark abstract painting by Goodnough and commented on the crimson spot in the upper right area. "There's no such spot," I said, having looked at this painting every day for two weeks. "Yes, there," he said, pointing, "in the upper right about eight inches from the corner." There it was, a small red spot about the size of a dime. "Probably it was a mistake, a drip that Goodnough ignored," I countered. "I don't think so," said Schapiro. "It might be called a tension point to relieve the black; keep it from going inert." I looked carefully and realized Schapiro was correct. More important, I learned a quick, once-over-lightly would never do, and further, I learned the importance of memorizing, as best one could, images in their entirety. As a dealer I enjoyed playing this game with viewers. I would ask them to look at a painting for one minute, turn away and then describe what was visible. They would often be astonished at how much they had missed, even getting colors wrong.

In January 1954, after much cajoling, I convinced my patron Dwight Ripley to put together an exhibition of some forty of his color drawings. All of them were satirical—they poked fun at modern painting. No one delighted in modern art more than Dwight, but piety was not one of his attributes. There was, for instance, a highly baroque drawing of a fancy Victorian easel, replete with tassels and velvet swaths, in the middle of which sat an austere Mondrian. Having accidentally spilled some green ink on white paper, Dwight added *palazzi* and gondolas tossed to the sky and called this drawing *The Bomb Hits Venice*, a sly reference to his one-time fiancée, Peggy Guggenheim.

In front of the gallery, at the window, Dwight placed his favorite object, a birdcage within which was a terrarium, and within that, a fish tank. A finch, some mossy plants and a goldfish—all live—completed the ensemble. Each day I had to feed and water this elaborate *fin de siècle* construction. But one day the bird escaped, dashed wildly around the gallery, headed straight toward the window and broke its little neck on the glass. Dwight felt badly and so did I. We used a stuffed bird for the duration of the show. The show was much admired. Saul Steinberg, for one, found it amusing, but only a few pieces sold.

When summer came, Herbert Machiz rented a theater in Lake Hopatcong, New Jersey. It was called the Lakeside Summer Theater. The rent was low, the possibilities were exciting. The Lakeside venture was not the usual straw-hat outfit, using visiting stars to pull in the public. Herbert aimed for plays of good quality, mostly revivals: *Chéri* by Colette, *I Am a Camera* by Van Druten/ Isherwood, *The Grass Harp* by Truman Capote, *Ring Round the Moon* by Jean Anouilh, for instance. But there were some new works as well, such as *Eugénie*, Randolph Carter's dramatization of *The Europeans* by Henry James. Several years later Herbert directed Tallulah Bankhead in the title role. Tennessee Williams gave us two short plays for tryout, *Something Unspoken* and the touching *Talk to Me Like the Rain*.

Alfred Leslie was hired to design and build the stage sets. There were sixteen apprentices to help him—most of them girls between the ages of fourteen and seventeen, all from terribly respectable middle-class families. Alfred, in such a position (the apprentices lived in the theater dormitories along with the paid actors), suddenly became a new personage—a combination of Mr. Chips and Simon Legree. With gimlet eye he "imprinted" the novitiates; the resulting fear and adoration became a drama in itself. As the summer wore on, this theater-within-the-theater grew ever more intense. One day, while standing unobserved outside the scene dock, I overheard Alfred weaving his magic. He was stretched out on a beat-up chaise longue dressed as usual in a tiny bikini. The girls stood and sat around him while he described a film he was planning to make. "This is the plot," I heard him say. "A stranger comes to a small town. He is so handsome that all the women go mad for him. None resist. This, of course, gets all the other people, the husbands and boyfriends, in a frenzy of hate and jealousy. A meeting is held, a vigilante committee is formed. The men march to the house where they know the stranger is with a certain girl. They are carrying torches, and when they get to the house they throw rocks. All of a sudden the door swings open and a figure stands there ablaze with light." Alfred stopped, got up, went into a Mr. Bronx body-building pose. "The stranger," he cried, "is none other than Apollo Belvedere!"

The girls were beside themselves with delight and scurried after him as he went into the studio to work on his stage set. No wonder Alfred believed art began and ended with him.

The following summer Herbert hired another scene designer and took in only a few apprentices. This time the going was difficult—actors got ill and had to be hospitalized, the expenses rose, there were problems maintaining an adequate staff. The last production was very fine. It was Gian-Carlo Menotti's *The Medium*, marvelously sung and acted by Annajean Brown, a singer Herbert had worked with in Vienna. On the second-to-last day of the performance the hurricane of 1955 hit

New Jersey. The Lakeside Theater was ruined beyond repair. Our lawyer had forgotten to take out the proper papers necessary for corporate organizations in the state of New Jersey, and for several years Herbert and I were held responsible for paying the resulting losses. It was a summer of disaster, saved by the presence of a new love in my life—the superb golden cocker spaniel, William.

One of the theater's leading actresses, Jane Hunt, had found William in a nearby kennel, and, since she had been raising dogs all her life, she instantly knew when she saw him that this was no ordinary dog. She bought William and gave him to Herbert as a present. Throughout the summer he served as the theater's mascot, attending rehearsals daily and keeping an eye on the box office in the evenings and at matinees. Oddly, William never watched a performance on stage. When I returned to the city I took him to the gallery and from then on William became a gallery dog. This irritated Larry Rivers. At his next exhibition Larry demanded that William be removed. "No one looks at my pictures when that dog is around," he cried. I left William home for one day, since I knew Larry seldom came in once his show was launched. He was quite right. Many people preferred my cocker spaniel to what was hanging on the walls. A few years later, when Herbert directed *Street Scene* by Kurt Weill, William was hired as the dog that gets walked in several scenes. On opening night, while the soprano Elizabeth Caron was singing her big aria, William faced the audience and "pointed" exactly as would a trained show dog. All eyes turned to observe his magnificent color and stance. The soprano was furious, but William was mentioned in the New York *Times* review the next morning. He was replaced soon after because of naughty goings-on backstage. William resented performances on stage, even as he did at Lake Hopatcong.

The season moved ahead. Two things occurred that ended our tenancy on East Fifty-third Street. The first happened on a day of gray dreariness caused by a heavy, unremitting fall of rain. No one came into the gallery. We were on the first floor, ten steps up from the sidewalk. Suddenly the door opened and a man lurched in, drenched by the rain, muttering and moaning, and fell in a heap in the middle of the front gallery. He was a derelict—sick and almost unconscious. Even from where I sat I could smell the vomit that stained his clothes. I'll let him stay, I said to myself. If I call the police they'll throw him into the ward for vagrants at Bellevue Hospital. If I urge him to leave, he'll lie on the sidewalk getting sicker. The day went by slowly—the poor man urinated and emptied his bowels. The stench was dreadful; the storm outside worsened. Needless to say, no one came in to reproach me. At about four in the afternoon I went into the storeroom to check some drawings and when I came out my sad guest had departed.

A few weeks after this depressing incident, while I was addressing announcements at my desk, a wide hunk of the plaster ceiling directly over me came loose and fell on my head. The plaster dusted the desk, the floor and me a disgusting white. I wasn't hurt, not even scratched. But I looked at the gallery—"these rooms in a tenement!"—and was filled with rage. Ordinarily such an incident would have given me the giggles, but this time my sense of humor vanished.

I telephoned Tibor de Nagy and said we were leaving East Fifty-third Street.

20

WE MOVED TO AN ELEGANT OLD MANSION ON THE CORNER OF EAST Sixty-seventh Street and Madison Avenue. Upper Madison Avenue was increasingly becoming the new gallery area. It was fashionable; we made it more so.

The Viola Woolf School for Ballroom Dancing was situated on the second floor, with a wide staircase curving upward to the top floor. The gallery was on the third, but it was simple to have paintings carried in and out of the building, not only because of the stairs but because of the large ornamental iron doors at the entrance. The music for the dancing classes didn't start until three-thirty in the afternoon, but Saturdays it went on all day—not loud enough, however, to unsettle nerves. Mr. Woolf was always on hand attending to details, but his wife, Viola, was impervious to his vaguely officious manner. She embodied charm, good manners, gracefulness, the much-prized cool decorum of the prosperous Jewish *haute bourgeoisie*. She even *looked* that way.

Soon after we moved in, Mrs. Woolf met me in the hall, introduced herself and said, "I understand you exhibit the paintings of Helen Frankenthaler. Such a lovely girl. Did you know she and her sisters Marjorie and Gloria learned their dancing steps with me when they were little things? Really darling girls and so handsome?" I was reserved but interested, and as it turned out the Woolfs were good neighbors, often helpful when there were problems with the building.

We had one large room, a smaller one that served as an office and three storage spaces—none of them big enough to store the many large canvases that the artists liked to paint and for which I had an abiding affection.

In October 1955 we hung the work of Paul Feeley, head of the art department at Bennington College, a handsome, dashing fellow, popular at the school. It was Feeley who encouraged the college to open its doors to outstanding artists to serve on the faculty, and recruited controversial critics for lectures. Many of the most celebrated avant-garde personalities spent time teaching at Bennington; this tradition continued for a long period. A chronicle of who did what and when at Bennington would be a valuable addition to the history of modern art in America. Feeley's own paintings were radically reductive, utilizing Arp-like, rounded forms similar to dumbbells or spools; he stained unsized canvas in primary colors. I didn't really like them, but I felt that I should.

Journal, 1956

The ugly versus the beautiful. The awkward versus the slick. I increasingly experience these dichotomies when I'm looking at new paintings and sculpture. Old art by dead masters doesn't raise these questions for me in the same way. My responses are more simple, based on less complex likes and dislikes. Lack of understanding is usually the result—in the case of past art—of not knowing enough, for example, about the subtleties of Romanesque stone carvings or the conventions of Sienese primitives. I am, however, attracted to what might be called "the ugly" even in past art—the grotesques of Bosch, the "crudity" of Uccello, Goya's horrendous disasters of war. Reevaluation of past art goes on from generation to generation—but in general the consensus of taste is obvious and the positioning of this work or that changes only a little, rarely drastically. El Greco comes to mind here, and the music of Bach.

Confronted by brand-new work, artists as yet unknown, the dichotomy becomes very real. It has occurred to me that I am still in the shadow of certain Surrealist notions that I believed I had shed. Have I thought through the implications of "automatism"? Automatic writing, for instance, in Breton's poetry, would be a more plausible technique if there was no doubt as to his use of free association to create what we think poetry is. But Breton's language tends to be literary and worked-over in order to give the impression of high style. Roditi was not alone in pointing this out.

Is it possible for painting to be "automatic"? It seems to me that the use of such materials as paints, pencils, brushes, paper, canvas, are tools and properties that must be manipulated with skill, and this use contradicts the notion of "automatism." One cannot paint, I suspect, while in a trance. No hypnotist could induce a nonartist to become an artist, or even a good artist to create a masterpiece automatically.

Reading a text recently on Chinese watercolor painters I was not surprised to learn that a skilled delineator of the flowering peach branch had done this subject so many times that it became *almost* automatic. But I don't believe that this is anything other than achievement through regular practice, like practicing scales on a musical instrument. A further difficulty is presented by the forms when looking at an abstract painting; even in the most minimal works these forms seem to stem from a long and ancient history, a "genealogy" that can be traced to dimmest precivilization. The manipulation of what goes on to a surface, the arrangement of forms and colors, may be claimed to have sprung from the "unconscious" but I am very skeptical about this.

And what in the world did Breton mean by "beauty must be convulsive"? I have yet to see good art by catatonics or so-called schizophrenics. Certainly Van Gogh's art, even his swirling cypress trees or fields of corn, is not "convulsive." The evolution of the art I like can be easily traced from Cézanne to the Cubists and to the development of further plastic ideas and visual experiences, even in the art I am getting to know and exhibiting.

Lastly, I simply don't believe in the Surrealist encouragement of "art by all"—certainly not as a vocation that everyone is capable of, thus erasing the difference between dedicated professionals and happy amateurs.

Perhaps my taste for the "ugly" is a preference for what I detect as energy in a work of art. It is a revelation of will, and a capacity for *bona fide* concentration; it is the energy necessary for committed action—no matter which art is involved. I distrust art that is easily "understood," charmingly decorative, propagandistic or quickly merchandized.

Perhaps I am rationalizing the fact that collectors are not breaking their necks to acquire the unknown artists in our gallery.

As though to bear out what I was writing in my journal, in November an exhibition of paintings by Manny Farber was presented. I had been reading the movie criticism of Farber in the *New Republic* for a long time and I admired his peculiar responses to American movies that were not classed as highbrow. Give Manny a B movie like *Cat People* or

The Invasion of the Body Snatchers and his imagination expanded like a dirigible. If, following the insights Manny had projected into his criticism, you went to see the movie he liked, it was transformed by his vision of it—a real gift, I thought. I was only too delighted when Manny invited me to see his paintings. They were in the "ugly" category—even uglier than I knew—with deliberately rough and crude surfaces composed of areas that were like dissonances in music. Manny's work could never be called pretty. It was raw but sophisticated. Even though I wasn't enjoying his show, I decided it was good for the people who came in. Perhaps Manny was runnning interference for my other abstract painters? I imagined a situation where a collector might not be pleased with Goodnough, Hartigan or Frankenthaler, and I would say to him, "Well if you don't like *them*, wait until you see Manny Farber."

On the heels of Farber came Paul Georges. Originally from the Northwest coast, Georges had been living and working in Paris, had married a French girl and, upon returning to the United States, settled in New York. His paintings were big, strong, colorful, abstract and distinctly *à la mode*. What I liked was his flair, quite forgetting that only a few years ago it was exactly this trait that had excited me about Harry Jackson. Unlike Harry, Paul Georges was a lovable, big, burly fellow—no monkeyshines about him. Other artists commented on how remarkable it was that Georges had kicked off the dust of Paris and his strongly trained academic post. Surely he would arrive in time; all he needed was time.

Skipping ahead to the following season, Farber had another exhibition and so did Georges, and this time both shows left me ice cold. It was my opinion that having decided an artist was a member of the gallery group, a dealer doesn't start censoring and advising that artist about what he should show or not show. A dealer should take what he gets. How can he know what might develop? What might be the seed of a new idea? Only occasionally did I exercise my veto. The artist produces the product; the dealer is a merchant.

Yet I knew in my heart that I would never admire Farber's pictures, much as I liked him as a brilliant human being. But with Georges my response was different. It took me three days of *seeing* his new work to realize that not only did I not like what I saw but that it was awful. It was big, colorful and abstract—but quite devoid of substance. It was insincere and lacked presence. It meandered aimlessly over the walls. I recall that Grace Hartigan expressed shock, and even Larry Rivers, who tended to have a good word for everybody, shook his head. Good Lord,

I said to myself, this is like Kirsten Flagstad trying to sing like Jeanette MacDonald. Poor Paul Georges, as sensitive as a barometer when the weather changes, soon detected my negative feelings. "What," he asked me, "is the matter?" Feeling wretched and stammering a little, I answered, "What I see is a 'failure of nerve.' " The fashionable phrase of the time. "Paul, you simply are not and never can be an abstract painter."

Both artists moved out at the end of the season. A few years later Manny Farber moved to California but continued to exhibit his work— one boisterous show at the Kornblee gallery before he left. Paul Georges did not hold a grievance against me—but slowly began another aesthetic life, going down into the well of painterly experience he had accumulated during his years of learning. I was delighted when I received an invitation to come see his new work in another gallery. Gone was the abstraction. This later work had authority—a bravura style. Paul had found his true self, painting the human figure.

In 1980 Manny Farber was honored by the Guggenheim Museum with a showing of work that was praised by the New York *Times* critic John Russell. A reproduction of one painting indicated Farber had stuck to his guns.

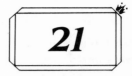

21

"*I* THINK," SAID HERBERT ON A SNOWY SUNDAY MORNING IN FEBRUARY 1956, "it is shocking that you have never been to Europe. Or anyplace else of consequence."

"One doesn't need to go anywhere if one lives in New York," I answered. "I've already been to Cleveland, Washington, Philadelphia, Boston and New England. I hate everything west of the Hudson—and airplanes, too." The truth was that the idea of traveling frightened and confused me. "Molnar the playwright has the right idea, living at the Plaza and never leaving his block. He has the park, good delicatessens, Bergdorf Goodman and a nice fountain in front."

"Well, like it or not, we're going to Europe at the end of May."

"I don't see how we can go. We don't have that kind of money; at least *I* don't."

Herbert looked at me as though he were directing a scene. "Promise me," he said, "that if we *do* get the money, you'll go." What could I say but yes? Within an hour I'd forgotten the conversation. But not Herbert. In early April he insisted we go to Rockefeller Center for passports. I was certain I'd never get one because of having, in my Rimbaud period, been a member of the Young Communist League. I called a lawyer friend and asked him how I should reply to the questions on the application form about my political past. I was told to answer truthfully, which I did, stating time and place. I got my passport in one day; Herbert had to wait a week. I still, however, did not believe we would go. Early in May Herbert came home one day to announce we had reservations, round trip, on the *Île de France*, departing the last week of the month.

I told Tibor that the gallery would have to put up enough money for a four-month trip to Europe. "It is most important for me to look at galleries abroad," I announced, "and attend the Venice Biennale." Tibor naturally had to approve my departure, since it was actually my money. Herbert had taken on extra teaching assignments and also had two directing jobs—in this way he too had raised enough cash to take off.

The gallery was at last beginning to move work out into the world. There had been sufficient publicity surrounding the artists to create a public that came to see shows regularly, and a few collectors were evincing enough interest to buy what they liked. Joseph Hirschhorn had taken an office upstairs from the gallery, where his curator Al Lerner was ensconced. Both men would stop in to look and chat. Hirschhorn was particularly interested in Rivers. Al Lerner liked Freilicher and Porter. My best customers were people in the middle-income bracket—doctors, teachers, lawyers and other such professionals who could afford to spend from $300 to $900, often on an installment plan. Drawings were priced from $50 to $150; other artists and students found these attractive. Gallery expenses were kept to the minimum by using inexpensive announcements, which we addressed and stamped ourselves. Advertising was also kept down, since space in magazines and newspapers could be a drain. Also, we had our doubts that advertising was of much value. It seemed to us that word of mouth was more efficacious. Buying ads did not guarantee getting reviews from the critics despite some people's contention that it did. Since our rent and electricity bills were manageable, we were closer to Hans Hofmann's prediction of a seven-year initiation period. Two more years of trial and error, I thought, and then we would succeed, little knowing that running an art gallery was perpetually a question of trial and error. There was enough cash in the exchequer for me to go to Europe, however.

"What you need," said Herbert, "is the Grand Tour, since this will be your first time over. We will go to a lot of places, see many different things—so that you get the hang of it." To go on a journey was Herbert's idea of heaven. He knew all about tickets for trains and planes, and how to obtain the most by spending money shrewdly in restaurants and hotels. He was well acquainted with all the places we would visit: England, France, Italy and Spain. "We will restrict ourselves to major works of art and monuments; we will see great architecture everywhere—no side trips this first time for you." (Herbert could be schoolteacherish.) "We have so little time to do all we want to do."

We were to stay with Peter Watson when we were in London. His friend Norman Fowler met us at the airport with a cab; he was to take us back to Peter's flat in Palace Gate. The minute we looked at him we knew something appalling had happened. "Peter is dead," he told us. "He had some kind of attack while he was in the bathtub and fainted; the water came up over his nose." Poor Norman burst into tears. "The whole thing is so grotesque—and to complete the nightmare, I'm under police surveillance." I knew that Peter had picked up a severe case of jaundice in North Africa, and that he had not been well. Norman had gone to bed early and did not know Peter was going to take a bath before retiring. A few hours later he was awakened by the sound of running water and went to the bathroom. The water was coming under the door. The door was locked. He called for help; the door was broken down. Peter was dead—a strange death by drowning. Stephen Spender came to the apartment immediately and defended Norman's character and close relationship with Peter to the police inspectors.

The next day I telephoned Cecil Beaton and told him I would come at noon to Pelham Place and sit with him. I knew that Peter Watson had occupied a central and frustrating place in Cecil's emotions; there he sat in his drawing room hunched in grief. As we talked, Cecil broke down in sobs. I held his hand as he tried to articulate his passionate and frustrated love of many years. "And to think he's gone and that we will never be together . . ."

That afternoon I took a portfolio of works on paper to the Institute of Contemporary Art to which Peter Watson had donated money and advice; he had suggested I bring to London a selection of work by artists I was showing. Included were drawings and gouaches by Hartigan, Leslie, Frankenthaler, Rivers and Goodnough. Ushered into the office of the I.C.A.'s director, Lawrence Alloway, I told him why I had come and why Peter had thought my selections would make an interesting exhibition for Londoners. Alloway's face was a study in frost. He quickly assured me that the I.C.A. would have no interest whatsoever in my Americans. I was ushered out. A few years later the name Lawrence Alloway would loom large in the New York art world. Sponsored by Betty Parsons, Alloway arrived in Manhattan, ostensibly to write Mrs. Parsons' biography. Instead, he quickly gained repute as a critic; it was he who invented the phrase "Pop Art" and he, along with Richard Bellamy and Ivan Karp, who became the major propagandist for the most publicized work of the 1960s. A "Pop" exhibition mounted by Alloway at the Guggenheim Museum sealed his reputation as the most articulate defender of the new direction.

Poor Norman Fowler was soon inundated with the problems of inheritance. Peter Watson had left him all his pictures, books and recordings—but no money. I suggested, since he had no desire to live in England, that he summon a book and record dealer to buy those items and put all the artworks that didn't interest him up for auction, and in this way pay the death taxes. "But what will I do with the pictures I like? I haven't decided where I will live." I suggested he loan the work he was keeping to a good museum, not in New York, for a five-year period. The best one might be the Carnegie in Pittsburgh, and I would happily write a note to its director and my former teacher at the Albright gallery, Gordon Washburn, to see if the Carnegie was interested. There were some fine Picassos, Giacomettis, and a Juan Gris—as well as the superb Pavel Tchelitchew portrait of Peter Watson dressed in medieval armor. All of this was done and Norman had no worries for five years; the Carnegie was delighted to have the collection on display.

We stayed a few days with Cecil Beaton in his country house near Salisbury. I learned to understand Constable by looking at the cathedral and the countryside. We looked at Windsor Castle, we looked at Oxford; we went up the Thames to Greenwich. We looked at the buildings of Inigo Jones and Christopher Wren. I saw Uccello and Piero della Francesca at the National Gallery; Blakes, Bonningtons, Richard Wilsons and the glorious Turners at the Tate. I was overwhelmed by the collection of art, artifacts and design in the Victoria and Albert. We dutifully visited galleries showing contemporary art and went to the theater every night that we could.

Herbert knew Paris as well as he did New York and took pleasure in showing me his favorite places. We often sat in the Café de Flore or the Deux Magots, continually surprised to encounter so many old friends. I looked at the Medici series in the Louvre as though I were Grace Hartigan, and the Courbets as though I were Larry Rivers, Monet's *Water Lilies* as though I were Helen Frankenthaler. Again and again, as I looked at the old masters, I compared them to the painters back home. Rodin *in situ* was a revelation, particularly the work in the garden of his beautiful house.

We went to Spain via *wagon-lit*. We absorbed the Prado. I discovered Zurbarán, whose paintings were to change my feelings about "realism." The best were in the School of Fine Arts on the third floor. I saw my first Gaudi building. Our mentor and guide was Mrs. Henry Jarrel, who lived on Covarrubias Street.

Janet Jarrel was the wife of an unbelievably handsome naval officer, now an attaché in the United States Embassy, and the mother of two daughters. Janet had known Herbert Machiz since the days when he lived in Paris. A Jamesian survivor, she seemed to me the incarnation of Milly Theale. She spoke very slowly in a low voice, the expression on her face grave; then, at exactly the right moment, she would break into a smile as warm as a sudden sunbeam. On our second day in Madrid we were summoned to lunch in a large, airy, many-shuttered apartment, through which the light filtered into the rooms. The long, high drawing room astonished me, for it was furnished with old American antiques, lemon-oiled to a fine polish. Over the fireplace was a portrait done in the early nineteenth century of a high-collared, somber gentleman. "That is my great-great-grandfather Thompson," Janet explained. "He was the first mayor of Buffalo." I could barely believe my ears. Buffalo! The early mayor had lived in one of the splendid houses at the foot of Porter Avenue, where the patrician city founders resided. Wherever Janet lived, many times in the Far East, the Navy would loyally ship the family heirlooms to wherever "Hank" was stationed. They had retired to Madrid because, "We are used to servants and I don't think we could live in the States anymore." But the Jarrels weren't confined to the city; they had a *finca* about thirty miles out in the country, an old mill that Janet had done over. We went there for Sunday lunch and met Duarte lo Pinto Coelho.

Duarte, a Portuguese aristocrat, was to Spain what Cecil Beaton was to London and New York—a frivolous, warm-hearted designer and decorator, owner of Madrid's most fashionable boutique—and as kind and generous as Janet Jarrel. Of course, neither of them had a brain in their heads when it came to politics and both thought General Franco was a blessing. When I confessed to them that I had been and still was an ardent supporter of the Spanish Republic, they explained what an error this seemed. Said Duarte, "Oh, you Americans! You are so naïve, so childish. We forgive you because you never understand *le monde.*" Janet shook her head sadly. "If it weren't for Franco, we would not be able to live in proper style—and that is *so* important, don't you agree?" Happily we never discussed politics again.

It was Duarte who introduced us to his circle of artists and writers—the most fascinating being Luis Escobar, a great director in the theater, who, despite his ambiguous political ties, had been able to go on producing fine plays—even the work of his dead friend García Lorca. "Ah," we were told, "you are going to Barcelona, so you must call upon Signora Ruiz, Picasso's sister." And we were given a letter of introduction to an old contessa who was close to the signora.

It was lovely having a room in the Hotel Colón; we didn't mind the racket of the bells in the cathedral across the street. In the municipal museum we saw the frescoes of ninth-century Catalonia. We walked in the Parque Güell where Gaudi had set his stamp, observed Gaudi's unfinished cathedral and his fantastical apartment building where all the balconies seemed to be wearing dominoes and the roof resembled a children's playground.

"Isn't Gaudi wonderful?" observed Herbert. "But wouldn't it be much of a muchness if the whole of Barcelona were designed by him? It would all look like the witch's house in *Hansel and Gretel!*" This was said as we got off the funicular at the top of Mount Tibidabo, which overlooks the city and harbor—a magnificent panorama.

A few days later, Duarte's friend telephoned to say that she would take us to visit the Ruiz family. They lived in a large, old-fashioned house in a very respectable quarter of the city. One of Signora Ruiz's daughters-in-law met us at the door and we were taken into the parlor. Picasso's sister was seated in a commodious wheelchair; she was paralyzed in her arms and legs—but the extent and force of her personality was instantly apparent. Her eyes were like Picasso's, round as buttons and dark, and she had an expression on her face so full of good humor that one instantly loved her. She spoke no English, nor did any of the Ruiz sons and daughters-in-law know more than a few words. Luckily Herbert knew a little Spanish and the contessa translated when necessary. There was much joking and laughter. A tray of candies and cigarettes was passed around, and little glasses of sherry.

First we must see the work of the signora's sons, both painters—and the old mother made several little speeches about their talent, inherited, of course, from their grandfather who was a great professor at the Academy. I carefully, in my mind, tried to enjoy the Ruiz brothers' paintings for what they were and not compare them to the work of their uncle. Luckily they were charming. At last Signora Ruiz asked to have Picasso's work shown to us. "These are all family things," she said. "Pablo did this one [a bird] when he was four." Then we were shown pictures he had done when he was six, seven, nine and finally a large canvas he had done when he was about twelve or thirteen. It was a picture of a man dying in his bed—surrounded by doctors and family all in grief. "Pablo was a genius from the day he was born. How could he be otherwise, being the son of such a distinguished father?" Having seen the *pièce de résistance*, we were shown nothing else. By now the signora was tired and it was time to leave. I really wanted to kiss her hand, but unfortunately her arms were wrapped in shawls and all that Herbert and I could do was make a low bow and thank everyone for so much kindness.

We took a Turkish boat up to Genoa and from Genoa a train to Venice. It was late afternoon when we arrived; a *motoscafo* took us to the Hotel Europa, which overlooked the Grand Canal and Santa Maria della Salute. It was not until after dinner that Herbert led me to the Piazza San Marco. The orchestra was playing, the lights were glowing, and as I drank my espresso I knew that I had found the city I would always regard as the place where one breathed and moved within a total work of art. For the next twenty years I went to the Serenissima annually; its splendor never faded for me.

22

Journal, October 16, 1956

I've been back in New York for over a month and I have not put together the experience of Europe. It swirls in my head. I should have been continuously happy—but I wasn't. In Naples I got word that my father had died three weeks previously. There was nothing I could do about it. No one knew where I was, since Herbert and I did not follow a schedule and there was no way to get the message to me.

I have since asked my sister Evelyn how my father died; he was eighty-three but always healthy. "I think," my sister said, "it was because of the automobile license. He had gone to City Hall to get it renewed, and some clerk in the license bureau decided he was too old to have a new one. Since driving around, visiting relatives and friends or going fishing was his greatest pleasure, to have this freedom taken away was a blow for him. He went into a state of grief; within a few days his breathing became difficult. His lungs were clogged, and they put him in an oxygen tent. I went to see him in the hospital the day he died. 'Evelyn,' he said, and two big tears rolled down his cheek, 'the jig is up.' And soon after that he was dead. I asked the doctor what he died from and the doctor said, 'I don't really know. Some kind of congestion.' "

My own sadness is hard to formulate. I have seen very little of my family for several years. Even as I write this I know well what a help my father had been to me when I was young—encouraging, amused and sensitive to my physical and emotional frailties.

It was in Venice that I read about the death of John Latouche—suddenly, at only thirty-eight years of age—from a massive coronary. Shortly after this I heard of the death of his charming friend and patroness Alice Bouverie—once the wife of Prince Serge Obolensky, sister of Vincent Astor, mother of my friend Ivan Obolensky. The world that Herbert and I knew surrounding these two had passed away. They were a gay and beguiling company, those people in the musical theater: Jerome Moross, Lena Horne, Josephine Premice, Sono Osato, Carol Channing, Kaye Ballard—all the delightful entertainers we had enjoyed at Latouche's gatherings on East Sixty-seventh Street. They were the artists Latouche wrote for and worked with in *Ballet Ballads, The Golden Apple, Cabin in the Sky*; and for whom he had written many memorable popular songs.

Standing in line outside the American Express office in Rome, waiting to get lire for travel checks, I bought the Rome *Daily News*—but didn't read it until we were on the train going to Florence. When I opened the pages I discovered that Jackson Pollock had been killed in an automobile accident two days before.

Journal, November 1956

Death is new to me. I can't take it in: Peter Watson, and John Latouche, and Mrs. Bouverie, and Jackson Pollock and my father. On the train reading the newspaper between Rome and Florence I startled the other passengers in our compartment by letting out a wail. Herbert had already been through a couple of my *crises de nerfs*, but the oddity this time was the exaggeration of my reaction; it was as strange to me as it was to Herbert. "You are thinking of Lee Pollock," he said, knowing that as we were en route to Florence she would have arrived in Paris. Jackson and Lee had decided to separate for a while to gather perspective on themselves and their relationship. In the twenty years they were together they had seldom been separated except for Jackson's hospitalizations. Lee had never been to Europe and had decided this was a good time to go. Both of them needed time to think about what they expected from each other and what they wanted for themselves. The crisis was not brought on by one of Jackson's drinking sprees. He had been in a period of abstinence from alcohol. Their problem was essentially spiritual, an exhaustion stemming from too many struggles, both financial and artistic.

I have since spoken with Lee several times. Aside from the shock and grief, she already has to deal with lawsuits caused by the accident. There were two women passengers in the car; one was killed, the other slightly injured.

Soon after, the season was in full swing. A journalist from *Fortune* magazine called on me at the gallery. "I am writing a piece that discusses what causes changes in taste, and who brings this about," he explained. "The answer to that one is easy," said I. "Artists bring about changes in taste; their work creates the taste by which it is to be appreciated."

"Quite so," he replied, "but often the artists produce work the public doesn't immediately understand; furthermore, if the work isn't seen, how can anyone appreciate it?"

"Alas," I said, "some of the finest work has had to remain in storage for too long, which is a misfortune for the artist. All work of good quality should be seen and enjoyed."

"There's such a plethora of art, someone must cull and select. Nowadays it's the dealers."

I was silent for a moment, and then said, "Actually some of the best art was brought to the attention of the public by critics. Clem Greenberg, for instance, has encouraged today's interest in the Abstract Expressionists."

The journalist remained unsatisfied. "Many people don't read art criticism in *Partisan Review*, the *Nation* and other such magazines, since they are published for a small, educated readership."

I suddenly recalled Ananda Coomaraswamy's lecture I had heard years before at the Albright gallery in Buffalo. Coomaraswamy had spoken of the maker, the receiver and the purveyor who acts between the two; the agent of kings, princes or rich tycoons was the middleman. The history of modern art from the mid-nineteenth century also included a history of art merchants from Durand-Ruel to Pierre Matisse.

I was flattered when the *Fortune* writer said, "It's people like you who bring about changes in taste and that's why I'm here for this interview. A whole new generation of artists seems to be getting attention and you show several of the most interesting."

"Are you pulling my leg?" I asked. "There's more activity surrounding the new work than ever before, and more galleries, more collectors and better art publications. I'm just one of the many new enthusiasts." (Don't be self-serving, John, I warned myself.)

The interview went on rather too long; I got bored. In a day or so I dismissed it, forgot it. But, astonishingly, *Fortune* did publish the reporter's findings, and I found myself in such company as Julian Beck and Judith Malina of the Living Theater, John Cage and a few other "taste" benders. Who was I, however, to ignore an unexpected almond in the cake when least I expected it? But would it change anything in a spectacular way? Of course it didn't, but it did add fuel to the fires of my conceit. I could now privately fancy myself as a number-one "taste maker," forgetting that other art merchants, like Charles Egan, Eleanor Ward, Leo Castelli, Grace Borgenicht, Betty Parsons and Sidney Janis, held similar views of themselves. They, however, were entitled to experience such felicity.

Innovation, newness were in the air. Eleanor Ward found a ruin of a stable on the corner of Seventh Avenue and West Fifty-eighth Street. She renovated it into the Stable gallery, keeping most of the old timbers and planked floors; the smell of horse manure remained. It was certainly unlike any other art gallery in Manhattan, suitable in every way to Eleanor's adventurous spirit. We became good friends after I asked her if she would allow a show of Larry Rivers' plaster sculptures in her spacious basement. The show was a *coup de théâtre*. Rivers' sculpture never again looked so well. She then won my admiration for mounting a small show of Joseph Cornell's "Celestial Theaters" in a back room— all of them among the finest boxes Cornell ever devised. Cy Twombly and Robert Rauschenberg both gave exhibitions that fit the equine spaces like saddles to ponies. But perhaps the event that won Eleanor Ward her largest fame was the Stable Annual, a large-scale group show utilizing all three floors of the building. This event had in truth been inaugurated in 1951 as an effort of the Artists Club and presented in an empty store on East Ninth Street. Older artists selected younger ones, the so-called Second Generation. The Stable took over the show in 1953.

A committee of artists still decided which painters would be included. It was possible, attending any one of these exhilarating jamborees, to see the full gamut of avant-garde directions called the New York School. Much of the taste was for abstract painting and sculpture; a certain percentage was given to coteries (friends of the artist doing the selecting). Some of it was outrageous junk. But none of it was boring. Eleanor loved to sit in her little office listening to the heated squabbles outside her door. Nor was she above promoting a few. She loathed dreariness. She adored chic and was the epitome of high style in the way she dressed, lived at home and entertained. After the Stable was abandoned due to obsolescence and sheer expense, Eleanor found a duplex on East Seventy-fourth Street in a grand old mansion. This was finely renovated by the architect John Biedenkapp. It never occurred to anyone to think it peculiar that a place where no horse ever champed continued to be called the Stable.

New spaces, new faces was Eleanor's creed and she proceeded to discover Andy Warhol, Robert Indiana and the new Marisol sculptures (as opposed to the old, small bronzes). Joan Mitchell was one of the few of her former artists who remained with the gallery. Sculpture was shown in the garden to great effect. Eleanor had done it again.

The older, more famous painters were shown by Parsons, Kootz, Janis and Egan. But Sam Kootz was much appreciated by the young because in 1950 he had invited Meyer Schapiro and Clement Greenberg to select a show called *New Talent*, which consisted of twenty-three of the Second Generation, all unknown newcomers. Formerly an advertising executive, Sam Kootz had an immense flair for publicizing his shows and attracting prosperous buyers. Part of his prestige had to do with a Picasso exhibition, the first in New York after World War II, which created a sensation and ensured the prestige of the Kootz gallery.

The art critics on the newspapers were at that time a tedious lot. Edward Alden Jewel and later Howard Devree of the New York *Times* were impervious to what was going on in the art world. Worse was to come: the appalling Emily Genauer on the *Herald Tribune* and then the scary John Canaday replacing the suetheads who had preceded him on the *Times*. At the beginning of the 1950s a forceful, sharply articulate critic became the defender of the new artists, Thomas Hess. When Alfred Frankfurter resigned as editor of *Art News*, Hess took over and made of this magazine an important organ propagandizing for the Abstract Expressionists and their eclectic followers. Many of the feature writers and reviewers were poets, among them James Schuyler, Frank O'Hara and John Ashbery. Some of the other contributors were artists—for instance, Ad Reinhardt, Elaine de Kooning, Fairfield Porter, all of whom were skillful and witty writers.

Tom Hess was the ideal editor to pump life into a moribund publication such as *Art News*. Educated abroad and a Yale graduate who had studied philosophy, Hess was both worldly and intellectual. A sense of humor, a comfortable private income and innate kindliness made him an ideal arbiter of taste. Most important, he liked the company of artists and moved among them with ease; some of them became his closest friends.

Herbert and I were particularly fond of Tom's wife, Audrey. She was seriously involved in liberal politics, serving on many committees, working for candidates. Audrey was a Stern from New Orleans, and as cultivated and intelligent in her way as Tom was in his. They lived in a grand house on Beekman Place overlooking the East River, where they often entertained members of the art world, the most amusing party being on the night of the annual election returns. When Audrey, who had never given a speech in public, had to do so, she hired Herbert to give her lessons in public speaking. They got along very well and when Audrey finally made the speech she got through it splendidly. But as her mother, Mrs. Stern, told me years later, Audrey had been a semi-invalid since childhood, and her illness, a heart condition, was a cause of deep concern not only for Tom but for her three children. However, signs of doom and gloom in the Hess ménage were discouraged; Audrey was not one to complain and Tom did not exploit his distress.

Throughout the 1950s, *Art News* kept a lively and knowing eye on the growing art scene. It encouraged controversy, took unpopular positions, defended the outrageous from time to time and infuriated staid conservatives. An editor of an art journal who doesn't go in person to see as much of what is going on, and involve himself in the myriad activities of a volatile conglomeration of ambitious artists, cannot comprehend a scene so labyrinthine as the New York art environment. Tom had the energy and curiosity to do so. More than that, since Audrey and he had the means to buy pictures and sculpture, they built a fine collection of works they both enjoyed and admired. Putting oneself on the line can produce both love and odium. Neither Tom nor Audrey had the time or patience to worry about outside opinions. They too were tracking the marvelous.

23

THE NEW, SINCERE MONEY FOR GALLERIES STARTED FLOWING INTO NEW York about 1953. One of the newcomers was a rich collector from Buffalo named Martha Jackson. The money was apparently from chemicals. She had been a Kellogg, and for a long while I thought her income came from cornflakes and other cereals. Mrs. Jackson liked to buy pictures directly from the artists; she went with cash in hand—greenbacks—and there were few artists who could resist the sight of greenbacks. Joan Mitchell was one artist who did resist, but then, she was rich herself, which is always a good position to be in when overcoming temptation. Martha did not care to buy pictures through dealers and in the end opened her own place, first on East Sixty-fifth Street, later in a large town house on East Sixty-ninth Street, which she remodeled from top to bottom. I might have been more amused by Mrs. Jackson's shenanigans had she not poached on what I considered my territory. Thus begins the story of how artists move about.

What was described as "the game of musical chairs" is probably just as true for artists as it is for writers, actors or musicians as they go from one management or publishing house to another. The reasons for this process are sometimes quite simple, but more often complex. An example of the latter was the sudden migration away from Betty Parsons of all the "stars" of the early 1950s to the Sidney Janis gallery, including such Abstract Expressionists as Pollock, Still, Gottlieb and Rothko. As a group they demanded that Mrs. Parsons flush out of her galleries the thirty or so artists they considered below par. Many were women. Ad Reinhardt refused to join with the dissenters on the grounds that it was no business of the artists to dictate to the dealer what was to be exhibited and what was *verboten.* Mrs. Parsons refused to meet their demands; as a result, they all moved next door to Mr. Janis. It should be pointed out that the prosperous Janis gallery had a large stock of excellent French moderns and a good-sized working capital. Since the artists were hard-working and earned little money, they felt that the idealistic Mrs. Parsons dispersed her energy over too wide a gamut of second-raters and that concentration on a few artists would produce better financial returns. I don't believe the artists who moved out were in the wrong. They were concerned with survival.

Several years later the same kind of exodus occurred from the Charles Egan gallery, where de Kooning, Kline, Tworkov and others exhibited. Here the problem, according to the artists, was again money. Pictures were sold, but the artists were kept waiting endlessly for their share in the sales. Sometimes they would receive no pay at all because the gallery, which had little capital and no stock of blue-chip pictures, was inundated with the expenses of keeping its doors open. The problem was compounded further by Charles Egan's genius complex; he viewed himself as a combination of Diaghilev and Svengali and quite believed that it was his inspiration, his perfect eye, his leadership, that had invented the artists and guided their work. Some, like Kline, were rather amused by Egan's ego; others were not. Everyone agreed that while it lasted the Egan gallery was a local treasure. It was to continue for several years in different spots. One sculptor remained adamantly loyal, Reuben Nakian, who never made a move without Charlie at his side. In a curious way Charlie was undone by his own intransigent Irish charm.

The first major defections from my gallery took place in 1958 and 1959. Martha Jackson had taken a shine to the big, stylish abstractions of Alfred Leslie and produced the usual dollar bills to acquire one from his studio. By the time I found out that Leslie had done this, he had spent the $1,200, and there wasn't even a bone left for the gallery. This threw me into a rage of such proportions that I declared him excommunicated. "Go to that Martha Jackson if you think more of her than you do of me," I yelled. Which he promptly did. Apparently some of the artists told Alfred that he had given the gallery a dirty deal, whereupon, to salve his conscience, he gave me a large canvas I didn't particularly want. Later on I was glad that I had it, since I sold it to pay some bills.

The next farewell was Proustian in its underlying motivations. One day Helen Frankenthaler came to see me and confided that she was going to marry Reggie Pollack, the artist brother of the dealer Lou Pollack, both good friends of mine. "But Reggie is already married to some Israeli girl," I commented. "That's over, they're getting divorced," said Helen. She and Reggie would be going to Europe for a while; the key to her studio was with her lawyer in case anything was needed in an emergency. Several weeks later I left for Venice. It was 1958, a Biennale year, and as usual a great round of parties was in progress—the largest and grandest given by the Marxes of Chicago on the roof of the Hotel Danieli. During a lull I went out on the terrace overlooking the lagoon. The boats of the Lido Casino were twinkling in the distance. A misty rain began to fall. Someone stood nearby, head in hands. It was Reggie Pollack, tears running down his cheeks. When he saw me he threw his arms around me in grief. "Why, why did Helen leave me?" he wanted to know. What answer could I give him? Helen had changed her mind abruptly and just as abruptly had married Robert Motherwell. I had attended the wedding luncheon.

A few months after my return from Europe it was my turn to grieve. At eight-thirty one evening I received a telephone call from Helen in which she briefly explained that she was no longer with my gallery. When I asked why, what had gone wrong, her answer was simply, "Of course you understand why," and that was that. I didn't understand, but some time afterward a mutual friend who was at the Motherwells' house told me that Motherwell did not approve of his wife being in the gallery of someone with my kind of private life. By this time Helen had moved into André Emmerich's new ground-floor gallery. It was cold comfort to notice that most of the pictures sold for the following year or so went to clients of mine who were considering acquiring a Frankenthaler. Yet it was a fortuitous move for Helen. In a few years Emmerich made what is called in Manhattan a "good marriage" to a young woman of means. The gallery expanded and grew. Someone told me it was a "Tootsie Roll" fortune, but I never asked André if candy was the telling ambrosia. Perhaps it was an unfolding of his skill.

The third goodbye was agreeable. "My paintings have become too large in size and scale to fit into the gallery," explained Ken Noland. "I've been invited by Clement Greenberg to show with French and Company." It was true; Noland's latest large-scale targets were taller than our ceilings. The new gallery, which opened the following season, would be located on the top floor of Robert Dowling's latest structure, the Parke-Bernet Building on Seventy-sixth Street, across the street from his other property, the Hotel Carlyle. Dowling let it be known his new building would be only six stories high, so that his view of Central Park and beyond would not be cut off. French and Company, a venerable dealer in old masters and antiques, had rented the space. Spencer Samuels would be the director; he had become bored with the traditional family concern and wanted to run an up-to-date contemporary gallery; he had chosen Clem Greenberg to advise him on what to show—a far cry from the services Mr. Samuels *père* had rendered William Randolph Hearst for many years in the furnishing of the celebrated Hearst *palazzo* called San Simeon. Noland felt sad to leave our gallery and gave me a departure present of a large five-by-six-foot early painting, very colorful, reminiscent of Robert Goodnough's clock- and counterclockwise images.

The new French and Company gallery opened in 1960, designed by the sculptor Tony Smith. It was an impressive space and Noland's new work fitted in very well. One of the other painters chosen by Greenberg was Barney Newman. Spencer Samuels hadn't quite reckoned with the histrionics that awaited him. One of the Newman canvases was so immense it had to be put on stretchers in the gallery. A day or so before Newman's show closed, this particular canvas slipped off its hooks and fell to the floor, straight down, about six inches. It did not fall forward. Spencer's secretary, Marjorie Hensen, made the mistake of telling Newman what had happened, whereupon Newman was transformed into a raging last-act Othello. Whipping out his trusty magnifying glass and climbing a ladder, he inspected every square inch of his canvas until at last he came across a small patch of tiny cracks. "Aha!" he cried. "If this painting isn't restored exactly to its former perfection, I shall call my lawyer!" Poor Marjorie quickly got in touch with the restorer whom we all called "Mr." Moro, who arrived the next morning with his valise of equipment. The noxious spot was pointed to. The restorer checked the pigment of the surface, got out a little bowl, mixed the necessary medium blue thinly—and with a paint blower and a single blow, returned the surface to its former pristine condition.

When Newman arrived later in the day, again with his magnifier, he could not find the offending area. He turned his attention to more important matters. "How," he wanted to know, "do you people intend to get this important work *out* of the building?" Poor Marjorie made the mistake of innocently telling the truth. "Why, the same way we got it in." "No indeed," said the Master of the Single Stripe, "the windows will have to be removed and the picture will be lowered to the sidewalk on ropes. That is what Ben Heller had to do with Pollock's large *Blue Poles,* and that is what I demand also."

"What *did* you do?" I asked Marjorie several years later, after she had come to work in my gallery. "Soon after Barney left the premises," she confided, "I called in two excellent framing technicians who took the canvas off the stretchers, carefully rolled it, took it downstairs, re-stretched it and there it was the next day, ready for Newman and his magnifying glass. When he saw it in the exit hall leaning against the wall, ready for wrapping, he demanded to know how we had gotten it there. I smiled as sweetly as I could and answered, 'I'll never tell.'"

By the end of the first season Spencer Samuels had learned that contemporary avant-garde art was not for him and he closed the gallery before he lost his shirt. Arne Ekstrom moved in shortly afterward, revised the space and for several years the Cordier-Ekstrom gallery, pursuing a modern direction far different from the taste of Clement Greenberg, managed not only to keep open but to run a prosperous business.

Each of my three defectors subsequently had one success after another. Obviously this can only be a cause for satisfaction. However, one of them, Ken Noland, managed to enrage me many years later when he was given an important retrospective show in Cambridge, Massachusetts. The catalogue boasted a thoughtful introductory essay by the critic Michael Fried. As was my wont I checked the list of Noland exhibitions, all of which were duly noted except the two that had taken place in the Tibor de Nagy gallery. Since Fried was a careful scholar, I felt this was an ignominious omission and I could not resist challenging him on such sloppiness. "But I received this affirmation from Noland himself," explained Fried. "It was he who composed the list of acknowledgments and I followed his directions, naturally thinking it would be correct." I was nonplussed and, of course, inquired of Noland what had happened. He was quite cool about it. "I do not," he said pontifically, "recognize any of my work before 1960." I suppose this was the prerogative of true genius, but I had to wonder about future complications in auction rooms.

24

WITHIN A FEW DAYS OF EACH OTHER, TWO TOTALLY DIFFERENT ARTISTS had stopped by the gallery and mentioned a new young painter whose work they admired. The first was Robert Rauschenberg. "Have you been down to Delancey Street," he asked, "to see Red Grooms' production called *Fire! Fire!?*" I thought that some sort of Off-Off Broadway extravaganza was being praised. "No—it's not that—quite; it's not a play or a dance piece—it's a 'Happening.' It's like seeing three-dimensional painting or sculpture, only the figures are real people costumed, made up and running around in a house that's on fire. It's quite wild and wonderful." Parlor games, I thought, and forgot about it. But a couple of days later Fairfield Porter, not a man to take an experience lightly, also asked me if I had heard about Red Grooms' show downtown. Porter was even more enthusiastic than Rauschenberg. This time my interest was aroused.

Although various books about Happenings have been published, usually giving credit to Allan Kaprow as the artist who invented them, it was Grooms, who, in the summer of 1958, had put together his living "pictures" in Provincetown—and then some months later remounted the show in a space available on the Lower East Side. His partner in this enterprise was his wife, Mimi, an artist in her own right, daughter of the sculptor Chaim Gross. It was a dashing event, with fire engines and fire fighters responding to a calamity. The only real fire was a few lighted matches. I got in touch with Grooms and asked if I could see work that might be exhibited in a gallery, on a wall. "Of course," said Red. "I paint and draw and will be happy to bring you a few things." There were not many—Red and Mimi were so busy on a number of projects that there hadn't been enough time for easel and drawing board.

When I saw the Groomses I was instantly taken with them. Mimi with her big eyes, brunette hair and soft voice seemed a petite sprite out of Titania's retinue; and Red looked like Li'l Abner, very tall, with a thatch of red-blond hair and an ingratiating smile. His accent was pure Nashville, Tennessee. The fictive persona was soon dispelled when I learned how very busy they had been in the last few years. They had their own puppet theater, they toured Italy in a horse-drawn gypsy wagon performing circus acts—and, in fact, had joined a small one-ring circus as clowns. They made paper theaters with rolls of painted scrolls—but both of them were basically painters. I said I would try to sell what I could from the back room of the gallery until there were enough finished works for a show.

I had to wait until 1962 before we could launch a full-scale exhibition. It took place in our East Seventy-second Street gallery, which we would occupy for five years. It was a beautiful space designed by the architect Robert Brown, who had installed a vaulted ceiling and invisible spotlights. The pictures, all by Red, were an explosion of high spirits. *The Banquet Years*—Roger Shattuck's book about Paris artists and poets at the beginning of the twentieth century—was the inspiration of many of the pieces, several of which were in three dimensions. One construction depicted the banquet given by Picasso for Le Douanier Rousseau at which, among other guests, sat Gertrude Stein, Marie Laurencin, Rousseau playing the fiddle, Picasso dunking a donkey's tail into a can of paint, the poet Max Jacob. (It was bought by Carter Burden, then a student at Harvard and later a well-known politician.) Other constructions showed Alfred Jarry in bicycle costume, Max Jacob drinking an apéritif at a little table and a man walking through the Latin Quarter with a long loaf of bread. There was also a big canvas of the roller coaster at Coney Island, one of the cars looping out of the top of the picture and back in.

The show was a hit and Red was on his way to stardom. By now a group had assembled around the Groomses—the Ruckus studio. There were a few more Happenings and then a spate of film productions, the first being *Shoot the Moon*, followed by *Fat Feet* and *Tappy Toes*. The props and backgrounds for these short movies were so colorful and attractive that we included them where possible in many of the exhibitions presented between 1965 and 1974.

But the big blockbuster shows began in 1967 when Allan Frumkin invited Red to do a gigantic construction of the city of Chicago. It filled not only the Frumkin gallery but our own space at 29 West Fifty-seventh Street. There was the Second City, with Hugh Hefner and Mayor Daly striding its wide boulevards, the elevated riding through the Loop, hundreds of cars and people, Mies van der Rohe skyscrapers. There was the elevated line and Mrs. O'Leary's cow that kicked the lantern; there was Palmer House, Jane Addams and even Chicago's celebrated gangsters.

"What a shame," said my old Chicago friend Maggie von Maggerstadt Rosner, "that *Chicago* isn't where it belongs!" "And where would that be," I asked. "At the Chicago Art Institute, of course." Whereupon Mrs. Rosner purchased the whole construction and donated it to the Institute, where it has been popular with the young ever since. But before it went to its permanent home, *Chicago* traveled first to the Venice Biennale, then to Nebraska, Washington, D.C., and finally to the Museo de Arte Contemporaneo in Caracas, Venezuela.

The Groomses and Ruckus were in full cry. An invitation from Minneapolis inspired another jumbo-sized construction—this time, *The Discount Store*. It was six times the size of *Chicago,* and depicted life in a typical supermarket, the kind that offered a vast variety of merchandise. It was shown, however, not in a museum but in a large empty area of Dayton's department store in Minneapolis, and, of course, created a sensation.

But how to unveil *The Discount Store* in New York? First I went to the Museum of Modern Art, where William Lieberman tried hard to convince his colleagues to present Red's supermarket. But to no avail. Living as I did on East Seventy-third Street not far from Madison Avenue, I noticed one of the stores between Seventy-third and Seventy-fourth on the west side of the street was for rent. The owner was also my gallery landlord and it took very little to persuade him to rent the space to us for five weeks. Price: $3,800. Red had made it clear that his construction could not be sold in parts—only the whole thing—which consisted of over two hundred and fifty separate pieces.

By now the Ruckus group had grown to a dozen and a half young men and women who were also artists. To see the group descend on the empty store was like watching Mr. and Mrs. Santa Claus busily engaged in their celestial Christmas workshop. It was not an easy task.

The store was over two hundred feet deep but only twenty feet wide. The ceilings were a bare eleven feet in height. The din of construction could be heard all the way to the Whitney across the street, a museum that had not as yet taken an interest in Grooms; but then, New York museum directors had done no more than lift their noses.

The opening day was pure bedlam. The local precinct sent a police car over to keep an eye on us. A crowd collected on the sidewalk—the space was so jammed that viewers had to go through single file and the people in line came in as others went out. I stood at the entrance shouting over a mike, "Get your brand-new Red Grooms poster while we still have them!" Since there were half a dozen schools within a six-block radius, the largest part of our audience was kids. But if you were a casual passerby or on a bus going up Madison, our store looked like a real supermarket, a cause for both confusion and hilarity. One woman came in, her chauffeured car waiting at the curb, to see what she could buy. When she heard nothing was for sale except the whole thing she was incensed. "This is a fraud," she shouted as she stamped out.

The Discount Store traveled to a few more cities, always raising the same hubbub. It, too, went to Caracas for the large-scale retrospective held there in 1974. The occasion was the opening of a new museum. Included in the show were the huge *Astronauts*, the bizarre *Mr. and Mrs. Rembrandt*, and almost every important piece created by Grooms up to that point. In the period during which the show was on, over half a million people came to see it, most of them never having heard of the artist before. But word had gone out that the show was great fun. Perhaps many were attracted by the big billboard located on the main highway leading into Caracas that Red and the Ruckus group had painted in the brightest colors.

It is easy to see why Red Grooms has been so well liked by a very big public, both highbrow and lowbrow. It is less easy to explain why his work is neither cute nor commercial, why it isn't, above all, "Pop" art. (The term had been coined by the critic Lawrence Alloway—a gentleman I had come across a few years previously in London and who did not take a liking to anything I showed in my gallery.) When that brand of art came into prominence in the early 1960s, it occurred to me I should get in touch with whoever was organizing a Pop exhibition and suggest Grooms as a participant. Obviously I did not understand what the "Pop"sicles were about. In every case Red was excluded. When I asked why this should be so, I was told Grooms was too "romantic", "not serious"—even "too popular." After seeing the first big Pop show presented by Sidney Janis I was instantly aware that indeed he did not belong in the same category as Warhol, Rosenquist, Segal, Oldenburg, Lichtenstein, Wesselman and the rest of the crew who gained so much notoriety and who made instant art history. For me the newest trend was heavy, gloomy, earnest, a mere repetition of Abstract Expressionist techniques *without* the subject matter. It was neither funny nor satirical—it was kicky.

"Would you call Grooms 'Pop'?" asked a visitor in my gallery. "Certainly not," I snapped back. "What would you call what he does?" I thought for a second. "A fantasist, America's foremost fantasist!" I quickly telephoned Red and told him what he was going to be from then on. "Wow," said Red, "Gee whiz—that's *great!*"

Thus the march of art went on throughout the 1960s, much and brilliantly publicized, not only by Alloway but even better by the incredibly buoyant Henry Geldzahler—who by now had become the youngest curator at the Metropolitan Museum. My distaste turned me toward the most austere and intellectual visual creations—first with what became known as "minimum" painting and sculpture and then what was termed "color-field" painting. I proceeded to mount, in the Seventy-second Street gallery, the first exhibition of the new "Reductionists," as one critic called them. The show included Larry Bell, Robert Murray, Donald Judd, Larry Zox, Darby Bannard and Carl Andre. Several months later Kynaston McShine, a curator of the Museum of Modern Art, mounted a second but much larger "minimum" show. A whole new avant-garde had come into existence that would become increasingly prominent in the next decade. Its influence spread through the art worlds of Germany, France, Sweden, Italy, England and of course, via the art schools, throughout the United States. The passion for reduction reached its apotheosis at Kassel, Germany, in the huge international show called *Dokumenta.*

Quite innocently my delight in "minimum" was evinced in a series of exhibitions throughout the 1960s. Carl Andre, for instance, did not so much fabricate sculptures make "installations." The first startler was an arrangement of fourteen-foot long, two-feet-by-two-feet thick, Styrofoam beams heaped log-cabin style in my Seventy-second Street gallery. The entire space of the gallery was so filled that viewers had to sidle through the aisles left free. Another show in my Fifty-seventh Street gallery consisted of about seven hundred white bricks laid on the floor in big rectangles. As it happened, a dear friend whom I had tried for some time to get to come to the gallery—the actress Cathleen

Nesbitt—appeared one morning. She wore a fine hat and beautiful gloves, looking as always like someone out of *My Fair Lady*. She stood at the door, peered at the empty walls and said, "But, John, *where* is the show?"

Then there was a vogue for working in large formats of fiberglass. Ron Davis, from California, constructed trompe-l'oeil–shaped pieces in which geometrical designs were so placed as to give a sharp sense of depth and solidity but were actually quite flatly constructed and deceived the eye by their tricks of perspective. Not so Sylvia Stone, whose regard for large, cut sheets of fiberglass, again in geometric forms, was uncompromisingly straightforward, no legerdemain, a pure distillation of translucent grays and blacks, free-standing at various heights on the floor. One that I particularly liked I bought for myself and foolishly loaned to a museum down in Pennsylvania; I did not know the museum was on the skids financially. I had a good deal of trouble getting the piece back, but when it finally did get returned, someone had scratched a deep four-foot mark with a nail across its surface. The piece could not be repaired. I called the insurance company for restitution. The adjuster, a supercilious and uncivil fellow, arrived, listened to my complaint and asked what I thought my compensation should be. "Fifteen hundred dollars, the cost of the sculpture," I replied. The man looked at me aghast and said, "Why, anyone could make that article; its simply a sheet of fiberglass. We'll pay you the cost of the material—seventy-four dollars." I never collected—despite the tonguelashing I delivered. "Miserable philistine!"

The most reductive painter I showed was Patricia Johannsen, whose passion for geometry and the golden mean was central. One of her paintings, about twenty-four feet long, was plain canvas with a single black line four inches wide. It ran horizontally through the exact middle from end to end. This particular exhibition caught the fancy of the very young revolutionaries who were committed to the Weathermen. They were mostly about sixteen to eighteen years old, lived away from their parents in communes, and somehow had found the pleasures of my gallery, where they would sit on the floor, eating sandwiches and drinking orange soda. I, of course, enjoyed having them and liked to hear their stories of how they were tumbling the bourgeoisie.

Pat Johannsen's father, who had helped invent the lethal Polaris submarine missile, came to the gallery to stretch his daughter's vast canvas. A jolly man, he was certain that Pat was outstanding, and he must have been in seventh heaven when Pat did a single piece of metal sculpture one mile long on an abandoned railroad track bed. It was thrilling to see it photographed from a helicopter.

The color-field painters were, of course, much more alluring than the reductionists. The ideological leader was Darby Bannard. Formidably intelligent and informed, handsome and determined, he was the product of Ivy League schools. He had, in fact, known Frank Stella at Princeton. I always felt that it was Stella, more than any other artist, with whom he was competing. Whatever Bannard painted, he had an idea behind it: for instance, the scale must be within the artist's arm stretch, left or right, top or bottom. Or pictures worked within a system of grids or a series of arcs, thus eliminating randomness or old-fashioned "composition." However, Darby's major interest was the science of color and for this he relied on the United States Bureau of Standards, which had studied the naming and numbering of colors more carefully than is commonly known.

"Did you know that the human eye can detect a million different colors?" Darby asked. "Of course, only a few colors are used by most painters. Perhaps a couple of dozen—for instance Léger or Mondrian—use even less. I am trying to employ color far beyond what is ordinarily utilized."

"But how can you do this if it's so hard to see the difference between them?"

"I don't need to. The paint companies have elaborate color charts and formulas, a wide selection of color chips. Using house paint, I go to a paint-mixing machine, indicate by setting the values which color I want—let us say a very pale lavender at the higher end of the spectrum—and out comes the exactly mixed pigment. I then label each can with its formula and it is ready for use."

Many artists who read *Art Forum* were quite struck by Darby's brilliant article on the possibilities of color. In this sense it could be declared that he was the foremost theoretician as well as practitioner of color-field painting.

Oddly, Bannard never moved away from the area of his alma mater, Princeton. During the years he showed with my gallery he shared a splendid property with his good friend, Barbara Johnson, who had amassed what was then the best-known private collection of scrimshaw and whaling memorabilia in the world; Bannard had also become an expert. In the garden was an arch made of whale jawbones, the perfect symbol of the owner's enthusiasm. A hundred-and-fifty-year-old tortoise, which had once belonged to Queen Victoria, wandered freely about the house.

Two of my other artists carried the banner of the color-field method—Kendall Shaw and Check Boterf. Shaw had for some time been painting almost posterlike panels depicting, in silhouette, celebrated athletes at peak performance—track stars, baseball players, swimmers. During the summer of 1968 Shaw designed a production of Vladimir Nabokov's satire *The Waltz Invention* for the Artists Theater Festival. He constructed the sets and costumes of felt, celluloid, silver Mylar and other extraordinary materials. Even more sensational was his production of Jean Cocteau's *Knights of the Round Table*, full of magical transformations. It was after this that Shaw began doing his color-field panels—some as wide as twenty-eight feet—in which color worked as the sole agent for structure and emotional effect. They were beautiful and hard to sell. Once again Shaw did an Artists Theater production using color-field conventions—a production of Gertrude Stein's last work, a children's book called *First Reader*. It was a funny, heartwarming musical review performed first in Southampton, then at the Astor Place Theater, and later at special children's programs for the Museum of Modern Art, and lastly at the Metropolitan Museum, where Henry Geldzahler graciously hung Picasso's superb portrait of Gertrude Stein at the entrance of the auditorium. Few artists I've known have projected such maximum effectiveness with such minimum means. Shaw's fourteen-foot rod puppets for the Nabokov play were fabricated with simple masks on poles and black fabric hanging from the heads to cover the puppeteers inside the figures. As they lumbered in, the audience burst into applause.

Check Boterf was both a painter and a sculptor, and his means for combining these two elements was stretched canvas over geometric wooden armatures. Like Léger, Boterf's taste was for a few primary colors and black and white. Boterf liked large pieces, usually six to eight feet wide and high; all were installed on walls, including a forty-foot piece for a bank in Texas—completely white. The great tastemaker of the Museum of Modern Art, Dorothy Miller, was particularly fond of Boterf's work, perhaps because Boterf humanized the austerity of the many modern buildings where most of them ended up.

One last enthusiast for the resources of color was not an abstract painter but a landscape artist—John Gundelfinger. His lyrical vision was satisfied by his major subject, the rolling hills and meadows of the Delaware Water Gap area of New Jersey. The early hours of the dawn or the crepuscular light before nightfall were the tonalities and hues Gundelfinger searchingly analyzed as he shifted his place of looking from high land to valley with the sky sometimes engulfing all—or seen only as a thin strip. "Is this a return to Monet?" I was sometimes asked. And my answer has been the same: "No, it is a deeply felt response to nature with all the painterly lessons remembered from the Impressionists, Turner and Willem de Kooning." Living as I do with several Gundelfingers on my walls has been a continuous source of pleasure and contemplation.

When the 1960s came to an end, so did my relationship with Tibor de Nagy. I moved to a new space at 50 West Fifty-seventh Street. Some of the artists went elsewhere—Porter to Knoedler's and later to Hirschl and Adler; Goodnough to André Emmerich; Jane Freilicher to Fischbach. Red Grooms and a few others remained with me. I continued making exhibitions until 1975 and then closed shop and said goodbye to art dealing.

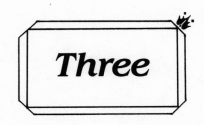

Three

25

*T*HE STORY OF MARK ROTHKO AND WHAT HAPPENED TO HIS ESTATE AFTER his tragic suicide in 1970 was important not only because it involved an artist of great talent, an artist whose career was on the rise and who was beginning to attain great stature and recognition, but also because it was the first conclusive evidence to the public of the great sums of money now involved in the New York art scene. It was, of course, the money problems and the financial dealings of all those involved that the newspaper headlines concentrated on and that kept the public reading. These headlines conveyed figures that only ten years earlier would have seemed staggering to anyone involved in the New York art scene. Nowadays, these figures seem low because of the unprecedented rise in prices of New York School pictures in the seventies. But the Rothko case was the first time that high prices, and a debate over those prices, were publicly associated with contemporary Abstract Expressionist works.

The Rothko story is a personal one as well, and because it involved Rothko's friends, advisors and dealers, it is one that had a profound effect on the art world. Among those involved were Rothko's friends and fellow artists Theodoros Stamos and Herbert Ferber, the art world accountant advisor to Rothko, Bernard Reis, and the director of the powerful Marlborough gallery, Frank Lloyd. The disposition of Rothko's estate, and the bitterness and recriminations it provoked, were occasioned not only by the complicated state in which Rothko left his affairs, but also by the incredible growth of the art scene and the big money interests that were then beginning to enter the field. Big money changed not just the workings of the New York art market but even how art was perceived.

The expansion of the art market in New York began rather slowly and there was not a noticeably strong upward trend until about 1954. Paintings by the Abstract Expressionists began to sell for prices between $3,000 and $7,000, a big advance over the previous decade. It was considered "not bad" that in 1954 Pollock's *Blue Poles* was sold by Sidney Janis to a Dr. Fred Olsen in Connecticut for $6,000, of which Pollock received two thirds. Adolph Gottliebs were being purchased by private collectors at decent prices. Franz Klines, William Baziotes and Robert Motherwells were reaching a variety of museums and individual collectors. Mark Rothko would not sell his work except occasionally, perhaps one a year. Clyfford Still refused to sell his work except under certain conditions.

One can, at best, only speculate why certain pictures bring large sums of money and others do not. In the late nineteenth century, Frederick Church, a Hudson River painter, and the French painter of nudes Antoine Bougereau caught the fancy of the American rich, newly rich and saloon keepers. Their work sold for phenomenal prices, while some of the best painters of the period (for example, Monet, Cézanne and Van Gogh) were barely making enough to cover their living expenses. At the present moment such disparate painters as Andrew Wyeth, Andy Warhol, Jasper Johns, and Roy Lichtenstein have caught the attention of art buyers in a manner not too different from the enthusiasts for Church and Bougereau. An *afficionado* of nineteenth-century art such as Robert Isaacson, now an expatriate art dealer, would say, "Not to be compared! Of course, both Church and Bougereau are far superior to the likes of Warhol, Lichtenstein and these other upstarts." Who is to say?

Whenever a museum such as the National Gallery or the Metropolitan purchases a picture costing two or three million dollars, a queue forms instantly, and continues for weeks. The line-up for *Aristotle Contemplating the Bust of Homer* by Rembrandt (to name one such piece of real estate worth an executive's ransom) enticed several thousand art lovers, all astonished and bemused that a piece of canvas with some paint on it could cost *that* much. Pictures that are demurely absent from the passions surging around the market are, at best, put up with, smiled upon, ignored. Is it not possible that some of Bougereau's paintings (and some of Frederick Church's) have something to tell us? This would seem to be substantiated by the fact that only recently a large Church set a new auction record for an American painting. One would hesitate to say that Bougereau's reputation will never be revived as well. Remembering the enthusiasm of Baudelaire for many painters who are all but forgotten today, perhaps we should pause and consider the evanescence, the ups and downs of taste, and at least the possibility of other points of view. I recall Willem de Kooning once saying that there were few paintings, old or new, that he didn't enjoy in one way or another.

The question, however, of who creates the "market" for high-priced contemporary painting is not as simple as it would at first seem. Perhaps the most widespread view is that it is the result of favorable write-ups by critics and reviewers. It is they who give people certainty of taste and knowledge. If enough writers say an artist is superior, then he no doubt is. Thus, there are those who maintain that the fame and fortune of the Abstract Expressionists, among them Pollock, Rothko, Gottlieb and Stijl, were created by Clement Greenberg, a no-nonsense critic with a firm sense of his own taste. But a careful reading of Mr. Greenberg's writings (one must say careful, because he is more often than not misquoted and quoted from other quotations) would show that he has liked a wide variety of painters and sculptors, many of whom did not achieve either fame or fortune. Few critics have been so aware of the way taste functions and the way it changes; Mr. Greenberg makes this abundantly clear in essay after essay. He seems to believe art is a kind of steeplechase and that some people have the ability to predict the outcome. (If that were possible, it might be more profitable to go to the racetrack.) The truth is that Mr. Greenberg's criticism was and is constructed along certain philosophic-aesthetic lines that include a "success" syndrome. It is not necessary to name the artists whom Greenberg has liked who have not been a success; he would be the first to admit that certain artists, such as de Kooning, for whom he has felt little enthusiasm, have enjoyed enormous success.

Journal entry, March 1968

I am constantly aware of the difficulties of coming to terms with Clement Greenberg's critical views. They seem to me increasingly narrow and authoritarian. Oddly, I like most of the artists he likes—for instance Jules Olitski, whom I discovered in 1959 and sent to Ellie Poindexter's gallery, where he was shown steadily. Again I agree with Clem about the splendor of David Smith and the yeasty talent of Morris Louis, Hans Hofmann, Ken Noland, Darby Bannard. I agree with him that both Rauschenberg and Johns are at best minor painters. On the other hand, his complicated rejection of de Kooning, whom he considers a traditionalist and not a *bona fide* modern abstract painter—seems to me wrong headed and prejudiced. I cannot accept his "categorical imperative"—a Kantian notion that essentially ends up with "it's good because *I* say so." In short, it's Greenberg's taste as opposed to other tastes, and it is there that I balk.

Clem cannot know what "history" will decide or what consensus there will be as to which artist will continue to be liked and remembered and which ones forgotten. Yet he writes as though he were certain. Since I believe that if good artists are individual and unique, then the experiences that are offered to viewers will be individual and unique with each work of art.

Still, whatever the reason for my differences with Greenberg, it is a fact that his criticism has aroused intensive argument—pro and con—and it gives the New York art world its edge, its liveliness.

The question then arises: does the New York *Times*, for instance, heavily influence the market? In short, do write-ups by Hilton Kramer, John Russell or Grace Glueck turn the tide of artists' careers in terms of the market? It is hard for me to believe that these critics have—or even want—this power. Like everyone else, they have their likes and dislikes. They are overworked, never have enough time, must attempt to be just and, at the same time, honest—a large order considering the huge number of exhibitions that open month after month in New York. Hilton Kramer has written positively and with perception about artists such as Anne Ryan and Mary Frank, yet collectors did not rush to the gallery to buy their works. The same could be said about the other critics who have also written well of their favorites.

Journal Jotting, November 1959

A man came into the gallery to see the work of a new artist named Ralph Humphrey, who is an advocate of monocolor paintings. (Humphrey has already been imitated in France by Yves Klein.) At any rate, I showed the gentleman one lovely small work about fourteen-by-twenty inches and told him, upon being asked, that the price was $125. The man said he wouldn't pay that much; would the artist reconsider the price? I said I would ask Ralph Humphrey, which I did. "Bring the price down to eighty-five dollars and I won't take a commission," I suggested to him. "In this way the ice may be broken." A few days later the man returned. I found from reading the guest book that he was Mr. Robert Scull, the taxi king. "Have you spoken to the artist?" he wanted to know. "Yes, I have," I replied. Before I could say anything more, he said, "Good, I will pay you twenty-five dollars."

This is the only time I've asked a client to leave the gallery and not come back.

There are other clients who set my teeth on edge, although in general I'm rather lucky. One, certainly, was the "buyer" for Sears, Roebuck—the actor Vincent Price, who has been casing the galleries where new work by unknowns is shown. "I buy pictures in quantity," he explained, "to be sold retail in the original pictures department of the Sears chain."

"And what," I asked, "do you pay for pictures wholesale?"

"We pay between twenty and sometimes fifty dollars—but, of course, we buy in large amounts."

Thinking how long and hard most of my artists worked at a single canvas, I said, "There are two places where you can go and find exactly what you want. One is the outdoor show at Washington Square and the other is on the Spanish Steps in Rome."

Another bargain hunter is the Seventh Avenue tycoon Larry Aldridge, who likes to buy, at $14 or $15 each, two or three dozen "small things" to give away at Christmas. "It's very good for the artist," he explains. Since it is impossible for him to ask the price of a picture or a sculpture without going into a merry-go-round of bargaining, I dread his visits. On the one hand, I want him to purchase my artists for his collection, and, on the other, I do want to make some sort of profit.

Because the market for art is many-layered and highly diverse, it is always a good idea when speaking of it to indicate *which* market is being referred to. The purchase and sale of masterpieces of the first magnitude is carried on almost completely within the offices of a handful of private dealers. This has been more or less the system since the beginning of World War II. In the late nineteenth century and well into the twentieth, the famous art dealers kept establishments that were more or less open to the public. Durand-Ruel, Wildenstein, Knoedler and Duveen all had galleries on both sides of the Atlantic. A truly great dealer like René Gimpel, essentially European, maintained a reputation for honesty and excellence unrivaled anywhere. Few books have been written on the subject of art dealing that have the clarity and directness of Gimpel's memoirs. His book is a mine of information, a mirror of the fashions in taste as they occurred in a changing society. We can, for instance, discover how Rembrandt's portrait of his son, Titus, was sold to the financier Jules Bache for $40,000. A man of charm and erudition, gifted with an almost perfect "eye," Gimpel moved among the Fricks, Rockefellers, Carnegies, Rothschilds and the remnants of the rich European aristocracy with the ease of a man who neither overvalued or undervalued himself. In 1940, when the Nazis took Paris, Gimpel, a loyal Frenchman, refused to leave and was interred in a concentration camp, where he died four years later. His *The Diary of an Art Dealer* is without doubt a unique document and perhaps the only such record to candidly tell exactly what occurred in a specific market—the where, the why, the what, the how much.

But, of course, Gimpel wrote what few other men would have dared, probably because he lived in a world where taxes and incomes had quite a different meaning than they have today.

The story is told of how Miss Frick, after brooding for many years about a Cézanne she had purchased in 1919, decided she would no longer keep it in the collection and would return it to the firm from which she had bought it, Knoedler's. "I don't like this picture," she is reported to have said, "and I want a check for exactly what I paid for it." The management instantly granted her wish. There were those who thought the action wildly eccentric—and those who thought Miss Frick quite prudent to avoid such a huge capital gain, since the painting had increased in value many times over. Miss Frick, of course, was and is of that former society in which taxes and income had a different significance. It is interesting to note that she thought of the Cézanne as a picture rather than as a dollar sign.

The role of art dealer in the market for the very rich tended to be that of a merchant prince, since he must of necessity possess the panache of a man quite familiar with the idiosyncracies of the upper classes without being disturbed by either their foibles or brutality.

René Gimpel was not so unlike many other gifted and honest art dealers. He was, of course, perfectly aware that such colleagues as Lord Duveen and Bernard Berenson were scamps, but he had taken their measure. Like others, Gimpel felt a certain distaste for Berenson, whose ethics and scholarship were not always unclouded. Gimpel was connected by marriage to Joe Duveen; he did not, however, emulate Duveen's tricky business practices. He was also aware of some of the dealings of George Wildenstein, another art merchant to whom he gave a wide berth when possible.

The popular image of the art dealer as an oily character with a thin mustache played in the movies by Vincent Price is, of course, absurd. Many *bona fide* dealers are civilized, decent men and women whose living very much depends on their characters, and though they are sometimes mistaken or do foolish things, they are not much different from professionals in other fields.

The biggest problem faced by dealers is not collectors or the critics or the public. The biggest problem is the artists. Many artists, probably the majority, if they exhibit in galleries, can be unhappy with the gallery they are with, and often resent and dislike their dealer. Why this should be is a subject that might be dealt with by sociologists, psychologists or in some cases psychiatrists. The answer usually given is that the artist always needs more money and will, therefore, go where he can get more. This is a spurious argument, since the public and the critics and the collectors will go wherever an artist may be showing, if that artist is of sufficient interest to them. There are examples of artists who simply never moved. Edward Hopper remained throughout his professional career with Frank Rehn, a dealer who was neither fashionable nor famous; Picasso was loyal to Kahnweiler through several decades; and Ad Reinhardt remained with Betty Parsons even during the exodus of 1953. But many more artists hop about.

The question of money is important, and when a dealer simply cannot handle the volume or size of a given artist's work, it may be proper for the artist to go to a gallery better able to handle the enlarged product. In Europe this was never a problem; the artist tended to spread his work among several galleries. This was particularly true for graphics. Most large European cities had a number of galleries specializing in prints and drawings. Prints, however, did not become popular in America on the same scale until the late 1950s. The 1960s saw the emergence of a vastly expanded market. But by then the market as a whole had expanded, whereas in 1952 there were not more than a dozen serious galleries, most of them quasi-serious.

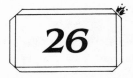

26

Journal Jotting, November 1959

Mark Rothko stopped by the gallery to see the Ralph Humphrey show. Ralph is the roommate of Rothko's close friend Theodoros Stamos. It was cold and there were snow flurries outside. Mark, pink of cheek, entered the gallery like a hearty Russian coach driver who has just driven his *troika* for twenty versts. I almost wished I had a steaming samovar and could say, "Won't you have a glass of *tchai*?" for the pleasure of watching him drink his tea through a cube of sugar held between his teeth. There was a mischievous gleam in his eye as he said, "I understand that the man who runs a fleet of taxis was in trying to buy a Humphrey." Obviously Stamos had repeated my story of Robert Scull. "Humphrey has some talent, wouldn't you say?" asked Mark. "Would I show him if I didn't think so?" was my reply.

Mark sat down, smoking a cigarette out of the corner of his mouth. It is difficult to capture exactly the tone of his speech. He has, for instance, the faintest of accents, neither foreign nor domestic; sometimes I think it must be an intonation from the state of Oregon, where he grew up. Sometimes I think it is an echo from Minsk or Pinsk or wherever his Russian Jewish ancestors came from. He then launched into a speech against collectors.

I, who depend upon the good will of collectors to keep my gallery going, find it difficult to understand the anger of certain artists toward their patrons. David Hare, the sculptor, for instance, gave his dealer, Sam Kootz, instructions that not only did he *not* want to meet the buyers of his work, he did not even want to know their names. With Mark the anger is more pronounced. He is convinced that collectors are exploiters, that they buy works of art to enrich their pocketbooks and social position, that they have the instinct of vultures, and that their deepest feelings are based on the joy of mere possession. He believes their most dangerous attribute is caprice; the capricious need to be *au courant.* If all this is so, then the artist had best be wary of them and make it as difficult as possible for them to acquire serious work. "Who knows," he asked, "when, at what moment, any one of them is apt to become bored with a single painting or all of them? What happens to the painting? Usually the miserable embarrassment of the auction block, the hellish fumes of Parke-Bernet." Mark shuddered, then added, "I particularly loathe people like Ben Heller and Mr. Hirschhorn. Both of them think they are greater than artists, both of them are self-satisfied because they are so rich, and neither of them knows anything about art."

"Alas," I finally said after a respectful silence, "can any artist ever know the fate of his work?" It seems to me that the future of almost any movable work of art is totally problematic.

"Quite true," agreed Mark. "But the artist can make it as difficult as possible. That is why I would rather teach and scrounge for money than sell paintings. I sell as few as I possibly can."

Rothko had come to his career as an artist in a rather roundabout fashion. He had originally, as a youth, been an actor in Seattle in a stock company where Clark Gable had been the leading man. Mark, too, had wanted to be a leading man, but had to settle for "character" roles. My friend Herbert and I liked to hear him talk about his dear friend Irene Worth and what a great actress she was and how he tried never to miss any of her openings. I think Herbert was the one person to whom Mark enjoyed confiding his love and frustration with acting and the theater. He felt comfortable with Herbert because he never brought up his professional life as a painter. Herbert made it clear without saying much that his admiration for Mark's work was continuing and unfaltering.

It was actually Arshile Gorky who talked Rothko out of making the rounds to professional offices and auditions and into becoming a painter instead. This happened at the Blue Ribbon in the West Forties. He and Gorky went there often because of the free lunch provided if one bought a glass of beer. Both of them were very poor. Mark had a cold-water flat on Sixth Avenue, a walk-up.

Journal Jotting

The series of large mural-like canvases Rothko was to have sold for installation in one of the rooms in the new Seagram Building on Park Avenue was precipitiously withdrawn. Mark says he's decorating no restaurants.

Still, there were those who do not interpret Rothko's "epic décors" as an expression of religious sensibility or an emanation of the sublime. One such dissenter is the brilliant young abstract painter Richard Hennessy, who finds Rothko very worldly. "His work," he maintains, "projects a feeling for luxury, opulence, refined pleasures. Where better could such lush canvases look than at Mies van der Rohe's building, in the Four Seasons restaurant that Philip Johnson designed?

"It is not a surprise that the very rich people like the de Menils, Donald Blinken or Mrs. Paul Mellon feel at home with Rothko's sensuous colors and forms. Can't you imagine a pasha smoking his hooka while reclining on his divan of pneumatic pillows, contemplating Rothko's floating, elusive forms?"

"Yes," I concurred, "while all the time soft flute music caresses his ears."

Mark was never interested in galleries or dealers. He went from Peggy Guggenheim to Betty Parsons to Sidney Janis, showing rarely after 1958 and then not for several years. It would be difficult to say precisely what motivated Rothko's reticence. Had he seen too many reputations rise and fall because of overexposure? Was it his distrust of collectors and museums? Or did he feel his work was too valuable to allow easy access to it? At any rate, his stance began to change after his second child, Christopher, was born and his first, Kate, started to grow up. He had purchased a large town house on East Ninety-fifth Street and had taken over a huge studio in a carriage house on East Sixty-ninth Street, opposite Hunter College. People wonder how he managed. But no artist in New York was better at managing—Mark was a shrewd businessman who could never be "taken." Having lived a tough life, he was what is called "street smart."

I first got to know Rothko's wife, Mel, when she and Mark were living together in their cold-water flat on Sixth Avenue. She seemed to me then and later, a bit of a Midwesterner, the girl from Ohio with her vaguely flat A's. Only one thing struck me as odd: she never called Mark by his first name, she always referred to him as Rothko. I thought this was some old-fashioned Jewish trait, the way very old Jewish ladies refer to their husbands by their last names. But it is possible it was some kind of irony.

I could never seem to connect with Mel. She was awfully good-looking and I could quite see why Mark doted on her. She had a way of being there and yet not being there, surely tantalizing for someone as ardent as Mark. It was in the Sixth Avenue flat that I remarked that Mark's pictures were too big for the rooms they were living in. "Not at all," Mark replied. "Big pictures are perfect for small New York apartments. They make them seem larger." "But what about furniture?" I asked. "Get rid of it. Pictures first, furniture second." I must admit he was right. Eliza Parkinson always kept a big space in front of her Rothko and it did wonders for the room.

It must have been hard to be the wife of so large and urgent a personality as Mark. He could not compromise—it was anathema to him. To be loved by such a man must have been almost suffocating—Mark did not do things in fractions.

Therefore I was disappointed but not really surprised when in 1968 I mentioned to Mark that I had heard he was *living* in his studio on Sixty-ninth Street, and he told me it was true. Things were not going too well at home, he said, and he had moved into the studio. Somebody who came into the gallery told me Mel had a serious drinking problem and was spending a good deal of time with her "shrink." It was hard for me to put that together with the Mel I first knew. I was shocked when in 1971, while in Munich, I heard from Herbert of Mel's sudden death six months after Mark's. I had seen Mel just before I went to Europe at a party given by Rose Slivka for all the *Craft Horizons* contributors. She seemed all right, a little spaced-out perhaps, but in fairly good condition. She apparently drank very little at the party, but it was alcohol that was a factor in her death.

One of Rothko's closest friends and one who helped him a great deal during his period of domestic difficulty was Theodoros Stamos. Stamos was named by Rothko an executor of his estate, a mixed blessing indeed, considering what was to follow. I first met Stamos at the end of 1939. I was visiting New York and staying on East Twentieth Street with Nancy Wilder, who lived three doors east of Amédée Ozenfant's school. At that time it was the fashion to study with Ozenfant. Robert

Goodnough studied with him, and another painter, Sari Dienes, was very much an Ozenfant disciple and lived on nearby Irving Place. Sari Dienes had her own circle of young painters around her, one of whom was Theodoros Stamos, occasionally called Ted, but usually referred to as Stammie. He was only about nineteen at the time. He had studied sculpture at the American Artists School on Fourteenth Street—formerly the John Reed Club. The Young Communist League people were sponsors of the school. The poor of the area, the Lower East Side, were encouraged to study there, and many did.

Stamos came from the poorest of the poor. His parents were Greek immigrants of working-class origin who had literally fought for their survival and the survival of their children. Stamos eventually found painting more congenial than sculpture and was encouraged by friends to become a painter. Quite miraculously, at about the time we met, Stamos had gone uptown to the Wakefield Bookstore. He had heard there was a small gallery in the rear of the store managed by Mrs. Betty Parsons. After Mrs. Parsons had scrutinized Stamos' work, she suggested he join her gallery. Stamos was one of the first of the celebrated Parsons discoveries.

Stamos was, of course, delighted. He had found his vocation and never departed from it, although much later he would occasionally teach at the Art Students League and elsewhere. Few people have realized how young Stamos was when he first showed his work. His contemporaries among the gradually emerging Abstract Expressionist group were older than he, some by as many as twenty years.

Although he mellowed somewhat as he grew older, in his twenties Stamos was apt to lose his temper quicker than he should have, and his manners were occasionally appalling. He could be tactless in the name of candor and very rude when vexed. On the other hand, he had a great sense of humor and could quickly see the funny side of people and situations. No doubt because of a profound dislike of poverty developed in early boyhood, Stammie had a tendency to parsimony; his frugality could sometimes be hilarious. Again, this was balanced by a capacity for unusual kindness, especially with friends, or even acquaintances who were ill or in trouble. Students responded warmly to the generosity of spirit he could display in regard to whatever talent they might have, and he was often helpful in advising them how to solve problems both artistic and personal.

Shortly after the war, in 1946, Stamos met and became intimate with the poet Robert Price. Price had been stationed in Japan for many months and was an enthusiast of Japanese culture, especially the poetry and paintings. On his return to America he joined with his friends Ruth and John Stefan to publish a quarterly called *Tiger's Eye*, an elegant, beautifully printed review that became the "voice" of the emerging Abstract Expressionists, and, in particular, the artists, poets and intellectuals who frequented the Betty Parsons gallery.

Not long after they met, Stamos and Price decided to share an apartment on West Eighty-third Street, where they lived until Price's death in 1954 at the age of thirty-six. The friendship was a turning point for Stamos—both for his paintings and his personality. Price was as gentle, courteous and reticent as Stamos was extroverted, rough-and-ready and often rude. Stamos' social horizons in the art world widened, and he became friends in quick succession with Adolph Gottlieb, Rothko, Barney Newman, Ad Reinhardt, Pollock, Motherwell, and the rest of the artists of the new persuasion. Although Stamos had been close to Tony Smith, as well as the painter Milton Avery (both of whom he had met in 1944), Price now became Stamos' strongest influence.

Stamos' earliest work had largely been concerned with what was referred to as biomorphic images, which did *not* come, however, from Miró, but were simply the forms he himself had observed at the oceanside—jellyfish, crabs, starfish, and other marine creatures. Avery had taught Stamos the way in which such elusive forms could be pulled together. (It is well to remember that Avery influenced many young American painters who were searching for simplicity and clarity.) It was Robert Price, however, who exposed Stamos to the Orient, showing him an art that was strong yet elusive. Price also pointed the way to the use of color to release the lyricism that was the essential quality of Stamos' vision and—contrary to his personality—his innermost need.

The friendship between Stamos and Mark Rothko picked up momentum about a year after their meeting. By 1948 the two of them were exchanging ideas and know-how daily; both visited each other's studio regularly. Stamos was moving away from his biomorphic imagery, Rothko was abandoning the "mythic" image and tending toward fields of color.

Robert Price had sustained a serious injury to this right arm during the war. It had been pulled out of the shoulder socket in an accident and would regularly lose its "placement," causing him severe pain. It was this, perhaps, that was a contributing factor to his sudden and fatal heart attack, which occurred in 1954. Stamos was with Price at the moment it happened, and the shock was so severe that his friends Violet and Helen Mendelsohn worried that the trauma might be lasting.

Stamos did not recover quickly. At first he would see no one except Mark and the Mendelsohn sisters. Then he began to drink heavily. Work was impossible. When at last he came to, after about a year, Stamos went into a panic and decided that his enemy was Betty Parsons, that she was taking his money and not helping his career. In another panic he went to the Whitney Museum and convinced them to buy one of his canvases without consulting Mrs. Parsons. Naturally, the sale was quickly discovered because Betty Parsons had done business with the Whitney for years; they were one of her valued clients. Upon asking Stamos what he had been paid for the picture, he told her a lower price than the one that had actually been paid. Mrs. Parsons was outraged, not so much by what happened as by the fact that "Stammie had lied to me." It can be easily understood that Stamos occupied a special place in Betty Parsons' affections: he had been with her since the old Wakefield gallery; he had been like an adopted child, a member of the family. His behavior seemed to her to be cruel and unforgivable. They never spoke to each other again. Years later, when I asked Stamos why he had done such a dishonorable thing, he said, "I really don't know why I did it."

After the break with Betty Parsons, Mark Rothko began to occupy an important position in Stamos' life. There was a twenty-two-year age difference between them. Rothko began to act rather like a father— helpful, sympathetic, encouraging. Telephone calls, studio visits were, all during the year except summer, daily and uninterrupted. Rothko's career began to ascend; Stamos would have good periods, but they were intermittent. There was a clear-cut dependency of both on the other. They never moped, since neither of them was in any way an "underachiever." Later, when Mark's domestic life became unbearably unhappy, Stamos did what he could to pick up the pieces.

Ironically, it was Stamos, along with Donald McKinney of the Marlborough gallery, who discovered Mark's body on February 26, 1970. They had an appointment with Mark at nine in the morning. Donald was to select twenty-five or thirty pictures that would represent Mark at his best in European exhibitions. The studio door was open and they entered. They found Mark's assistant, Oliver Steindecker, who told them that Mark was lying on the kitchen floor in a pool of blood. He had slit his arms and wrists with a sharp instrument, probably six or eight hours previously. Stamos let out a cry and became so upset that the next day he had to be hospitalized.

After hearing that Steindecker had already called the police, McKinney then telephoned the Marlborough gallery and Bernard Reis,

Rothko's accountant and close friend. After the police arrived they closed the building. When the detectives came (having learned that a celebrated artist was the suicide in question), they told Donald that all works of art must be moved to a police warehouse for safekeeping. Donald knew the kind of careful handling Rothko's pictures required and he insisted that everything remain in place until properly inventoried. The police finally agreed to this measure and assigned watchmen.

Perhaps the hardest thing was to inform Mel. This duty was performed by a close friend, Mrs. Morton Levine, who had arrived at the studio, and immediately went uptown with Steindecker. Rita, Ad Reinhardt's widow, also arrived; she had been the last person with Mark the previous evening, when they had dined together. She was deeply shocked, saying Mark had been perfectly all right the evening before. Donald finally took her home. Although he had been sick all day with continuous nausea, it was not until five in the afternoon that he could at last go to his apartment and lie down.

Few suicides have ever seemed to me so unforeseen, so unimaginable. It's unbearable to think of the pain, despair and anger Mark must have felt.

Journal Jotting, one year later, 1971

A few days after Mark's death, the inventory was completed and it was found that three pictures in the inventory, oil on paper, were missing. There was a lot of art world speculation that the pictures were swiped by either Stamos or McKinney.

A year later, a man arrived at the Marlborough gallery with three works on paper by Rothko. He said he was a dentist and that a patient of his had given him the pictures in lieu of payment. He would not say who the man was; he said the man had left the country, and anyway he wasn't sure of the name. Bernard Reis and Donald quickly identified the pictures as those stolen from the studio. Since no one had been allowed in or out of the studio while it was being guarded, it is clear that one of the policemen stole the drawings. Thus, another nasty rumor has been quashed.

27

*F*OUR MONTHS AFTER ROTHKO'S DEATH A MAJOR EXHIBITION OF HIS WORK was held in Venice at the time of the Biennale of 1970, and I was fortunate enough to be in the city for the opening in June. A red-and-gold banner announcing the exhibition hung from the balcony of Cá Pesaro. When I got to the *piano nòbile* the room was jammed despite the odd timing: it was a Sunday morning. Peggy Guggenheim arrived in her gondola at about the same time as I did; her *gondolieri* were in full livery, sporting the Guggenheim colors. Bernard and Becky Reis were with her—both seeming rather more grave than usual. It was such a short time since Mark's death and I had the certain feeling that they were sad, although deeply pleased by the splendor of the show. It was a magnificent memorial.

I didn't quite expect the show to come off. The rooms are very large with high ceilings, great windows, a luxuriance of baroque architectural detail. Donald McKinney, who had supervised the exhibition from the beginning, had hung the pictures with absolute tact, however. Nothing was crowded, no canvas pushed or cancelled another out. It takes very fine pictures to compete with Venetian architecture and décor, especially in so beautiful a *palazzo* as Cá Pesaro. Miraculously, not only did the paintings hold their own, but they seemed as though they had been destined all along to be shown in a palace. They looked themselves; they did not seem out of place. The sunshine came pouring through the windows facing the canal, whose water reflected the ripples onto the ceilings and walls, an effect of purest magic.

Toute Venise was in attendance—the Volpis, the Cicognas, the Barozzis, the Curtis family, to name a few. The Venice Biennale directors, critics down from Milan and up from Rome, museum executives, collectors from both sides of the Atlantic, the usual freeloaders, were all there. Everyone looked very handsome and human as they moved in front of Mark's canvases. It reminded me of a saying of Mark's that his works looked best with people around them. I suppose it had something to do with his sense of human scale.

I had lunch with Donald McKinney at Harry's Bar a few days after the Rothko opening. He looked handsome in his, as usual, understated but well-made clothes. He had recovered from the fatigue of the Rothko *vernissage* at which he had seemed worn out. "Indeed, I was," Donald said. "Let no man imagine it is an easy task to install a show in a messy old palace in Venice." To his dismay Donald had found, after all the negotiating with the city fathers of Venice to receive permission for the Rothko exhibition, that he had obtained the walls and space, but had no one to help him hang the show. Cá Pesaro is a city museum, housing a very heterogeneous collection. Upon arrival, the director was nowhere to be found, nor did he make an appearance until later; he was "away." There were three old men, caretakers, who announced *pronto* that *"hanno fatto la guerra."* They were war veterans, and indeed, one of them was missing a leg. None of them quite knew where anything was (which reminded me of Mrs. Alfred Barr *trying* to see the sculptures of Rodin's great contemporary Medardo Rosso owned by Cá Pesaro). More than that, the walls, floors and windows were dirty. "I was particularly discouraged by the rags hanging on the windows," said Donald. "The Venetians are partial to those scalloped curtains called Austrian shades, but they had long outlived their capacity for use. I had to remove them." Since the old caretakers could barely walk, Donald found himself sweeping floors, then sending out for cleaning women in order to get the work done. Because the ceiling was very high (probably thirty feet), Donald was forced to use a ladder so rustic the bark had been left on the wood, the only one high enough to reach the metal pipes from which the spotlights hung. Most of the lights were without bulbs or had bulbs that had long since burned out. Frightened though he was of rickety ladders and of climbing to such heights, Donald had no choice but to mount the rungs and replace the bulbs while *i vecchi* held on.

Meanwhile Rothko's canvases were waiting to be unpacked and hung. But when the wrappers were off, Donald discovered that there was not enough space in the main salon to hang all of them. The director had to be found and convinced that the two smaller rooms running parallel to the great hall were necessary as well for a complete hanging, especially since some of the smaller canvases would be lost in the wide spaces of the large room. When the director was finally located, he instantly put forward a series of objections best described as mindless. It finally dawned on Donald that he wished to be paid off; *una mancia* was quickly arranged, a suitable number of lire that made for a happier atmosphere. The final touches to the show were made shortly before the guests arrived. Donald had worked through the night.

"Well, it is a triumph," I commented. "Rothko's international reputation has been established beyond a doubt." "I suppose so," said Donald. "No other artist we've ever handled has cost us such a large investment. But who knows how long the market will last? Who knows how long any reputation will hold up?" We were both silent. I was thinking of Dufy, Bernard Buffet, the Neo-Romantics, Vlaminck, Utrillo, the Mexicans, Marie Laurencin . . .

A few days later I asked Donald to have a drink with me at my hotel, since he had been so kind as to treat me to lunch. Anyway, it's pleasant to sit on the Cipriani terrace and watch the boats go by. "I understand," I said, "that you are leaving Venice tomorrow." We were settled at a table near the bar; it was about six o'clock and a few people had come down from their siestas. "Yes, I am, and God willing, I'm to have a two-week holiday in my house at Barrytown."

I asked Donald about the timing and the production of the Rothko memorial. As recently as the first of June, virtually no one had heard anything about such an exhibition. It seemed to have come as a surprise, and not only to me.

Donald explained there had been no possible way to announce the exhibition, since it was not a *fait accompli* until May 19. I then wanted to know how in the world the catalogue, the poster and all the publicity could have been made ready in so short a time—it seemed to me very unlike Marlborough to dawdle in making such a decision and then have to rush everything. Donald told me the story.

Until May 19 Frank Lloyd, the head of Marlborough, refused to give permission for a memorial show unless an absolute agreement was reached between the gallery and the Rothko executors. Lloyd had insisted that his gallery be granted exclusive rights to sell *all* paintings in the estate from the same period of time, eight years, in which he had contracted to pay for the paintings purchased in 1969 and 1970—in all, a group of 205 paintings. The profits from these paintings to be sold on consignment, would, of course, go to the estate and the Rothko Foundation. Quite rightly, Lloyd realized that the value of the estate's pictures (many of them of poor quality) might easily drop if they were sold at random. This seemed to me a reasonable and highly sensible stance, since the expenses of the Venice exhibition and other necessary shows would be high. The public does not realize that in order to sell pictures at blue-chip prices, very large sums of money must be spent in developing a blue-chip market. Lloyd was too prudent a businessman to proceed in a venture that was not totally safe; an exclusive contract must be guaranteed. The lawyers for the executors and the estate had come to the mistaken conclusion that the Marlborough exclusivity was binding, thus fulfilling Mark's own wishes in the will that he and Bernard Reis had drawn up. It was not until May 4 that these lawyers reached their conclusion after careful research on the enforcibility of Marlborough's contract. (These negotiations were carried on with the executors Stamos and Morton Levine; Bernard Reis, also an executor of the estate, felt it improper to participate as he was a part-time employee of Marlborough.)

"But my dear Donald," I said, "it is not possible to get a show ready in three weeks. Something would have to have been done long in advance, especially if you are dealing with people so elusive as the city fathers of Venice and the directors of its Biennale."

Donald nodded. His headaches of arranging the memorial show had begun shortly after Mark's death. The agreeable *la piccina* contessa, Carla Panicali, director of Marlborough's Rome branch, had almost immediately proposed the memorial. Being in Italy and knowing how to cut through the red tape, she took on the job of preparing the groundwork despite Frank Lloyd's refusal to give a definite go-ahead. "After all," said Donald, "we could always cancel the show if negotiations with the executors failed.

Carla Panicali did proceed. Remembering the mess of the 1958 Biennale, when Rothko's work came off badly in the hideous American Pavilion, she decided to have it in a prominent location in the middle of Venice. Several locations came under consideration. Lloyd rather favored the Palazzo Grassi, a huge and impressive edifice owned by a Milanese businessman, Count Marinotti, and utilized for educational purposes. The city fathers hesitantly offered Cá Pesaro and wrote a somewhat ambiguous letter to Carla Panicali to that effect, but also made it clear that they would not finance the show. The situation became a game of cat and mouse, with Carla saying in elaborate and ambiguous language (Italian lends itself magnificently to such discourse) neither yes nor no. "It was a hanging-in process," said Donald. Thus, it was not until May 23 that Carla wrote to Guido Perocco, the director of Cá Pesaro, saying the Marlborough gallery would definitely rent space for the duration of the Biennale. She had also alerted her printers to be prepared for a rush job.

Twenty-seven paintings were finally sent, but not until the second week in June. The insurance for the four months of the show came to a bit less than $7,000.

"You see," said Donald, "it wasn't only the printers who did a rush job. The one nice thing, however, was Frank Lloyd's telegram saying, 'Do the best you can and don't worry about spending money.' He was never one to be, as they say, penny foolish."

Journal Jotting, January 1975

Reading the post-trial memorandum of the Rothko trial at the Surrogate Court, I was amused by the prosecution repeatedly suggesting that the exhibition in Venice had been planned, and as they say in legalese, "finalized" long before Carla Panicali's telegram from Mr. Lloyd.

Being in Venice again and seeing the Rothko memorial exhibition inevitably brought back memories of the 1958 Biennale, which included Rothko's work. Mark and Mel and their six- or seven-year-old daughter, Kate, arrived and took rooms in a house near where I was staying in San Travaso. The Rothkos were being entertained by Peggy Guggenheim and her entourage.

The house the Rothkos stayed in was one where Modigliani had once had a studio. The landlady was a nice old woman, a *marquesa* fallen in the world who did her best to keep up appearances and to hold body and soul together. I went there in the late afternoon one Wednesday for drinks and was received in the garden. It was not a bad garden but neither was it a good one. There were a lot of fig trees, but the Italians are not keen about groomed gardens, and the weeds tend to burgeon. I was nicely received, however. Mark looked pleased to be in Venice, Mel looked distracted. In the middle of the scene was this perfectly awful child, Katie. I soon realized Mel had reason to look distracted. In general I like all children, but this kid was a terror. No one could open his mouth without being turned off. She whined, she complained, she didn't like this, she didn't like that—and in a crescendo of nonstop activity she repeated, "When are we going to go home? When are we going to go home?" They had just arrived.

Since we are trained to think kindly of children, to be sensitive to their problems, I looked at Katie carefully and realized that she was rather large and overweight for her age, and maybe this might not be very pleasant for her. But I also had the feeling that both Mark and Mel were intimidated by Katie. I couldn't help thinking that perhaps Mark had had a child too late in life, that perhaps Mel had no talent for being a mother. At any rate, the whole scene was distinctly undelightful. But then the burdens of parenthood are beyond me.

One nice thing—little Katie was delighted by finding a real fig, one that could actually be eaten, growing on a fig tree.

It was only after his death that I accidentally discovered some facts about Mark's early life. I was dining with a friend who told me Mark's name originally was Marcus Rothkowitz, that he had been born in Russia, and transplanted to the Northwest coast when very young. My friend told me, "I was a pupil at the Center Academy of Brooklyn in the 1930s. My teacher was *your* Mark Rothko but *my* Marcus Rothkowitz." The school was attended by the children of rising Jewish merchants. Marcus Rothkowitz's wife, his first one, taught crafts. "Rothko was a terrible artist who made little woodcuts among other inept things," my friend told me, "but my mother bought one out of sympathy. It's still in her closet."

Rothko remarried, a gentile from Ohio, a commercial artist who supported him for a few years doing freelance jobs. I sometimes wondered if it was gratitude combined with guilt that formed the nexus of his marriage with Mel, the source of what became a swelling and perennial incompatibility, a conflict that never ceased.

Mark and Mel never seemed happy. They raged and shouted. Bob and Abby Friedman, who lived in the next house in Provincetown during the summer of 1969, found it deeply embarrassing to hear the yelling and screaming of their Rothko neighbors. In the late 1960s Mark was drinking as heavily as his so-called alcoholic wife. Provincetown, where they were spending the summer, was too small a resort for the other artists not to know how disturbed the Rothkos were. By this point one assumes the two children, Kate and Topher, as Christopher was called, must have set up defenses against the permanent war raging between their parents.

Immediately after Mark's death, Stamos had called Mel and offered one of three plots that he owned in East Marion, Long Island. After some discussion with her advisors, Mel accepted the offer and it was in East Marion that Mark's body was interred. It was decided that a large boulder with Mark's name and birth and death dates carved on it would be a suitable way to mark his grave. A similar boulder had been used for Jackson Pollock's grave in the Springs near East Hampton, in the same cemetery where Frank O'Hara and Ad Reinhardt are buried.

In April 1972 Stamos was very surprised to receive a letter from Kate Rothko's lawyer, Edward Ross, demanding that the body of Mark Rothko be removed from its present burial spot and transferred to Columbus, Ohio, where Kate's mother is buried.

I asked Stamos a few years later if Rothko's body had ever been removed from East Marion. No, he said, it had not.

28

*I*N 1971 KATE ROTHKO BROUGHT SUIT AGAINST THE THREE EXECUTORS OF her father's estate, Theodoros Stamos, Bernard J. Reis, and Morton Levine, and against the Marlborough gallery. At the time, Kate was a minor and her legal guardian was the sculptor Herbert Ferber, a friend of the Rothko family. Although the legal proceedings were enormously complicated, in the main the suit contended that the executors had conspired to defraud the Rothko estate and the Foundation by making deals with the Marlborough gallery that greatly undervalued Rothko works sold outright to the gallery, thereby benefiting the gallery at the expense of the estate. It was claimed that these deals were made out of the self-interest on the part of the executors, since Bernard J. Reis, an accountant, had been in the employ of Marlborough, and Stamos was at the time of the suit represented by Marlborough gallery. The suit asked the court to remove control of the estate from the executors.

In order to understand the trial and its ramifications it is necessary to understand the role of Bernard J. Reis, who was a central figure in the trial and in Rothko's life as well. He was not only Rothko's accountant but one of Rothko's closest personal friends, attested to by the fact that Mark named him as an executor.

The arrival of accountants in the art world was an event that evolved rather slowly. Few American artists of the so-called avant-garde made their living from their work and in the 1940s few needed accountants to take care of their affairs. However, accountants and lawyers for artists were increasingly a part of the scene after 1950. At that time the accountant's bills were often paid for with an artist's work of art, as had long been the case with doctors' and dentists' bills. Several dentists around New York accumulated rather impressive collections in this manner and, of course, made extraordinary profits when their pictures were later sold. One dentist in particular became quite rich from the sale of his de Koonings. None of these people ever offered to share his gains with the artists. Why this behavior should be considered more acceptable than that of a dealer who buys pictures outright and then sells them for a profit is not easily understood.

Most dealers sent the artists who showed in their galleries statements every few months, usually quarterly, and when pictures had been sold, a check for the sales was enclosed with the statement. As the American market grew, the artists found it too difficult to cope with problems involving taxes and there was a scramble to find accountants. Some of them proved very helpful, but many would drop the artist after a few bad seasons. Hence many artists (and dealers) were always on the lookout for a good accountant.

Bernard Reis became the most celebrated accountant in the art world as far back as the 1940s. His character and career were remarkable, first, because he was highly successful in his business and spent a major amount of his earnings on the purchase of artworks, and second, because his chief interest in life was the history of art and to that end he put together an excellent library of art books, and also read them. He was astonishingly erudite. Traveling abroad with his wife, Becky, Bernard Reis had early realized that to know art from books was useless; you had to actually go and see it. The Reises traveled a good part of every year, rarely returning without objects or pictures they had found in Tangiers or Paris or Rome or wherever else they had been. Whenever I told Bernard I was going someplace, he would immediately give me instructions as to what to see, where to stay, which restaurants were best. "Be sure to look for the Zurbaráns in the Scola delle Belles Artes in Madrid. They're on, I believe, the third floor and perhaps the most dramatic of his white ecstatics. Also in Madrid, don't miss the Museo Romantico; it's a beautiful town house kept exactly as it was in the 1820s and reminds you of nothing so much as the romantic world of Joseph Cornell. And the great thing in Barcelona is the museum of Catalan art, particularly the frescoes brought down from ruins of monasteries that existed between the ninth and eleventh centuries."

The Reis collection was not simply a reflection of a certain taste, but solidly backed by careful study. Unlike a Joseph Hirschhorn, Bernard bought slowly and shrewdly, rarely making snap decisions or capricious choices. Thus, his Matisses, his Soutines, his fine little Courbet landscape, the Degas, the Daumier, the Picassos, were acquired as thoughtfully as were, at a later time, the works of the so-called New York School or the splendid masks and totems of primitive Eskimos and Africans. There were probably about 300 items in the Reis collection, but this does not include the remarkable *éditions de luxe* of many of the greatest artists and poets of the twentieth century; it was a library that only a few collectors possess.

Bernard Reis began his business from scratch in 1918; in later years he had ten to fifteen other accountants working for him. When he retired in 1970 he was a rich man. It was not books and pictures that formed the core of Becky and Bernard's life, however; the living artist engaged their attention far more. When I first met the Reises I was still the managing editor of *View*. I attended a party at the town house of Peggy Guggenheim, who lived in the East Sixties and entertained often. I took quite a fancy to Becky Reis, for she was carrying a lorgnette through which she would peer with the amused eyes of a tiny owl. The lorgnette was part of her style and a distinct aid to her shortsightedness. A petite lady, she always wore huge primitive bracelets and necklaces of gold or ivory that she carried with the same panache as her lorgnette. Bernard, pink-faced, often smiling, smoked constantly, his cigarettes in a plastic holder. It was he who associated with André Breton, Robert Motherwell, David Hare and other Surrealists who worked on the magazine *VVV*. He served as its treasurer and accountant. From 1939 on, when the émigré artists began filtering into New York, the Reises took an active role in helping whenever they could. They were active with the French rescue committee and fund-raising activities to help the refugee artists. A list of exiles they helped serve is a list of many of the most distinguished artists of the twentieth century.

The Reis town house on East Sixty-eighth Street became one of the favorite gathering places for the European poets, painters and intellectuals. Becky was celebrated for her food. She was an enthusiastic cook whose cookbook, produced many years later, was the subject of heated discussions. She thought nothing of serving dinners for twelve or sixteen and even less of inviting eighty to a hundred people to her cocktail parties.

The Reises were more than casually involved in the New York art world. They were, in a sense, a part of its essence. It must be stressed how small the art world of New York was at that time. At a single opening of Pierre Matisse or Julien Levy it would not be an exaggeration to say that most of it would be in attendance. Everyone seemed to know everyone else—a state of affairs that continued well into the 1950s, when, precipitously, divisions between groups became increasingly marked. By 1960 there were several disparate art worlds. By 1970 the polarizations were complete, and in a sense it became futile to use the phrase "art world." It had come to mean nothing.

Did the artists seek out the company of Bernard and Becky Reis because they were rich collectors and hosts? Did they seek out Bernard because they needed his professional services? Or did at least some of them rely heavily on the advice and friendship of two people who were both worldly and affectionate? In the case of Mark Rothko, the reliance was largely of an emotional nature, even more than was his relationship with Stamos. If he hated museums, Mark hated lawyers even more, and in his mind what he needed most was an intimate friend who could also manage his financial, legal and domestic affairs. Bernard Reis thus became the central person in Rothko's life. They shared a certain conservative outlook. Mark was morally an old-fashioned puritan, a Jew outside of Judaism, but with many of the characteristics of a conventional Jewish family man. Bernard, of course, lived an even more conventional life—promiscuity and bohemianism were beyond him, so much so that those who lived that way seemed to him mere curiosities, sometimes interesting, sometimes tiresome.

Rothko's reliance grew greater with the passing of time and his increasing success: he came to depend on Bernard for almost all decisions. Thus, it was the Reises who went house-hunting for Mark until one was found on East Ninety-fifth Street that was both suitable and a good investment. Bernard arranged the mortgage. When Mark began to receive orders for paintings that could only be created in a well-appointed and commodious studio, Bernard made the arrangements for the large carriage house on East Sixty-ninth Street, which became the workshop for all the late, large-scale "series" canvases on which Rothko's fame may rest. It was Bernard more than anyone else who initiated the first profitable sales and brought Rothko together with the dealer Frank Lloyd, who would be responsible for his becoming a multimillionaire. Until Rothko met Lloyd, his works had not made any serious dent on the market.

I never really knew the third executor of the Rothko estate, Morton Levine. Mark apparently met him through Robert Motherwell, and took it for granted that Levine must be a brilliant man because he was a "scientist" who taught anthropology and was married to a fine concert pianist. I have no idea if Levine was brilliant or not. (I have never taken anthropology seriously as a science.) In any case, a few years after his son, Christopher, was born, Rothko began worrying about what would happen to the boy if he died. Mel was getting progressively worse, despite regular psychiatric treatment. Topher was fond of the Levines, and when he was old enough for music lessons he went to Mrs. Levine for instruction. The Levines were always delighted to have Topher with them and gave him a good deal of affection. Mark then asked Morton Levine to be the child's legal guardian. Later, when Rothko made out his will, he again asked Levine to serve with Bernard Reis and Stamos as an executor of his estate.

It was at one of Mark's Christmas Day parties that I first heard about the Rothko Foundation. Mark was fulminating about young artists—how spoiled they were, what terrible paintings they were doing, how wicked the museums were to give them so much attention while older artists, men of his generation, were being ignored and passed by. "I am setting up a foundation whose purpose will be to help men over fifty years old if they are sick or in trouble or just plain need money to keep going," Mark said. I asked who would decide who needed help. "Never mind about that. I'll have two or three good people who will know who the artists are that are talented and deserving. For instance, someone like your artist, Robert Goodnough." "But he's doing quite well," I replied a bit huffily. Mark laughed and said, "You never know what might happen."

When the foundation did come into existence in 1970, Mark's wishes were carried out quite as he wanted them to be. Until the funds were cut off by the litigation, over $300,000 was dispersed in grants to artists and writers in need. Among the recipients were John Ferren, who was dying of cancer and desperately needed money for his hospital bills; Stanley Boxer, ill with tuberculosis; Parker Tyler, after a massive heart attack. The list is a long and deserving one.

When Kate Rothko brought suit against the executors of her father's estate, seeking to have them dismissed, Morton Levine promptly divorced himself from the other two executors. He set up a separate defense for himself with his own lawyers representing him in the Surrogate Court. This proved harmful both to himself and the others, particularly since he presented evidence that turned out to be confused and ultimately destructive to all the defendants. By the time the case was actually being presented in court, he had lost his teaching job and his wife had divorced him. Topher was sent off to Ohio to be looked after by an aunt.

Any litigation surrounding the estate of an artist has the power to be ruinous to the market value and reputation of that artist's work. The lawsuit over the Bonnard estate prevented any of his work from being sold for many years. The absence of Bonnards on the market caused his prices to drop precipitously. The long, ten-year lawsuit over the Raoul Dufy estate, which dragged through one court after another, was disastrous to Dufy prices. Out of sight, out of mind, as the saying goes. It took years to rebuild the Bonnard market. It is unlikely that Dufy's reputation will improve, except possibly for his early Fauve pictures. Since it is well known that a lawsuit involving the estate of an artist is imprudent, such litigation is fairly rare.

When she brought suit against the executors, Kate Rothko was still legally a minor. After the death of her mother, which occurred six months after her father's suicide, a will was discovered made out by Mel Rothko in 1959. In this will, which Mel had neglected to change, the dentist/sculptor Herbert Ferber was designated as Kate's legal guardian. It must be remembered that because of her drinking problem, Mel Rothko did not always function consistently or clearly. This is made clear by the fact that Mark instantly changed his own will after the passionate quarrel that took place between Ferber and the Rothkos in 1968. At that time, Mark excised Ferber as an executor of his own estate. Mel had apparently given little thought to her own will in years, and therefore, upon her death, Ferber became Kate's legal guardian.

Socially, Ferber was both elegant and amusing. He was very much at home with the painters and sculptors who were emerging in the forties and triumphing in the fifties. Ferber was friendly with Pollock, Gottlieb, de Kooning and Motherwell. Rothko constituted a more central position in Ferber's life. Indeed, for several years, they were quite close.

If Mauriac's definition of art as "the work to be done" were used as the measure of Ferber's production, anyone would have to be impressed; he was prodigiously prolific. Group shows, one-man shows, museum shows, traveling shows; the work was regularly on view. He worked hard and persistently. No one was surprised when Ferber was invited to become a member of the prestigious André Emmerich gallery, for by that time he had built a considerable reputation for himself.

In 1962 an incident occurred that strained the Ferber-Rothko friendship. But in the 1950s Mel Rothko had been sufficiently fond of Herbert Ferber to ask him to serve as Kate's legal guardian if anything should happen to her or Mark. In 1959 Mel made out her will to that effect, but when the relationship with Ferber changed after their falling out, neither she nor her lawyer, Gerald Dickler, did anything about changing the will. Mark, however, did excise Ferber from his own will.

Thus, after her mother's death and until she was twenty-one, Kate was the legal ward of Herbert Ferber. This was for a period of several months, during which time Ferber suggested she file suit against the estate executors and Marlborough gallery. He urged Kate to hire Stanley Geller to represent her. Geller was eventually dismissed and Ed Ross, an extremely aggressive extrovert, replaced him. In Ferber's opinion, the executors were cheating Kate out of millions of dollars.

29

*T*HE ROTHKO EXECUTORS WERE CONCERNED THAT THE MARLBOROUGH GAL-lery was perhaps emphasizing the work Frank Lloyd had purchased outright form Rothko while he was alive, and their principal concerns were the security of the children and the maintenance of the Founda-tion. At any rate, late in 1970 the executors exacted a firm promise from the gallery to unload, at the least, thirteen pictures before the end of the year, for a guaranteed minimum total of $250,000. Stamos kept using the phrase "at good prices" to me, meaning as near as possible to the prices Marlborough obtained for the Rothkos they owned and sold. From my professional standpoint, I, of course, wondered how the gal-lery could possibly fulfill its commitment. How can any gallery ever know who is going to buy what, and when?

It was Bernard Reis who had been instrumental in linking Rothko with the Marlborough gallery initially. Reis was uniquely qualified to advise an artist as to the choice of a gallery. He had come to know most of the collectors and dealers intimately, and he tended to be rather hardboiled professionally when representing his artist clients. Moving often between New York and Europe as he did, Reis was sharply aware of the values of the international art market and its ongoing process. No one knew better than he that the art market had for generations tended to be international in scope, and that the best art always transcended national and regional boundaries. Reis was aware that the American art market was changing into an international art mart.

One of the ways quality works of art can be judged is by how understandable they are in places far from where they were produced. There are, however, vast numbers of paintings that enjoy greater appreciation in their own countries, for instance, still lifes and landscapes of the seventeenth century in Holland. English art of the eighteenth and nineteenth centuries is continually popular in auction rooms and galleries in England. Most American art has been bought by Americans. Needless to say, there are exceptions to this tendency. There are eccentric collectors who will buy anything that hits their fancy. There was a Manchester businessman who enjoyed mid-nineteenth century Italian genre pictures, a Texas oilman who bought nothing but English sporting scenes, a West German industrialist who was single-mindedly enthusiastic about American Pop art and bought it by the carload.

After World War II a greatly enlarged number of collectors with fairly modest means began buying little-known or unknown artists' works. But here again, the trend was for the buyers to purchase from their respective countries or regions. The prosperous middle class of Milan supported a rash of new galleries featuring "new" and "advanced" works (the "new" and "advanced" being a reflection, by the way, of the art magazines, of what was going on in New York; the Milanese avant-garde let no grass grow under their nimble feet).

But if there were more people in the middle class with extra money to buy luxury commodities, it must be remembered that numerically there were also more extremely rich people (worth over five hundred million dollars) than ever known in previous epochs. This is true after most wars; it was certainly the case with the Americans, the West Germans, the Italians, a new kind of Spaniard, and certain internationals— for instance, Gulbenkian in Portugal, the Gettys in England, the Greek shipping and oil people, all of whom bought great quantities of art and art objects.

The very rich, of course, have the opportunity to buy on the international market and therefore are likely to acquire the finest works. For example, Norton Simon bought Rembrandt's portrait of Titus for $2,234,000, and Gauguin's *Still Life with Apples* was sold to Stavros Niarchos for $297,145 in 1957 (a price that would be much higher now). The acquisition of a Cézanne landscape by Mr. and Mrs. Paul Mellon for $800,000 in 1965 was, again, of a work that would now be worth far more.

During the 1960s there was an influx of dealers from Europe to New York. The new demand was for Pop art; pictures by Roy Lichtenstein and Andy Warhol sold for unbelievable prices in places such as Düsseldorf and Cologne (I use the word "unbelievable," since I know what I could have acquired by Picasso, Miró, Braque and other artists for the price of one Warhol *Campbell's Tomato Soup*).

It became increasingly clear that art collecting, art appreciation, even art making had become a substitute for religion. The followers of Art have become true believers, lay contemplatives. To watch a disciple staring transfixed at a Jackson Pollock (after a sale of *Blue Poles* for two million dollars) is like witnessing one of Zurbarán's saints receiving the stigmata. To observe a new collector displaying his prized Monets or Vuillards is to see beatitude on a mortal face. One longs to raise the cry "Hosanna!"

Can there be any correlation between art appreciation and the overall price index of twentieth-century paintings in general? Between 1951 and 1969 Picasso had multiplied his prices thirty-seven and a half times, Braque twenty-two times, Bonnard thirty-five times, Chagall fifty and a half times, Vlaminck thirty times. As the profits soared, more and more art galleries opened in New York. They enjoyed one advantage that those in France, Italy and England did not: there were almost no restrictions on the trade of artworks. Part of the reason Paris lost its dominance over the world market was restriction on exports.

Paintings and sculptures by Americans, however, were slow in reaching customers beyond its borders. Sam Kootz and Sidney Janis tried in the early 1950s to interest Europeans in the importance of Abstract Expressionists. They did not succeed. When Picasso saw the paintings of Pollock he made a wry face and dismissed them as idiotic. Whatever paintings by Americans were sold at the time were at prices not unlike those at home. Nobody knew when or if the Americans would pass through *il portale d'oro*—the golden door. The resistance to "American-type" painting is now forgotten, although even in the late 1960s the French minister of culture, André Malraux, told the directors of the Venice Biennale that if a French painter did not receive the top prize, the French would withdraw. The directors acquiesced.

Why none of the big houses such as Durand-Ruel, Wildenstein, Knoedler, Paul Rosenberg or Duveen had been able to make an international market for the Americans is hard to say. All of them, of course, handled American painters for the American market. Knoedler, for instance, did a brisk trade in cowboy pictures by Remington; it was the favorite gallery of rich Westerners.

The first dealer of consequence to break the barrier and carry

Americans into the world arena was a Viennese who had changed his name from Levine to Lloyd. Frank Lloyd started in London after World War II with nothing and emerged in a comparatively short time as the most powerful and efficient dealer of modern art in the world. As the head of the Marlborough gallery, it was he, more than anyone else, who put the Americans firmly on the map and in the forefront of the contemporary art market.

This was at a time when the reputations of the Abstract Expressionists were beginning to fade in their own country as a consequence of the landslide of much younger artists appearing on the scene in the early 1960s. It seemed momentarily in New York that the older artists were losing their position. The truth is, however, that they had simply passed through the "golden door" and were, in effect, international commodities. It was largely Marlborough that took over the Abstract Expressionist school. Lloyd skimmed the cream, acquired sovereignty over the best work and, to a large degree, obtained contracts of exclusivity. The big money was now in New York.

In a curious way an art gallery is a mirror image of the person who creates it. There is a distinct difference between the informality of Betty Parsons, the intimacy of Jill Kornblee, the warm elegance of Pierre Matisse, the hodgepodge of Ivan Karp's O.K. Harris gallery in SoHo. The moment Frank Lloyd opened the New York branch of Marlborough in the Fuller building in 1963, it was immediately clear that the gallery space reflected power, sophistication and international money. Nothing like it had ever before been seen in New York among private galleries. It was not, however, quite satisfactory to Frank Lloyd. There was too much trouble moving work, especially large sculptures, in and out of the building. The ceilings were too low and the floors, foolishly paved with gray slate, sucked up light and created a vaguely dismal ambience. Thus, when Sam Lefrak announced his new Squibb Building at 50 West Fifty-seventh Street, Lloyd got hold of the plans and entered into negotiation for the whole second floor. He got it.

It was Frank Lloyd himself, looking like a happy cherub, who showed me around a few weeks before the new gallery space was opened in 1972. The architect, Ed Barnes, whose Walker Art Center in Minneapolis I admired, had done what I thought was an excellent job of designing the space. More than half of it could be used for exhibitions; the rest was designated for viewing rooms, offices, storage, receiving and packing. The design by Barnes cost $50,000 and the construction another $100,000. "Surely," I said, "it must have cost much more?"

"Oh," replied Frank, "Sam Lefrak paid the rest." He grinned, which made me realize that Lefrak had spent at least as much, if not more, than Frank Lloyd had.

Although I had seen most of the great art establishments both in New York and Europe, I realized there was nothing to which I might compare this vast enterprise, certainly not Maeght in Paris or Wildenstein or Knoedler in New York. The storage room bulged with pictures and statues that I knew represented only a small part of the Marlborough "stock"; there was much more in warehouses. And this newest Marlborough was only one branch of the international organization. There were two more in London, others in Zurich, Tokyo, Toronto, Montreal and Rome. Lloyd's family trust was located in Nassau; its financial operation in Liechtenstein.

I was curious as to how much it would cost to operate the New York gallery on a yearly basis. My guess was certainly more than a million, counting the expenses for the large staff, insurance, rent, publicity, storage and the rest of the costs any gallery encounters. I did eventually find out that in order to "break even," the gallery needed to sell at least two-and-a-half million dollars worth of work a year.

My own little gallery on Fifty-seventh Street cost $4,500 for each monthly exhibition—which meant, with a 50-percent commission on consigned work, I had to sell $9,000 worth of work a month simply to keep the doors open. Two or three exhibitions in a row that did not sell (and this sometimes happened, since I showed so much work by totally unknown artists) would cause the gallery great concern. Then, of course, I had to reckon with the reality that the art season was of nine months' duration—July, August and September were hopelessly dull, a time for closing. The rent, however, had to be paid twelve months a year.

What happens at the new Marlborough, I could not help but think, if Robert Motherwell, Beverly Pepper, Philip Guston or Franz Kline don't sell? Even with the rest of the "stock," the risk seemed to me large, daunting.

But then, of course, there *was* the rest of the "stock," as Frank Lloyd himself was only too pleased to show me, in his private office. That day the stock included two Picassos, a wondrous Pissarro, a Chagall, two Feiningers and a superb Munch. All of them had been bought recently, and all of them would be gone very soon. Lloyd had just sold an expensive Van Gogh. If Charles Merrill was a genius in the investment business, certainly Lloyd was a genius of art merchandizing.

When I later heard that Pope Paul was buying pictures for the Vatican collection from Frank Lloyd, I could not register surprise.

Lloyd, as might be expected, was a controversial figure, and there were many who loathed him. He was a screamer and a yeller, and many Marlborough employees came and went in quick succession, unable to stand the pressure. The intense competitive workings of a vast organization such as Marlborough were the antithesis of the genteel, relaxed pleasantness of old-time galleries; I often had the feeling that I, too, would last less than a week if I worked at Marlborough. And, of course, it was Lloyd himself who set the style and pace for his own gallery. I once heard his persuasive charm described by Jane Wade, a former employee, as "whipped cream on top of a spiked helmet."

Donald McKinney, who was appointed president of the New York Marlborough, not only survived but thrived. Collectors were very fond of him and he had a phenomenal sales record. He was also blessed with nerves of steel, and for whatever reason, Lloyd seemed never to upset him. Actually, Lloyd seemed to scream and yell far less around his new president.

If Lloyd was generally considered a shrewd operator, however, there were those who sometimes felt they had gotten the best of him. I remember in February of 1969 my friend Herbert Machiz, while out walking the dog, encountered Rothko on Madison Avenue. "You look like a cat who has devoured a mouse," Herbert told him. Rothko wore an expression of satisfaction that, combined with much twinkle in his eyes, gave him the look of a naughty leprechaun, Herbert later told me. "Indeed, I have devoured a mouse," Rothko replied. "Which mouse?" asked Herbert. "Well, not a mouse actually. A large tiger. I've just finished negotiating my newest contract with my dealer. Nothing gives an artist more pleasure than getting the better of a dealer or collector." Rothko's dealer at the time was, of course, Frank Lloyd. "And how did you do that?" "Easy," said Rothko. "The gallery was buying a big batch of pictures from me and I upped the price on all of them." Herbert suggested Mark come back to the house to celebrate with a drink. There was no more art talk when they arrived. I was home, and the three of us were soon off on Mark's pet subject, Irene Worth and the world of the theater.

My own professional dealings with Frank Lloyd were both unusual and amusing. In the early fall of 1962 I accepted an invitation to visit Lee Krasner Pollock for a weekend in East Hampton. When I arrived she informed me that Frank Lloyd would be coming for dinner that Saturday evening. "Good heavens," I said, "won't that be an embarrass-ment? After all, I'm suing him." Lee became irritated. "Don't be silly," she exclaimed. "You're a grown man, and besides, you ought to know what he thinks about the Rivers affair." Indeed, I did want to know. Larry Rivers had broken a three-way contract with me, Gimpel and Cordier, and had made a deal with Marlborough. Our suit against Rivers and Marlborough was not going well, and my brother-in-law, a lawyer, had advised me to drop the whole thing before I met with disas-ter. Another lawyer had advised that suing an artist was hopeless be-cause the artist could always claim that his "muse did not burgeon."

As it turned out, the dinner was fun. Lee, in one of her good moods, told hilarious stories, thus baiting me into being more outra-geous than usual. Mr. Lloyd never stopped laughing. At one quiet mo-ment, however, I was able to talk to him. "You know," he said, "when Rivers came to see me in London, he assured me that he was with *no* gallery and had *no* commitments anywhere. Since I could not have known what his situation in New York was, and since I barely knew him, I took him at his word. He then signed an exclusive with me. I suggest you take for your gallery whatever pictures you feel would be a proper settlement for the expenses you've already accrued. As for the suit, it will cost us both an arm and a leg. Dealers never win and the artist's market is sometimes ruined."

I accepted the offer. Three days later Mr. Lloyd sent me a bottle of Courvoisier to seal the bargain.

In February 1974 I stopped off at the Marlborough gallery to pick up some material for an article I was writing. By chance, while I was there, I ran into two collectors who had been former clients of mine. They asked me if I would look at a small Bonnard they were consid-ering for purchase. Neither husband nor wife could make up their mind. I went into the viewing room and there was Frank Lloyd, who greeted me affectionately as always. He then left me with his clients. The Bonnard was a delightful small landscape, which I analyzed for my friends as well as I knew how. I commented that it was a wonderful picture. Then I left.

About three days later I received a charming note from Mr. Lloyd, thanking me for helping conclude the sale. He also enclosed a check as my commission. I was very touched. My gallery certainly needed the money, but it had never occurred to me that I should receive a reward for advising. It was an elegant gesture that gave me a sense of Lloyd's style as a businessman.

30

I HAVE NEVER UNDERSTOOD PRECISELY WHY A YOUNG GIRL WHO WAS LEFT a handsome inheritance made the decision to sue her father's three closest friends and the art gallery that had been responsible for making a large fortune for her and her family. No other lawsuit in the history of art was ever so expensive and it seemed fairly clear from the beginning that, win or lose, neither the petitioners nor the defendants could gain much. Only the lawyers for both sides would be certain to profit.

Certainly, in her statements to the press, Kate Rothko never clarified the matter. In an interview with the Washington *Post* in the winter of 1976, she told a reporter that the main thing she wanted from the lawsuit was to have her father's pictures. All she appeared to possess were a few posters, pointing to the Marlborough posters from her position on the sofa where she was seated. Yet at the time of her mother's death, there were approximately forty Rothko paintings in the house, which had been left to the family in Rothko's will. I wonder what happened to these works.

In the same interview, Kate Rothko told of her parents going to the Four Seasons restaurant and how angry her father was with the way his paintings looked, with waiters, people and tables blocking the view. Rothko fumed all the way home and continued to be disturbed after he got there, Kate remembered.

In fact, as has been pointed out, the Rothko paintings, although purchased for the Seagram Building, were never delivered, and Mark had returned the check. Several of these works ended up in the Tate Gallery in London. (It had always been a disappointment to Mark that Kate took no interest in, or care for, his art.)

One of the major disputes during the trial was the number of works in the Rothko estate and, a more sticky problem, their value. I remember I had asked Stamos about two months after Rothko's death how many pictures were left in the estate. At that point the executors were just beginning to take up the tasks designated for them in the will, and I was curious about how they would solve some of the many problems they would have to deal with.

Stamos told me that there were perhaps seven hundred items in the inventory, dating back to very early efforts and including work in a variety of media. The problem with much of it was its quality, ranging from downright bad or mediocre to excellent. Many of the pictures were in poor condition, and much restoration, including stretching and framing, would be required. I immediately wondered where the works would be stored and who would undertake the large job of acting as curator. The greatest number of works I had ever kept in my own gallery was about three hundred and fifty. Keeping track of them, as well as the other works scattered among museums, private collections, lending "libraries" and in artists' studios, was never an easy task. Overseeing seven hundred or more works struck me as a formidable and daunting effort.

Stamos told me that the pictures would remain in the warehouse where they had been placed after Rothko's death. He did not know what specific course would be undertaken; that would be decided after further negotiations. It could take several months, he told me.

I ventured the opinion that the estate would incur a raft of expenses. Stamos agreed, and added that the executors would follow the best program open to them. He was anxious that the activities of the Rothko Foundation proceed, as new applications were being submitted. The executors were, as before, discussing requests for grants. The immense task of compiling a *catalogue raisonné* of Rothko's work would have to wait until later.

"It is a shame," I commented, "that Mark himself did not initiate a catalogue. Lee Pollock began the identification and dating of Jackson's works a few years after he died. That task has been going on with well-trained art historians since 1960, but it is still far from complete." (The Pollock catalogue was eventually published in 1978.)

The market value of the works in the Rothko estate was a major point of contention throughout the trial, and one of the people enlisted by the petitioners to give an estimation of the value of the estate was, to my surprise, the collector Ben Heller. I suspected something was up when Ben called me in November 1972 to invite me to lunch. I had not seen him since the death of his first wife, Judy, in an automobile accident. I was surprised by his call and at the time I had no idea of his involvement in the Rothko case.

I had several fond memories of Ben Heller and his first wife. I had originally met Ben through his close friend B. H. Friedman, who had been buying works of art from me. Bob Friedman invited Ben to the gallery to see a handsome oil on canvas by Helen Frankenthaler he had acquired. At this point, Ben had been collecting tentatively, but he was becoming more serious. He and Bob Friedman were friendly rivals— both of them were highly successful professionally, Bob as a consultant engineer with the building firm Uris Brothers and Ben in his father's business, Heller Jersey, a fabric manufacturer. Both Bob and Ben had sufficient incomes to live well and to buy paintings and sculpture. They had a painter friend, Paul Brach, who sometimes advised them as to what to see and what to buy.

Ben Heller and his wife, Judy, became frequent visitors to my gallery and made several purchases. They were particularly partial to the paintings of Robert Goodnough. I remember Judy Heller coming into the gallery one Saturday with a bag of dried apricots, pears and apples. She and Ben were chewing them like Ojibwas chewing pemmican or Eskimos with blubber. Judy smiled so winningly as she offered me some that I quite forgot, as I took one of the apricots, how much I dislike dried fruit.

Once in the late fifties I called Ben and told him about the production of Lionel Abel's play *Absalom* for the Artists Theater I was producing. I asked him if he would help by donating enough fabric for the costumes, which he did. Several years later I agreed to help Nancy Macdonald on a fund raising campaign for Spanish Refugee Aid. She wanted to put together a cocktail party in the home of a collector with a really good collection—good enough to charge $5 admission. The Hellers, because they approved of Nancy Macdonald, were pleased to offer their home for the event. It was a huge success, for by this time Judy and Ben had acquired the fine collection of pictures and sculpture for which they became well known.

Despite the fact that Judy was chronically ill with sarcoidosis, a disease that made life cruelly difficult for her, she seemed to have an inexhaustible fund of courage and, when well, great energy. Before her untimely death she became active in the field of landscape gardening, not as a hobby but as a vocation. I was delighted with her herb garden, created for my friend Babs Simpson, then an editor for *Vogue*, whose house in Amagansett was itself a work of art. It is unlikely that Ben would have carried his passion for collecting as far as he did without Judy's continuous support and enthusiasm. She loved the collection. The Hellers always seemed to have a most pleasant domestic life. Once when I arrived early at the Hellers' apartment for an appoinment with Ben, I saw him come in pink-faced from the sharp air of Central Park across the street, where he had been teaching his children how to be better baseball players. Their summer house in East Hampton, formerly Leo Castelli's, had a trampoline in the garden, where all the Hellers loved to jump up and down, up and down, higher and higher.

For various reasons we did not see each other for several years. After Judy's death Ben remarried. Our "reunion" luncheon was at the City Athletic Club on West Fifty-fourth Street. The Fifty-fourth Street clubhouse is quite grand, and here wealthy Jewish men of affairs play squash and have lunch. It was obvious from the tone taken by the staff that Ben Heller was considered just such a man of affairs. It had been so long since I had seen Ben that I could now observe him from an altogether different angle than I had in the past. Physically, Ben looked about the same as he always had, perhaps a little heavier. But the face was not the same one that had formerly betrayed an ardor for the study of philosophy; Ben seemed to have become worldly in a new way.

Since Ben preferred monologues to dialogues, I settled back to hear why I was summoned to his club and given lunch. He explained that it had been his good fortune to retire early from the manufacturing of fabric and that he was now developing several other projects—one of them a wine business, another a development in the Bahamas. But his main concentration was now on private dealing. Collecting art was no longer his chief interest, nor was he as interested in contemporary work as he was in ancient and primitive art and artifacts. He lowered his eyes and said, "Like it or not, I have become known as a man of taste." As he said this I could not help remembering the rather fierce argument he and I had had in his apartment in the early 1950s in which he insisted that Hartung and Soulages, Mathieu and other French abstractionists were superior to all other contemporary artists—whereas I maintained that Pollock, de Kooning, Gottlieb, Rothko, Kline and other Americans were the seminal artists of the moment. Ben had not as yet acquired his Pollocks, Rothkos and other Abstract Expressionist works.

After I had started on my delicious corned beef on rye, Ben got down to what he wanted to say. First there was a preamble about my having a reputation for integrity in the art world, and then he suddenly said, "I understand that you are going to serve as a witness on behalf of Marlborough in the forthcoming court case." I could not have been more astonished. How in the world could Ben have known such a thing? He had raised his voice a little; it sounded somewhat threatening; he had succeeded in making me nervous. I explained that I had indeed been approached by former Judge David Peck, one of Marlborough's attorneys, asking if I were subpoenaed as a witness, would I serve? My answer to Mr. Peck was, as in any other case, that I would be happy to answer questions that were within my competence, but the prices and the sale of Rothko paintings were outside my experience.

This did not please Ben and he launched into a long diatribe on the wickedness of Rothko's three executors and the crookedness and profiteering of Marlborough. Of course, poor Ben did not know how much I already knew about him and his efforts to become an international dealer. I knew, for instance, that he had approached both Frank Lloyd and Carla Panicali in Rome to work with Marlborough for everyone's mutual benefit. He had been flatly rejected by both. Now, Ben continued, as a good friend of Mark and in the interest of correct and ethical business practices in the art world, he for one would not see Kate Rothko bilked out of "millions and millions and millions of dollars."

I hoped my eyes did not narrow, but it was difficult to control my anger. Surely Ben must have known why Mark Rothko had been furious with him before his death. Surely he must have understood that I knew about Mark's anger at Heller's manipulation of his own Rothko painting, *Four Darks in Red*, into the Whitney Museum, believing that Ben had made a profit on the deal. It could not have been possible that Heller was unaware of Rothko's loathing for the Whitney. But then, Ben probably did not know that Mark couldn't stand him personally, even long before the Whitney deal.

Finally, Ben informed me that he had volunteered to be a witness for the petitioners. To that end he had been studying the evidence for weeks to prepare himself as an expert on the value of Rothko's works. Indeed, later at the trial, Heller would present estimates of the market value of the works in the Rothko estate that were far higher than those presented by any other "expert" called by either side. For some reason, Heller's estimates seemed to hold great weight with the presiding judge, who seemed unaware of Ben's Rothko holdings.

What is strange is that Professor Peter Selz, who was curator for the Museum of Modern Art's Rothko retrospective in 1967 and was at that time responsible for the museum's insurance estimates, was attacked repeatedly as being in collusion with Marlborough. Stranger still, despite prolonged and detailed factual evidence by Donald McKinney, who had sold large numbers of Rothko pictures and was clearly informed as to their actual sales value, was the fact that he should be so snidely undermined by Kate Rothko's attorneys as an unreliable witness even though the billings and payments for his sales were exhibited and examined in detail. None of the other witnesses were grilled as savagely as McKinney. His evidence was not disproven despite the third degree to which he was subjected, both in the District Attorney's private office and in the courtroom. On the other hand, rather trivial evidence of sales coming from two dealers, Arnold Glimcher of Pace Gallery and the Swiss dealer Beyler, both of whom had few dealings in the Rothko market, was found plausible by Judge Midonick.

We left the club and walked toward Fifth Avenue. "Ben," I remarked, "don't you think you made a rather large profit on the sale of *Blue Poles*? After all, you only paid about thirty-two thousand dollars for it." "It's only a question of money," he replied. "But it's such a lot of money," I went on. "I think you could have used some of it to buy a painting by Lee Krasner." "Good heavens!" exclaimed Ben. "She certainly doesn't need the money." My last words, "Not for the money, my dear Ben, but for the morality," were apparently carried away by the wind.

Indeed, the sale of Pollock's *Blue Poles* to an art museum in Australia the previous year had been riveting. I was particularly interested in Lee Pollock's reaction. Two million dollars would be an immense amount of money to pay for a Rembrandt, a Cimabue, a Giotto, a Zurbarán, a Monet, even a Picasso. What, in effect, would this new record price do to the prices of the pictures left in the Pollock estate? It could not make Lee happy thinking of her financial status at the time the picture was first sold to Dr. Fred Olsen. Nor could it make her happy, after all her years of struggle since Jackson's death in 1956, that her own work must go on existing in the huge shadow of her dead husband's reputation.

A few weeks after the announcement of the sale, Lee received a telephone call from the second Mrs. Heller, who invited her to a "farewell to *Blue Poles* party." "It has made us sad to see it go," said Mrs. Heller. "After all, it's been in the family for a long time." "I know exactly how long it's been in your family," said Lee icily, adding that she would be occupied that evening.

The day after the party I was talking with Bill Lieberman, then a curator at the Museum of Modern Art, who told me about the party. "The centerpiece on the table was quite extraordinary. It was a large cake whose frosting was a replica of *Blue Poles*."

The evaluations of the Rothko estate later led to another unfortunate incident, this involving the Art Dealers Association and in particular two members, Daniel and Eleanore Saidenberg. In early 1976 a group of dealers began pressuring the officers of the Art Dealers Association to probe the evaluations given by Daniel and Eleanore Saidenberg for the Rothko estate. These evaluations, including all the pictures left to the estate and the Rothko Foundation, had been made in 1971 at the request of the executors of the estate in order to satisfy the demands of the Internal Revenue Service. The critics of the Saidenbergs felt that the evaluations had been made without the permission of the Association as a whole and without sufficient knowledge of Rothko's work.

Many felt that the decision to excommunicate the Marlborough gallery from the ranks of the A.D.A. in 1975 immediately after the conclusion of the Rothko trial had never been fully discussed with the total membership. This had also been the case with the decision to disallow membership to Joan Washburn because she had taken a job with Sotheby Parke-Bernet while continuing to operate her own gallery. There seemed to be arbitrary rulings as to who could attend the Association's annual banquet, not to mention who would be awarded the Association's annual citation. It seemed to many of us that the officers had, year in and year out, usually with pressure from Ralph Colin, the attorney for the A.D.A., acted in a high-handed manner.

The most startling stance of all, again taken on the advice of Mr. Colin, had been the refusal of the A.D.A. to support Stephen Radish, an A.D.A. member who had presented an exhibition by an artist protesting the Vietnam war. The artist had utilized the American flag in many three-dimensional objects displayed in what the New York police termed an "obscene" way. Mr. Colin was sharply opposed to aiding Stephen Radish on the grounds that it was "not a good case," even though the New York Civil Liberties Union had taken on his defense. Many members of the A.D.A. felt that a common front should be made with Radish to protect all art galleries against possible charges of "obscenity" or "disloyalty" in the future. The case went through the courts for five years and, in the end, Stephen Radish was vindicated on the grounds of his constitutional right of free expression.

If ever there was a situation in which the organization's treasury might have been well spent, it was this case. But it seemed to many A.D.A. members, including myself, that the officers and chief advisor were not concerned with liberty or freedom or even human decency; they were worried about keeping a proper "public image" for the sake of art evaluations and the I.R.S. Art dealers must be regarded as respectable professionals with high moral and ethical standards, and Mr. Colin was retained by the A.D.A. to ensure that the public viewed art merchants in this light.

From time to time, of course, some members of the A.D.A. had done foolish things, such as selling works illegally removed from other countries or taking commissions far beyond the standard 50 percent from artists whose work they had sold on consignment. There wasn't a member who, like most American citizens, had not tried to minimize his income taxes or sell a few things under the table in hard times. Above all, there wasn't one who hadn't at least once (and generally very often) made evaluations of paintings and sculptures. No one before had ever been threatened with excommunication.

Thus, the pending charges against Danny and Eleanore Saidenberg seemed to me particularly unfair. I had known them both for years. Danny had been a splendid cellist and orchestra conductor before his arthritis had made performing impossible. On several occasions he and Eleanore invited me to their beautiful house on East Seventy-seventh Street for chamber music parties. Eleanore, an enthusiast for the dance as well as music, had been on close terms for years with the great art dealer Daniel-Henri Kahnweiler in Paris and had shown some of the best of Picasso, Braque, Gris and other twentieth-century masters. The Saidenbergs were known both for their personal kindness and their honesty in dealing.

Jane Wade and Virginia Zabriskie filled me in on what occurred at the A.D.A. meeting on the Saidenbergs the morning after it took place. Danny was allowed to read a paper explaining exactly the nature of the report he had made to the I.R.S. on behalf of the Rothko executors. Their evaluations of most of the 700 pictures were, in most cases, higher than those I would have given—in fact far higher, since I would have considered many of the earliest works of no value, except possibly for study purposes. Most of the so-called "Surrealist" or "mythic" pictures were of extremely poor quality, since Rothko did not come into his own until he had worked for many years.

When Danny had finished reading his explanation, one which denied all culpability of collusion with anyone, he said that perhaps he and Eleanore had not given sufficient study to the pictures in question.

Almost immediately after this, Sidney Janis asked for permission to speak. He told the membership that during the period he had shown Rothko's works he had sold few pictures, but that he had often been called upon to evaluate his work. If he had been asked to estimate the value of the pictures held by the estate, he said, he would have evaluated them much lower than had the Saidenbergs.

A vote was taken. The Saidenbergs were unanimously exonerated from all guilt. Both Jane Wade and Virginia Zabriskie agreed that the discussion preceding the vote had been a good one because many of the issues that needed airing had been brought forward. Both felt that in the future the A.D.A. membership would have more power to shape the Association's policies.

The officers of the A.D.A. seemed to take a particular interest in the Rothko trial, and the charges against the Saidenbergs were not the only evidence of this. As soon as the trial was completed and Marlborough was forced to pay damages, the A.D.A. made public via the New York *Times* a statement denouncing Marlborough, its former member. I was never able to determine if Ralph Colin had actually prepared the statement sent to the newspaper by the A.D.A. president, Roy Newhouse. If so, he undoubtedly would not want it known. Ralph Colin had once worked for Marlborough and detested Frank Lloyd. In the end Colin had found it necessary to resign from Marlborough.

*L*IKE EVERYONE ELSE IN THE ART WORLD, I FOLLOWED THE ROTHKO TRIAL closely. Like everyone else in the art world, I got most of my information about how the case was proceeding from the New York *Times*. However, it seemed to me that the *Times* was slanting its coverage to the side of the petitioners and heavily against Marlborough and the executors of the estate. Because many people regard the *Times* as a sort of bible, general opinion ran against the defendants. It was easy for people to feel sorry for the helpless young daughter suing to save her father's estate. Even people in the art world who had not had the personal contact with Rothko, the executors and the gallery that I did were ready to judge harshly. The case became the prime subject of conversation at art-world dinner parties, and most of the facts bandied about at these dinners came from the *Times*.

However, there were several elements about the case that the *Times* reporters did not understand or did not present to their readers. Many of the pictures left in the estate were far from first quality. The general public does not understand how carefully an artist's market must be cultivated and how carefully a gallery must balance good pictures against bad ones. It was never made clear that many of the older works were in poor condition, rolled up, torn, or dirty—or all three. In my opinion the executors had acted quite prudently in having the estate pictures evaluated as modestly as possible. The *Times* also paid scant attention to the work of the Rothko Foundation, which the executors had undertaken so diligently and with a deep concern to fulfill Mark Rothko's express wishes to help older artists in need.

Of course the varying opinions of Rothko and his work expressed during the trial led to much exaggerated chatter. I did not agree with Meyer Schapiro and some of the other "experts" called in to express their opinion as to the magnitude of Rothko's genius. By comparison with such great twentieth-century masters as Picasso, Matisse, Mondrian, Miró and Braque, I had always thought of him as a splendid and alluring minor figure (major, perhaps, for American art). What Rothko achieved was limited in comparison with the "giants." As far as I am concerned, the only major painter America has produced is Pollock.

I, of course, knew about Rothko's, and later the executors', deals with Frank Lloyd and Marlborough, which seemed to confuse so many people and cast the gallery in a bad light. When I first heard of Lloyd's original guarantee to Rothko to sell over two hundred of his pictures within eight years, I thought he was taking a fantastic gamble. I did not see how so many could be sold within such a relatively short time. I knew, because of my professional background, exactly how much work and expense would be involved to move the paintings Marlborough had bought from Mark and taken on consignment from the estate. I understood the need to make a decent profit on each sale in order to ensure the continued functioning of the overall gallery operation. I also understood the need for the executors to sign an exclusive with Frank Lloyd on such a contract to protect the considerable time and financial investment he had made in Rothko's work, the Venice show being only one example. Lloyd would have been in a very bad position if inferior Rothkos were being circulated by other galleries in competition with the best work, of which Marlborough had a large portion. Thus, the executors had no choice but to offer exclusivity to Marlborough pictures in their consignment, and not to other galleries. Although these dealings seemed to me, as a gallery director, perfectly straightforward, they confused many people in the art world and added to the impression that Marlborough and the executors had acted in collusion.

There were, however, other actions on the part of the gallery that confused even me. These had to do with the two restraining orders, a temporary one of June 26, 1972, and a permanent one of September 26, 1972, issued by the court to prevent the gallery and the executors from selling any more of the Rothko pictures that the gallery had on consignment from the estate. Apparently, however, fifty-seven such pictures were invoiced *before* the first restraining order and shipped out later. What was not made clear was that an international chain of galleries in five countries shipping from one depot to another—in this case Montreal—would do so in large lots. Not just Rothkos were involved but many other kinds of sculpture and painting. It was a practical expedient for moving stock from one gallery to another in different countries. In short, the invoice would have to have been prepared months before the actual shipment in order to meet various regulations—customs, shipping, insurance and so forth.

According to the *Times*, it was argued during the trial that the dates of the invoices and indeed many of the sales themselves seemed phony and that anything that was delivered was in violation of the court's restraining order. The implication was that Marlborough had acted to avoid the injunction and that by creating fictitious purchases, the gallery made profits it did not share with the estate properly and fairly.

I knew most of the names to whom the pictures were sold: Beyeles, Marinotti, the Mellons, Glenway Wescott's sister-in-law Barbara Wescott, the couturier Hubert de Givenchy, Joseph Pulitzer, Jr., the Goulandris clan, Flinker. But I had no idea who some of the others were: A.E.K., MAG, Andros Compania Maritimas, Fumagalli, Galleria Berrini, "Gui Rochet Agt.," Arthur Pires de Lima, Yoram Polany, William Hallsborough. Of course, the intelligent very, very rich move smoothly and silently doing whatever they wish to do. Baudelaire taught us that one of the first tricks of the devil is to convince us that he does not exist. The truly rich like to convince Americans that they don't really exist and prefer not to cut figures in society. Alas, their children often do. They are known as "big mouths."

The judge in the Rothko case was Millard L. Midonick. It was only after the trial was over, in January 1976, that I discovered someone who actually knew Judge Midonick, my friend Ed Weisel, former Parks Commissioner of the city. We had lunch at the Westbury Hotel, and Weisel was unequivocal in his praise of the judge as a human being—kindly, thoughtful, earnest in the pursuit of his duties. "But does he know anything about art and the vagaries of the art world?" I asked. "No," said Ed Weisel. "During the legal proceedings he had to rely heavily on the experts who were brought in, from Meyer Schapiro to Peter Selz. But then, John," he went on, "do *you* know anyone competent in the fuzzy area we are talking about?" I had to admit I knew only one judge who had been around the galleries, but I had no idea what type of judge he was. I did, however, know quite a few lawyers who were astute art collectors and observers of the scene.

"I can only tell you one thing that struck me as very knowing on the part of Midonick, and this he told me himself. He said he had repeatedly urged a settlement to save the situation, and repeatedly the suggestion was turned down by Kate Rothko and her attorneys." Ed Weisel looked like a mischievous Buddha at this point.

"Oh," I said, "Frank Lloyd on several occasions tried to settle in ways that in my opinion would have been highly beneficial to the 'petitioners,' as I have correctly learned to say."

A strange little rhyme passed through my head as I pulled off my next artichoke leaf:

> Isn't it funny
> How a bear likes honey?

Kate Rothko, who had "exhibited such venom and hatred of the Foundation," according to one of the Rothko Foundation lawyers who testified during the trial, "that she is incapable of administering an estate in which the Foundation is the overwhelming beneficiary without running into conflict between her emotions and her duties," finally had her way. On December 18, 1975, slightly less than five years after her father's death, Judge Midonick removed the three executors of the Rothko estate and assessed damages and fines totaling $9,525,000 against the executors, Frank Lloyd and the Marlborough gallery.

As the New York *Times* reported the next day, the judge found that the executors had acted in a conflict of interest or negligently in the selling and consigning of 798 of the artist's paintings to Lloyd for much less than their true value and under terms that were highly disadvantageous to the estate. The Surrogate Court canceled the contracts for the transfer of the 798 paintings and directed their return to the estate. In his eighty-two-page decision Judge Midonick granted most of the requests of Kate Rothko and the state's Attorney General, Louis J. Lefkowitz, who had joined the suit because Rothko had left half of his estate to a charitable foundation.

The record damages included a $3.3 million fine against Lloyd and his galleries, which the judge said could be mitigated by the return of the Rothko paintings to the estate that Lloyd had sold in violation of the court order. Lloyd was also held in contempt of court for those sales. The judge found that Reis and Stamos had acted in conflict of interest and they were held liable with Lloyd and Marlborough for the total damages and fines "individually and severally." Morton Levine, who claimed that he had been "pressured" into signing the Marlborough contracts by the other two executors, was ruled to have been "negligent" and he was held liable for $3 million of the damages. These damages were to be paid to the estate. The judge also denied the three executors the commissions they were entitled to under the law of at least 2 percent of the gross value of the estate for each.

Because the executors had sold 100 paintings for an average price of $18,000 and had given the other 698 works on consignment for a 50-percent commission—paintings that one "expert" said were worth as much as $32 million—Judge Midonick wrote in his decision that the evidence showed a "curious absence of hard-bargaining, arm's-length negotiations, deliberate considerations, and the presence of improvidence and waste verging upon gross negligence on the part of all the executors as well as a breach of duty of disinterested loyalty on the part of the executor Reis and the executor Stamos.

"The acts and failure to act of the three executors were clearly improper," the judge continued, and the contract they had made with Marlborough had "unconscionably low provisions as to price and . . . unreasonably long payout terms . . . indefiniteness of minimum price provision." The judge ruled that Levine's lack of personal gain did not free him from responsibility, as he had assisted in causing loss to the estate. As far as Lloyd was concerned, the judge declared, "It is clear that this litigation was the occasion for a sale of consigned paintings at inadequate prices," and that Marlborough gallery had, "at the direction of Lloyd, willfully disposed of estate paintings in bulk resulting in falsely low prices at the time of such sales." The judge pointed out that many of the 100 paintings Rothko sold directly to Marlborough by the estate had been resold "at retail from six to ten times their purchase price." (In fact, only a couple had been sold for very high prices, the rest going at the usual rate.) The gallery and its affiliates were, the judge said, "certainly aware of the conflict of interest and as such are chargeable with notice that the executors were committing a breach of their duty."

At the time of the ruling, Kate Rothko was twenty-four and a student at Johns Hopkins Medical School. Christopher was twelve, away at a private school in the East, but visiting his sister and her husband on weekends. Bernard Reis was eighty-one, Stamos was sixty-two.

On the day Judge Midonick's decision was made public, Kate Rothko's lawyer Ed Ross told the New York *Times,* concerning the gentlemanly profession of art dealing, "It proves that they should at least be as honest as the people who deal in stocks."

This was only one of many statements Mr. Ross had passed out regularly to the reporters for dailies and weeklies. Some of this self-serving publicity reached rather fulsome and dramatic proportions. A few reporters wrote shamelessly lurid articles suggesting everything from perjury to the possibility of murder. Marlborough and the executors were smeared in various subtle and not-so-subtle ways—their reputations were ruined. "This is a case," said Marlborough's attorney, Judge David Peck, in his only public statement, "that was tried in the press."

The executor Morton Levine was given to attacks of acute depression—before and during the trial. He found it necessary to undergo psychotherapy. His emotional condition was exacerbated by a separation from his wife. The Levines were divorced in 1974, but before that he was denied tenure by Brooklyn College; eventually he found work at Fordham University, where he was granted tenure. He died of cancer in January 1982.

Theodoros Stamos was so distraught by the Rothko trial that he suffered severe emotional breakdowns. Because dealers were leery of handling his work, the market for his paintings was put in lasting jeopardy. Stamos' only real possession was his house in the West Eighties, which the petitioners proceeded to take away from him as part of the judge's decision. He thus lived in a state of constant worry and concern over his impending eviction. He began spending six months of the year on a remote Greek island when not teaching at the Art Students League in New York. His close friend Alan Thieckler, who had served as one of a group of restorers of Rothko's canvases, died of cancer in August 1973 in the midst of the trial. (Of the other conservators familiar with Rothko's work, including Barney Brown, Dewey Owen and Mary Todd Glazier, a paper restorer, only Gustave Berger was called upon to give evidence on the condition of the works in the Rothko warehouse. Evidently Judge Midonick did not regard the others as sufficiently "expert" to present testimony.)

Bernard Reis was so distrubed by the accusations made against him that he suffered a stroke, which made it impossible for him to appear in court as a witness for himself and the other executors. After two additional strokes, he died in 1978. When he, too, was slapped with a judgment of over $3 million, he had declared himself bankrupt. Mrs. Reis was put in the position of losing her home to the claimants (mainly the Reis lawyers) but she was fortunately able to buy it back with her daughter's help. Many of the pictures in the Reis collection were claimed by the lawyers in lieu of payment for their fees. These were then put on sale at Sotheby's and tastelessly advertisted in their catalogue. Common criminals receive milder punishment.

The Rothko Foundation could no longer help indigent older artists. It became, as a result of the trial, a center for the dissemination of Rothko's pictures to museums throughout the world, thus gaining appropriate tax credits to ensure the legacy of the two Rothko children. As yet, no *catalogue raisonné* of the Rothko *oeuvre* has been published by the Foundation.

But who was this Judge Midonick, the umpire who decided the fate of so many people in Surrogate Court, in what was supposedly a civil, not a criminal, case? I asked a lawyer who had attended many decisions in the Family Court, where Judge Midonick had presided for most of his career. Family Court is a very simple affair, legally speaking, having to do mostly with child support. Millard Midonick, closely allied as he was with many politicians in the Democratic and Liberal parties, was appointed to the Surrogate Court, where his only important case was to be the Rothko labyrinths—more complicated than most and unique in the history of art dealing. That Midonick knew nothing of the art world or art became irrelevant as he viewed the Rothko children as victims of social injustice and financial chicanery. Poor little Kate, poor little Topher, both of whom—lawsuit aside—Rothko had left quite well-off.

In August 1982 Judge Midonick resigned from the bench. His $68,-000 a year salary was not sufficient, he announced to the press, and he was returning to private practice.

As for Frank Lloyd, he returned a large number of Rothko pictures that miraculously reappeared from Europe. He thus covered much of the fine leveled against Marlborough. However, as a non-citizen and with possible further criminal proceedings in the offing, Mr. Lloyd discreetly left the United States for his residence in the Bahamas. For several years he was *persona non grata* in New York. In early 1982 Lloyd returned to America. He posted a $1 million bond and announced that he would answer the Attorney General's accusations of criminal malfeasance. He declared that he had collected incontrovertible proof of his innocence in all his business dealings.

There was talk, of course, that Lloyd might finally go to jail. Everyone expected the judgment to go against him—and, sure enough, it did. As the New York *Times* reported on December 5, 1982, "Frank Lloyd, the owner of the Marlborough gallery and one of the world's best known art dealers, was convicted yesterday on charges of tampering with evidence in connection with a lawsuit against him, his gallery and the executors of the estate of Mark Rothko, the painter." The *Times* concluded its story by reporting that "Mr. Lloyd, who could be sentenced to four years in prison on each of the three counts in the indictment, remained free on a $1 million personal-recognizance bond."

But if for so many others directly involved in the Rothko case, it had ended in tragedy or death, for Frank Lloyd it ended on a note of unexpected comedy. When Acting State Supreme Court Justice Herbert I. Altman handed down his sentence on January 6, it proved to be one of the most hilarious and bizarre decisions in the history of art-world litigation. It wasn't to jail that Frank Lloyd was sent, but on a mission to enlighten school children about the values of art. As the *Times* reported in its front-page story the next day: "One of the world's best known art dealers was sentenced on a criminal conviction yesterday to set up a scholarship fund and art-appreciation programs for New York City high school students." This must be the first time in history that spending money on art appreciation programs was officially acknowledged to be a form of punishment! One can imagine what Mark, with his disdain for such programs, would have made of this "happy" ending to the Rothko case.

Afterword

If you don't like the games they are playing, make up one of your own.

—PAUL GOODMAN

IN NOVEMBER 1975, AFTER SOME YEARS OF INDECISION, I CLOSED MY GALlery at 50 West Fifty-seventh Street. The question had been resolved six months previously; I would stay until my lease ran out in November. The last exhibition had been promised to painter-sculptor Check Boterf. After that I would deal privately from my apartment.

The events that led up to the final closing of the door were many and mixed. Some of my best-selling artists had left for greener fields; the gallery expenses had risen disastrously; it was difficult to compete with heavily capitalized galleries. But the real truth lay elsewhere: I was bored, not a little but profoundly. Museum curators, critics, collectors, the artists, the hangers-on, had for me become a disagreeable tedium. The "art world," I found, was becoming something I detested. When I realized that I didn't enjoy going to "work" I knew it was time to say goodbye. "Work" never rated high in my notion of how to live. Arguing with truckers, worrying about shipments; frustrations with printers and photographers; nightmares about insurance; headaches with city, state and federal tax bureaus; and above all the constantly rising expenses and the accompanying decrease of profits—well, art dealing is not all roses. In the past I had simply taken these problems in stride, ignoring the hazards and quicksands of art merchandising. They had seemed merely the handicaps on the track to the marvelous. The annoyances had been no more an aggravation than the buzzing of gnats—but no longer.

What I didn't foresee when I turned from public art dealing to private was that such marketing (anything from a Dürer print to a Maxfield Parrish) contains just as many frustrations and culs-de-sac. "Well," said a friend, "at least most of the pictures you're handling are by ghosts happily dwelling in heaven." He was not, however, counting the recently dead artists whose work is militantly guarded by widows, children, relatives and very distant cousins.

The main difference in private dealing, I discovered, was the people involved. And what a lot of go-getters there turned out to be—all over town. The most nauseating group was the young married women with time on their hands who specialized in "Art for Offices"—sometimes whole suites of offices where masses of brightly colored prints, drawings and gouaches decorated the walls of jerry-built high-rises. Some specialized in cheering up doctors' and dentists' waiting rooms or placing kinetic light-ups and movables opposite operating chairs. Other entrepreneurs engaged themselves in filling the lobbies, courtyards, plazas and terraces of the new glass-and-steel edifices rising along Madison, Park and Third avenues. Invariably this was done with tangles of bent cable, slabs of Corten steel, high-buffed stainless, or massive hunks of granite, both round and square.

Another group of my bushy-tailed colleagues specialized in tapestries to lighten the grimness of vestibules and stairwells. Somewhere, in Ecuador perhaps, natives were hooking away at big zigzags, arcs, circles, rectangles or polka dots of eye-filling intensity to soften the impact of elevator banks. New business was pouring into foundries in Long Island, upper New York State, or New Jersey to "fabricate" jumbo-sized constructions by artists—famous, near-famous or quite unknown— who prepared mole-sized maquettes for elephantine productions. These celebrations could be found on the lawns of benign industrial plants, secure amidst the expensive landscape engineering, visible proof of business supporting art and improving the community.

I, however, found myself quite incapable of such vigorous salesmanship. I was one of the rather timid pushers who serve a drink or take a possible buyer to lunch or simply get an appointment to see a would-be customer. Hours on end would be spent on and near the telephone, waiting for the return call that never came. Then, gradually, the timid ones start consorting with one another. One has a Masson but no client, the other has a client but no Masson. We all became quite friendly in a sheepish way. The calls one received were: "See if you can get me a 1929 wooden Arp." "But they're impossible to find." "Your friend Virgil Thomson owns an important Arp. Can't you convince him that this is a good time to sell?" "I've talked with Virgil about that. He doesn't sell *anything*. He likes his art works. He doesn't need the money all that much." "How about Jeanne Reynal's Rothko?" "She sold it years ago. And she gave up acquiring pictures." "And Mrs. Chester Dale? Surely she needs money." "But she doesn't. She's perfectly comfortable."

It was true that I had many friends and acquaintances who owned fine pictures and statues. Once in a while I would be called on to look at something. Once it was a Watteau—worth over a million dollars. I was led to believe by the silly old gentleman who owned it that he was interested in selling. Ah, I thought, if I could sell just this one canvas, I'll be in clover. And off I rushed, consulting a Watteau specialist, having X rays made, urging the work upon a large international art broker. The painting *was* indeed a Watteau, good as gold. The broker would pay a million and a quarter for this tiny piece of real estate. When I triumphantly returned to my de-acquisitioner, he exclaimed, "Oh good! And now I know what it's worth. I wouldn't dream of letting go of anything so beautiful."

When I told one of my private-dealer colleagues about my disappointment, she became agitated. "Get a lawyer! Sue him! Charge him for consultation services!" But I realized that such a lawsuit would cost me more than any fee I might receive and that my client, being very, very rich, had expert legal advisors. *Tant pis.*

Up and down Madison Avenue they run, the courtiers of the art world, making their 1 percent, 5 percent, 10 percent, occasionally 100 percent. Sometimes they make a real killing. For instance, my friend Jane Wade sold a gigantic Henry Moore to a Midwestern city and was able to retire from the business. But for a lazy person like myself, art jogging held no attraction and once again I wearied of a race I could not sustain—let alone win. Life, I believed, was more important than art dealing. Within a year, I knew I had done with it. Events bring about unexpected alterations.

In August 1976 my close friend of twenty-five happy years, Herbert Machiz, died of a sudden and massive cardiac attack. This happened at six in the morning while a dramatic thunder-and-lightning storm raged. A year later the family from whom I rented my elegant garden apartment on East Seventy-third Street suddenly sold the house to a corporation that immediately began proceedings to evict me. After a few mysterious break-ins and robberies, I knew it was impossible to remain in a building that was already being "recycled" into several apartments. Luckily I had a new house in the country and a new friend to share it with.

But my luck didn't last long. A physical examination I was fortunate enough to undergo in time indicated a cancer in the bladder. (Later another malignancy showed up in my right kidney, which was promptly removed.) "You know," said my doctor one day in response to my whining, "your life from now on will be very interesting. After all, many people never have this experience." Good heavens, I thought, the phrase "cold comfort" takes on fresh meaning. Be glad for your heart attack. What fun to have epilepsy. Brighten the corner where you stare. But the good doctor proved to be right. What was the verse I used to hear? "Oh life, life, life! I cannot hold thee close enough."

My friend Susan Sontag telephoned and sent me her essay on being ill. Her malignancy was far worse than mine but her courage and determination were boundless. She had learned to undergo and live with chemotherapy and I found myself learning to do the same.

Like Montaigne (a perfect writer to keep always nearby, since he's good for a lifetime), I say, "I judge of my condition only by what I actually feel, and not by my fears and reasoning. Would you like to know how much I gain? Look at those who behave otherwise." If Susan could do this, why couldn't I? It is a question of living from day to day and week to week as fully as one can. I wasn't surprised that as soon as she could Susan had turned out a few more books, directed a play, participated in symposia. Nor had she lost any of her sociability and innate gaiety. It's not so terrible to measure one's life with coffee spoons. One simply makes more choices as to what's worth the effort and what is not.

In truth I became busier than I had been in years. First there was *Parenthèse*, a little magazine of words and pictures. I asked the poet John Hollander to write a motto for the title page:

Parentithemi: I-put-in-beside, and thereby besides. Between the curving lines like thin angels of rhetoric come our afterthoughts, sidelights, and nervous disclaimers; the hedges that guard the truth; the necessary appositives too frail to stand unpropped; the logical friendships that banish the monster in (mock) (turtle soup). But in the end, between these cupped hands upheld, the special radiance of the in-between.

It was a magazine devoted to words and pictures, with no timely journalism, no criticism, no book reviews, no gossip. *Parenthèse* began in 1975 and came out intermittently until 1980. I financed the magazine with advertisements from art galleries, full and half pages. The printing was done at an excellent small press in Kent, New York. "Shall I call it *Parenthesis* or *Parenthèse*," I asked my old friend Pierre Matisse. *"Parenthèse*, of course," he replied. "More snob, more classy." Quite true; one can never be elitist enough when it comes to the arts. In the back of my mind was the brilliant presentation of the text and illustrations of *View*. The founding principle was my belief in "interaction." But of course, *Parenthèse* would be nothing like *View*, since the motto of the latter publication was *"Il faut être absolument moderne."* I knew that for *Parenthèse* I must find new artists, new voices, new ideas (or caprices). It must be serious, occasionally frivolous. Older talent would not be neglected, either, should something good come my way.

Once again the search for the marvelous was under way. During the eight issues that saw the light of day an astonishing parade of words and pictures came between the brackets—"the special radiance of the in-between." Two beautiful pieces of fiction by Guy Davenport; a story by Meyer Liben, the gifted Kafka of the Upper West Side; an essay on the songs composed by Friedrich Nietzsche by John Reeves White; a section from the journal of the great botanist Rupert Barnaby—all appeared in the magazine. Poems by rather well-known poets such as John Ashbery, Barbara Guest, James Merrill, Alan Ansen and John Hollander were presented side-by-side with such discoveries as Paul Auster, Judith Moffett, Alfred Corn, J. D. McClatchy, Douglas Crase, and Madison Morrison. I asked Walter Abish for a story with a happy ending and in came one called "Happiness." It might have been called "Bliss"—it was very funny. All of us were delighted when Abish received the Faulkner Prize for his novel *How German Is It?* a few years later.

As for the artists, I was once again gallery-going at high speed. There was a rich haul for the magazine: Leonore Tawney; Florencio Galindo, a new Spanish realist; Anne Dunn; Howard Hussey; Raymond Mason; Anne Arnold; Margaret Israel; the sculptor Robert White; Bryan Hunt; Deborah Butterfield; Margot Stewart; Ethlyn Hoenig; Dorothy Andrews; Ivan Biro; and Joe Zucker. Older established figures were not ignored, for instance, Miró, Gottlieb, Jean Tinguely, Al Held, Lester Johnson, Joseph Cornell, Dmitri Petrov, Eugene Atget, Cecil Beaton and Berenice Abbott.

How did the words and pictures connect? Only vaguely, I must admit, parallel perhaps in feeling and atmosphere. But, like Alice, I enjoy a book with pictures. In 1981 I decided that it would be more interesting to change the direction and content of *Parenthèse*, call it *Parenthèse Signatures* and publish one poet with one artist in a larger portfolio style, de luxe, limited to 150 signed and numbered copies. *Tongues on Trees*, a suite of ten poems by Alfred Corn with ten drawings by the landscape painter John Gundelfinger was the first. The price was $25, with proceeds from each publication going toward the next. The second was J. D. McClatchy's *Lantskip, Plantan, Creatures Ramp'd*, a bestiary with creatures drawn by Billy Sullivan. The design for these publications was in the skillful hands of the painter Arthur Cady. It was a pleasure to have such a modest publishing venture praised in the New York *Times* by its art critic John Russell.

Still, the governessy aspect of my character was not satisfied. After ceasing to be an art merchant, I felt the "call" to go out to the hustings and lecture on modern artists and their art. Besides, I needed the money. Word got around that I was ready to perform in public (for a fee) and off I went to Brown University in Providence, Rhode Island, where I lost my dog for an hour before the lecture; to Vassar College, where we all sat in a circle and ate cheese and drank wine while I described the fifties; to the University of Pennsylvania for a two-hour talk on Joseph Cornell—a lecture repeated at Yale with my slides being shown before and after the speech; to the Newport Art Association for four feet of snow and twelve people in the audience; then to the Hirschhorn Museum in Washington; the Cleveland Museum of Art for Edward Hennings' large Surrealist show; to the Heritage Foundation in Norfolk, Virginia; to the Whitney Museum in New York (the last being a few nightclub turns with the puppet act thrown in).

My greatest triumph, however, was to be invited to my hometown of Buffalo, to the Albright-Knox art gallery, where I was wined and dined and where, following my lecture, I attended a reception in a beautiful old mansion now occupied by the museum's director, Robert Buck. It was a house I had visited as a child, and entering it again was a strange, Proustian experience.

Lecturing in many places had another benefit; wherever I went people always turned up whom I hadn't seen for a long time or saw seldom, mostly artists. But even more delightful was getting to know so many students and learning what the young were dreaming about. This was a particular joy in the two visits I made to that most unique of art schools, Skowhegan in Maine.

But does an art dealer ever lose the itch to put on exhibitions? In my case, at least, no. Since I was a member of the board of trustees of the Southeast Museum in Brewster, New York, where I live, I helped organize many exhibitions. My two favorites were a show of very old wooden tools and a large-scale circus gala celebrating the fact that Brewster (*not*, as claimed, Bridgeport, Connecticut) was the birthplace of the American circus, very early in the nineteenth century. The farmers in the area had housed the circus animals in the winter—for instance, elephants in the barn behind my first Brewster house. (The barn cat was called Hannibal.) What made the museum show a delight was a parade organized by the painter Ethlyn Hoenig down Main Street, the lovely display of some of Ivan Karp's sideshow banners, and a large installation of objects and construction by Frank Lincoln Viner—plus one of Viner's puppet productions. Thanks to the generosity of Lily Auchincloss, the opening featured two performances of the Big Apple Circus in the museum's auditorium.

A few years later, Robert R. Littman, the daring director of New York University's Grey Art gallery and study center, invited me to organize a show that would be a revelation of my particular tastes in painting and sculpture. Carte blanche, no strings, two years to get it ready, a decent curatorial fee and a full-scale catalogue with all the works in the show illustrated, including eight in color—what gift could be more princely than such total freedom? A grant was obtained from the National Endowment for the Arts and other money came from private sources. The university administration viewed this operation from a benign distance.

Nothing I had ever tried to do turned out so well. The Grey gallery staff could not have been more professional or sympathetic, no matter how outrageous some of my selections might be. The problems of installation were many—a huge construction of string by Leonore Tawney; twelve-foot marionettes for Stravinsky's *Oedipus Rex* made of balsa wood, which had to be placed behind Plexiglas shields for protection; an enormous pile of bright orange Styrofoam beams by Carl Andre; a delicate life-sized reclining figure in ceramic by Mary Frank, lent by Mrs. Vera List not without anxiety for its safety; tiny, swipable collages by Anne Ryan and Joseph Cornell; very expensive oils by Jackson

Pollock and Willem de Kooning—and many other irreplaceables.

Champagne was served at the black-tie opening. Maybe it was the champagne that helped pack the room, but perhaps not. During the four weeks the exhibition continued, the University was pleased that over thirty-five thousand people came to see what was going on. The press had been enthusiastic; possibly word-of-mouth helped.

Encountering Carl Andre shortly afterward, I asked him what he thought of the show. "Interesting," he said, "but very eccentric." No doubt he was right. After all, I had chosen to call my spectacle *Tracking the Marvelous.*

Index

About the Author

Born in Buffalo, JOHN BERNARD MYERS has been an organizer of film societies, editor and publisher of little magazines, puppeteer, theater producer, student of art history, and, for thirty-seven years, art dealer for the New American avant-garde. This is his first book. He lives in Brewster, New York.